Sounds *from* Silence

Sounds *from* Silence

Graeme Clark and the Bionic Ear Story

PROFESSOR
GRAEME CLARK

ALLEN & UNWIN

Allen & Unwin
9 Atchison Street
St Leonards NSW 2065
Australia
Phone: (61 2) 8425 0100
Fax: (61 2) 9906 2218
Email: frontdesk@allen-unwin.com.au
Web: http://www.allen-unwin.com.au

National Library of Australia
Cataloguing-in-Publication entry:

Clark, Graeme M., 1935–.
    Sounds from silence: the bionic ear story.

    Includes index.
    ISBN 1 86508 302 X.

    1. Clark, Graeme M., 1935–. 2. Otolaryngologists—
Australia—Biography. 3. Cochlear implants. 4. Deafness—
Rehabilitation. I. Title.

617.882092

Set in 10.5/14.5 pt Weiss by Midland Typesetters, Maryborough
Printed by Griffin Press, Adelaide

10 9 8 7 6 5 4 3 2 1

Contents

Thankyou to my wife, Margaret. Without your love and unfailing support, there would be no story to tell.

To our children, Sonya, Cecily, Roslyn, Merran and Jonathan and sons-in-law Ian and Peter—thankyou for enriching our lives. Your love has been the best encouragement. Also to our grandchildren, Elise, Monty, Daniel and Noah.

Mum and Dad, you provided all the love and wisdom a child needs. I could not have wished for better parents.

To my sister Robin and my brother Bruce—thankyou for your selfless interest and for always being there.

Thankyou to my research colleagues for sharing in this adventure and for your commitment to making the dream come true.

Thankyou to the patients and their families for your faith and trust in our integrity and care.

Thankyou to the many donors and sponsors who have given of their time or money. Without their help, the bionic ear could not have been achieved.

My appreciation to all the staff of Nucleus and Cochlear Limited who have made the bionic ear a commercial success.

Acknowledgements

I would especially like to thank: Sue Davine for typing the text and so willingly undertaking the many other tasks required; Dr David Lawrence for his untiring help with the photographs and illustrative material; and John Huigen and Frank Nielsen for invaluable general assistance.

I would also like to thank my wife, Margaret, for patiently reading and correcting versions of the text.

I am grateful to Jenny Darling, Jacinta de Mace, Margaret Barca, Chris Durham, Linley Hartley, Judy Crake and my father, Colin Clark, for reading the early versions of the text and for their helpful comments.

Preface

This book is a personal account of the development of the Australian multiple-electrode cochlear implant (bionic ear). My research into helping deaf people hear by means of electrical stimulation of the hearing nerve has been a long journey into the unknown. The journey was motivated by a boyhood dream to help deaf people like my father; that dream became a mission to which the greater part of my professional life has been devoted. For years I was criticised for undertaking a task that many scientists and doctors considered next to impossible. Criticism is part of the scientific process and must be expected when an advance is radically new. The support of my wife, family and friends, and my faith in God, enabled me to continue with the work.

When I commenced my research in 1967, there were two frontiers in medicine—genetic engineering and the restoration of brain function. Youthful enthusiasm and the desire to restore hearing drove me to pursue the latter. It satisfied a creative urge to make discoveries. My quest for meaning in life also meant that studying brain function held a strong attraction. Furthermore, my faith in God had to be tried and tested through living life to the very limits of my capabilities.

The scientific questions requiring answers, and the bio-engineering problems needing to be resolved, have been discussed in many monographs, books, chapters, scientific papers and conference proceedings. But science depends on human endeavour. I have tried to tell here how events affected me, and how I was driven towards my goal.

It is hoped that this book will give insight into how a number of people have worked together on this great challenge. I have had the privilege of leading a talented research team that grew from a small group of young people to a large, scientific enterprise over a period of twenty years. It would also not have been possible without a quite unique interaction between research and industry. Cochlear Limited, the firm that produces the device, started as a small 'tiger team' and grew out of the pacemaker firm Telectronics by way of a holding company called Nucleus Limited. Our fundamental research supported its growth.

There can be few innovations in medicine that have required input from so many disciplines. These include electrophysiology, neuroscience, biology, bio-engineering, electrochemistry, materials science, toxicology, pathology, psychophysics, speech science, electronic engineering, communications engineering, anatomy, otology, audiology, speech pathology, and education of the hearing impaired. Knowledge in these disciplines had to be analysed, interrelated and focused on a specific outcome.

It is now an immeasurable reward to experience the gratitude of people who are able to hear again or, in the case of children, for the first time.

Miracles as such
Are not just a dream
Although in disguise
That is what they seem

Therese Kay, grandmother of Ari Fisher, Melbourne

1

Deafness in the family

Although my ears have never heard,
An accident of birth,
And although my eyes near sightless,
I celebrate my worth.
I'm older now and wiser too
And happier by far,
For someone reached inside the shell
And made me touch a star.

Excerpt from a poem by the mother of a deaf and blind child

SIAN NEAME

Anne and David Neame were looking forward with excitement to the birth of their third child. On 13 September 1987 they had a beautiful daughter they called Sian. She was a placid baby; in fact, Anne used to remark that nothing upset Sian. Not even the noise that came from the nearby kitchen and family room disturbed her sleep. She was alert and bright, and it never crossed Anne's mind that Sian, who had been routinely screened for deafness, might have hearing problems.

Anne started to worry that all wasn't well when Sian was eighteen months old and hadn't yet begun to talk. She remembered how talkative their two boys, Liam and Lachlan, had been at this age. She made an appointment for a speech therapy assessment, prior to which Sian had another hearing test. While the child sat in the testing booth, the young audiologist gradually increased the noise level. It became so loud it was almost unbearable, but Sian remained impassive. Anne's growing fears for her daughter were confirmed when the audiologist concluded that Sian was profoundly deaf. Anne was shocked by the news. What would it mean to have a child who was deaf, she wondered? Would Sian be able to learn to talk? 'It was as though my whole world had fallen apart,' Anne later explained. 'I had thought my life was all mapped out, and I couldn't cope at first with this sudden change.'

Anne had been brought up as a Christian in the Roman Catholic tradition, but she now felt angry with God.

> We were very angry. It wasn't fair that our friends had their life. I had just gone back to teaching on an emergency basis and was planning to work full-time to help with our finances. All that went on hold. I found it very difficult for a while to cope socially with our friends. They seemed not to have a care in the world, and we had a child with a profound hearing loss. This knowledge seemed to consume my thoughts and I had trouble at times coping with normal social situations. I also felt extremely protective towards Sian.

Anne went to her family doctor for counselling and felt encouraged when he said that hearing tests weren't infallible. Anne and David started to doubt the diagnosis. They were referred to an ear doctor who suggested inserting small tubes through the ear-drums to resolve any middle ear problems and restore some of the hearing. This sounded reasonable to Anne and David, who were clutching at any hope. Sian soon underwent the procedure, and the surgeon reassured them that everything would now be all right. It wasn't even necessary to fit hearing aids, he said.

As there was no change in Sian's condition, they sought a further opinion from the laboratories of the Australian Hearing Service, which confirmed that Sian was profoundly deaf. She was fitted with hearing aids.

Anne and David weren't sure what to do next. Everyone they spoke with gave them conflicting advice. Sian should learn to speak and to lip-read, said some. She should learn to listen and lip-read, and be taught English along with additional signs for the speech sounds she couldn't hear (known as total communication), said others. Still others were adamant that it was better to learn the Australian version of Sign Language of the Deaf (Auslan), a language that is quite different from English and spoken mostly within the deaf community. Anne didn't know what to do or where to turn for advice. 'It was just awful,' she said. 'All we wanted was for her to talk.' They didn't want her to have to rely only on Sign Language of the Deaf, as they wanted her to be able to talk to hearing people as well.

Finally, they decided that Sian would learn to speak as best she could using an auditory/verbal approach to education being evaluated at the Early Education Program for Hearing Impaired Children at the John Pierce Centre in Melbourne. With this method, which relies on audition alone, speakers cover their mouth when talking to the children, to encourage them to use any useful hearing. The Centre proved to be a wonderfully supportive environment for Sian and her family. Anne and David appreciated the love and concern shown by the staff, and the fact that they treated the loss of hearing as a family issue to be discussed and worked through for each family member.

At this time, Anne and David went through a grieving process for Sian.

> We really, really grieved. We grieved full-on. We felt that we had lost our little girl who we adored and loved, and who we thought could hear. When we looked at Sian, we had these hopes that parents have for their children. Then to be told that there is a problem or a difficulty that is profound—it really affects your life.

Sian wasn't the person they had thought she was, and they now had to discover who she really was. It was the caring of Sister Joan Winter, Helen Hill and the other staff at the Early Education Program for Hearing Impaired Children that helped to give them hope. Anne and David would talk well into the night after David came home from night shift. They were amazed that people could be so caring and loving and give so much of themselves.

> It gave me a new-found belief in God and I started to see it all in a different way. I couldn't believe there could be so much help from people who didn't know you. Much later I wrote a letter to Joan [Winter] saying I had been very disillusioned in my religion, but that the people I had met and the people who had held our family together restored my faith in God. It was just amazing. They restored my faith in God because they were so supportive. They were just there. And we really, really were in crisis.

At about this time, Anne and David started to hear talk of the bionic ear. One of the audiologists at the Australian Hearing Services knew about our progress through personal contact with our senior audiologist, Ms Pam

Dawson. Sister Joan from the John Pierce Centre had also raised it as an option. She and Sister Frances from St Mary's School for Children with Impaired Hearing had been very supportive of our early work with children and had seen its benefits at first hand. Although a genetic counselling professional had advised that Sian was far too young to be considered for a bionic ear implant, Anne and David were very keen to find out everything they could about the procedure. They came to see Pam Dawson when Sian was two years of age, just six months after diagnosis.

I was still reluctant to operate on a child as young as Sian. Although our studies had shown that there were no real safety issues to be concerned about, I wanted to be sure that we had gained enough experience in how to train young children and how to assess them. I arranged for one of our audiologists, Ms Louise Rowlands, who was experienced in speech and language as well as hearing assessment, to work with Sian. I wanted Louise to try and get the most out of Sian's hearing aids before we proceeded with the bionic ear operation. As head of the Cochlear Implant Clinic at the Royal Victorian Eye and Ear Hospital, I reviewed Sian's progress on 30 November 1989. Although she was profoundly deaf, she had shown remarkable progress in developing her listening skills and language. She seemed to be making rapid progress in using her residual hearing. There was much discussion about whether we should delay the operation because she might do as well with two hearing aids. However, we were learning that the longer we left the operation, the less chance there was of the patient achieving good speech perception. After also deciding that the blockage of the tubes aerating the middle ear had settled down and wouldn't interfere with the operation, I agreed that we should proceed.

We all spent a lot of time discussing the decision with Anne and David. It wasn't a simple one to make. I assured them that we had taken all possible precautions to ensure that the risks were minimal. Not only had we practised the surgery many times, but I had also set up a special unit in the theatre to blow sterile air over the operating table to reduce to an absolute minimum the chances of wound contamination with infection. In proceeding with the operation, we all believed we were acting in Sian's best interests in the long term. Her operation was scheduled for 13 March the following year, when she would be only two years and six months—our youngest patient.

Sian Neame with her mother, Anne, shortly after her bionic ear operation, 13 March 1990.
(Photograph courtesy The Herald and Weekly Times)

The day of the operation approached quickly. On the evening before, Sian and her mother were admitted to the hospital. Anne would stay over-night and be with Sian in these new and strange surroundings. Louise, as Sian's managing audiologist, as was our practice, helped mother and child to adjust to the new environment. The following morning, Sian was sedated and taken on the trolley to the theatre clutching her special toy, called Joey. The staff of Nucleus Limited had sent Anne an old bionic ear headset and speech processor which she had put on the little teddy bear.

Anne recounts, 'The lift opened and I could see you and Brian Pyman with your green garbs on, and it was horrible.' She knew then that Sian was completely in the hands of the doctors and staff in the operating theatre. In order to relieve the anxiety, Anne and David went to the nearby Fitzroy Gardens with Louise who reassured them that all would be well. The operation proceeded smoothly, and we were able to insert the electrode bundle as far as we could have hoped.

Sian was soon reunited with her parents in a drowsy state after the operation. As soon as possible, I returned to the ward where Anne and

David had been waiting and reassured them that the operation had been successful and we had cleared the first hurdle. By the next day, Sian was almost like her normal self apart from a head bandage and loss of hair on the side of the surgery. I went to see her daily and, four days after the operation, I was happy for her to go home.

Two weeks after her discharge from the hospital, Sian returned for the bionic ear to be switched on. With young children we only established stimulus levels for one or two electrodes at a time, so that they didn't experience any sounds that were too loud. We didn't want them to be put off by the experience. At each session a few more electrodes were switched on, so Sian would get gradually increasing experience of the different types of sounds she might hear. Initially, a strategy to process speech wasn't used. Anne really wanted it all to be processed immediately and became a little impatient that things were happening so slowly.

After one session at the hospital, Anne and Sian went to Parliament Station. As they were sitting waiting for their train, a woman walked by in high-heeled shoes and immediately Sian turned to listen. Anne's hopes soared. 'It was just amazing,' she said. 'I felt like crying with joy. I wanted to go and grab the woman and tell her what her high heels had done for me!'

Gradually, Sian's experiences of sound increased. Anne remembers the day she heard birds outside.

> It was beautiful that she could hear them twittering. Then she would respond to the phone ringing and the toilet flushing, and appreciate the noises made by her older brothers when playing games.

When the speech processor was switched on, Sian had to start to learn what other children absorb naturally when they are eighteen months to two years younger. She played with other children, and was able to participate with her older brothers in activities around the house.

During this time the family joined the Parents' Federation for Children with Impaired Hearing, which held camps that attracted people from all over the state. There were talks, they were told, and many opportunities to interact with other people. The family went along to a camp soon after Sian's implant. Her head was shaven, making it obvious that she had had a bionic ear operation. Anne and David were ignored by the signing deaf adults. Anne described it as 'not a nice experience'. David, however, was quite angry about the way they were treated. 'It was our decision for our child to have the operation, as we wanted her to have hearing,' he said. Their experience at that first camp indicated the attitude of many among the signing deaf community towards the bionic ear. However, they were happy with the choice they had made for their child and continued to receive considerable support and care from their teachers. Before long, Sian was making very good progress.

While all this was happening to the Neame family, news came through to me that on 27 July 1990 the US Food and Drug Administration (FDA) had approved our bionic ear as safe and effective for use in children from two to eighteen years of age. This was the first bionic ear to be approved by the US body, or indeed any world health regulatory body, for use in children. Following the announcement, Anne, Sian and I were interviewed on the Channel 10 program 'Good Morning Australia' on 29 July. I emphasised that this development was very important for Australian industry, and that it would give many deaf children the opportunity to communicate with normally hearing people. Anne said that, even at this stage, it seemed absolutely miraculous. 'Sian is more in touch with her environment and will come when her brothers call her from a distance,' she explained. Still, Anne thought that it would take ten to fifteen years for Sian to speak normally.

As Sian grew, she became aware that people would occasionally stare at her because she wore the external aerial of the bionic ear behind her ear, but otherwise she didn't think of herself as being deaf or in any way different from other children. She was treated by her older brothers the same as in most families and given no special consideration. Before long she was starting to chat to her friends on the telephone. Anne remembers how Sian and her brothers would fight for the use of the telephone. One day when Sian had been on the telephone for half an hour to her friend Emily, her brothers in the other room were becoming very impatient. Anne looked at David with tears in her eyes: their child, who had been deaf and who they thought would never speak, was now causing a row in the family over talking on the phone for too long! One of the blessings from the implant was that they didn't need to treat her in any special way.

Sian attends St Mary's School for Children with Impaired Hearing. However, most of her day is spent in the companion mainstream school,

Holy Trinity, with special assistance from St Mary's when needed. Sian has big ambitions to learn other languages, such as French, and hopes one day to become an actress, as she likes drama at school, or maybe even to become a television personality. Already Sian is achieving this goal through her role in a Telstra advertisement.

ELIZABETH ANNE DUNN

If anyone had told the young Elizabeth Dunn, known as Anne, that she would lose almost all of her hearing at the age of twenty, she would have been both shocked and unbelieving. And if anyone had predicted that thirty-five years later, she would be the grateful owner of a bionic ear that partly restored her hearing, she would have thought that sheer fantasy.

Anne, the daughter of an Adelaide medical practitioner, had a happy childhood. As a young adult studying at the University of Adelaide, she looked forward to a rosy future that included a scientific career and later, she hoped, marriage and a family. Her dreams were smashed when a sudden serious illness put her in the Adelaide Hospital for six months. During that time she received large doses of the antibiotic Streptomycin in over a hundred punctures of her lumbar spine, which eventually damaged her inner ears and caused almost complete deafness.

With her loss of hearing, Anne became resigned to the future. Luckily, David, her boyfriend of two years, stayed around to pick up the pieces and they married two years later. 'With the help of family and friends I settled into a happy home-making way of life. Then, after about six months, another surprise—we decided to go to London where David would do further study.'

Undaunted by the thought of living among strangers, and even though she was unable to hear, they set off overseas. They made new friends and travelled all over England. It didn't seem to matter too much that Anne was deaf. The pair spent an enjoyable couple of months in Germany. David watched, with great amusement, as their landlady, who spoke no English, and Anne, who spoke no German, conversed by way of lip-reading and a strange kind of sign language.

After two years overseas, they returned to Adelaide with their brand-new baby daughter. Over the next decade, two more children arrived.

Anne and David found that the children needed to be considerate of, and in close contact with, their mother, in order to communicate with her.

David became established as a consultant physician at the Adelaide Hospital, but also found time to retain his links with the Student Christian Movement and was the doctor for the Movement's national conference held in Adelaide in 1958/59. Margaret Burtenshaw, whom I married in 1961, attended from Sydney. Margaret had been living it up after her final university exams and her resistance was low. After spending all night on the train and several more late nights, she succumbed to pneumonia. She says:

> I was put to bed in one of the colleges and Dr David Dunn came to see me each day to give me an injection of penicillin. The conference ended and I still wasn't well enough to go home, so Dr Dunn said they would be able to have me at their place, and his wife would look after me—a big thing to do.
>
> My impression of Anne Dunn while she looked after me was that she looked like an angel. She was beautiful and had a lovely, serene smile and a soft voice. The children were delightful too—Elizabeth and John. I played with them a bit. I always felt embarrassed later, because I felt I never adequately expressed my gratitude, and the gift I gave them was a toy piano for the children. Although I had a toy piano when I was young and enjoyed it, it was a pretty useless gift. I was also sorry that I hadn't kept in touch with them over the years after they had done so much for me. But then, later, we were able to return the kindness in a way that I couldn't possibly have foreseen, with the gift of hearing from a bionic ear.

Although Anne had thirty-five years of almost complete deafness that brought problems and limitations, she considered she had a fortunate life. Her family and friends helped her to make contact with the world and kept her happy. Nevertheless, in October 1977 I received a touching letter from Dr Dunn saying that he would like to give his wife a bionic ear for her forty-eighth birthday. He had heard through the press about the bionic ear we were developing and wanted to give his wife the gift of hearing. He said in his letter that she had had meningitis (an infection of the membranes lining the brain) due to tuberculosis, and that it had been treated many years ago using the drug Streptomycin which, together with the illness, had damaged her hearing. He wasn't expecting a lot, he said, but any help would be a lovely gift. He also said that his wife lipread expertly, and spoke normally, but had monumental difficulty and wanted liberation from her frustration. He concluded by asking: 'If there is a list of hopefuls, can she join? Maybe the meek will inherit the earth, but they don't seem to get near the top of the list.' In a postscript, he wrote: 'I realise the naivete of expecting great things at the present stage.' I had to reply we weren't ready to implant anyone, and they should wait till we had results with our first patients.

Two years later, in 1979, I was surprised by a telephone call from Dr Dunn, who said that his wife was now nearing her fiftieth birthday. 'Could this be the time for a birthday present?' he asked. He had learned that we had operated on our first patient and had obtained encouraging results. Dr Dunn had also written to my secretary in the hope that when he and his wife were in Melbourne they could have an appointment to discuss the possibility of an operation. I explained that I was in the midst of testing our first patient and wanted to operate on a few more people in Melbourne before being able to discuss the pros and cons of surgery on a patient from interstate. I said that I regretted I couldn't perform the operation for his wife's fiftieth birthday.

I didn't hear again from Dr Dunn or his wife Anne for some time. We continued our work to evaluate the prototype device being developed at the University of Melbourne. Then, in 1982, the Australian industrial firm Telectronics, and its holding company Nucleus, produced a clinical trial device for world trials in the United States and Europe for the US FDA to see if it would be safe and effective for commercial application. The University of Melbourne team carried out the first evaluation of the Nucleus implant on six patients operated on at the Royal Victorian Eye and Ear Hospital late in 1982. I had nearly forgotten about Anne Dunn at this stage.

Word got around through the press and the professional societies about the benefits of our cochlear implant. I then received a letter from an ear, nose and throat colleague in Adelaide, Dr Bob Guerin, asking if we could review Anne's case. A letter also arrived from Dr Dunn asking us to reconsider Anne for an operation. I agreed this time to take a patient from interstate because I knew that if we needed to follow her up in Adelaide, Bob Guerin and Dr Dean Beaumont, who were very skilled ear specialists, could provide assistance. We could also see Anne from time to time in Melbourne.

I organised tests when Anne and David Dunn arrived in Melbourne, and found that she was so deaf there was virtually no hearing. We stimulated her inner ear with electrical currents by a wire passed through the ear-drum to see if there might be residual hearing nerves left after possible die-back due to deafness. The result was a little discouraging, although not contra-indicating surgery. I was also worried that the infection around the lining of the brain might have caused the inner ear to be filled with bone so that electrodes couldn't penetrate close to the hearing nerves. However, the X-rays were at least a little encouraging.

After our detailed evaluation, I considered it appropriate to proceed with a bionic ear operation. I thought that we had a chance of helping Anne to recover some useful hearing. I wrote to Bob Guerin explaining this.

There was another problem, however. At the time, there was no government funding for the device. Our first six patients operated on in 1982 had a free bionic ear because it was considered experimental. Anne and David would have to foot the bill themselves, as we had also not been able to get any agreement from the health insurance agencies that they would pay for such a device. The cost of the birthday gift for David was $10 000.

The date of the operation was scheduled around Anne's need to be with their youngest daughter who was facing her final school exams. 'At last a date was fixed—28 May 1985—and my adventure began,' Anne said.

Prior to Anne's operation, I had been approached by the Channel 9 television network to produce a documentary for the program 'A Current Affair', compered by Mike Willesee. I hadn't previously wanted to risk press coverage before and after an operation, in case it wasn't successful. But we now had experience with patients, so I agreed. Anne Dunn happened to be the next person being considered, and she was prepared to be the subject. Debbie Byrne, the reporter, talked to Anne before the operation, and Anne said that what she most wanted was to be able to speak with people more easily.

The operation was carried out at the Royal Victorian Eye and Ear Hospital by Drs Brian Pyman and Robert Webb, under my supervision. As the inner ear could have been filled with bone, it was a relief that fifteen of the twenty-two electrodes needed to stimulate the hearing nerves could be introduced. Anne recovered well from the surgery, and the following morning I visited her to see how she was getting on. The sun glinted on my hair and glasses. Anne said, 'I had this illusion that I had seen an angel.'

After the operation she had little discomfort—only a temporary taste disturbance, but no giddiness. On the tenth day after surgery, Anne returned with David for the bionic ear to be switched on. We were in my clinic room, with audiologist Alison Brown at the terminal of the computer. With her screen lit up, Alison prepared to press the keys to excite the electrodes in Anne's inner ear. She turned to Anne and said, 'Are you ready?' Anne lip-read the question, then sat waiting. A suggestion of a smile passed across her face and she raised her left eyebrow as though she heard something. Suddenly her face lit up with a big grin. She said, 'A scale!' and turned excitedly to David. Alison then said to David, as she handed him the microphone, 'Would you like to have the honour of saying the first word to Anne?' David took the microphone and said, 'We've got a lot of catching up to do, haven't we?' Anne replied, 'We have, and it will take us another thirty-five years.' Not only did Anne hear her husband's voice but also water running into my clinic sink, and she could tell which was which!

Because her time in Melbourne was limited, the early part of the training program was condensed into three sessions of instructions and tests. Anne then returned for more training and adjustments for just one day every four to six weeks until the end of the year. The facilities to do this hadn't been established in Adelaide.

On returning home, Anne especially wanted to hear the voices of her children and grandchildren. When she greeted her son and daughter-in-law, she said: 'You don't quite sound like I thought you would, but rather as though you are speaking underwater.' Her little grandson looked on with great curiosity as Grandma played with the little box that helped her to hear.

Soon after Anne's return home, Channel 9 ran the feature program. Normally I don't watch my television appearances, but I made an exception this time. Margaret joined me to watch the show. She exclaimed, 'That's Anne Dunn!'. Then she reminded me of the story of the Dunns' kindness to her years ago in Adelaide when she had pneumonia. This was the start of a renewed and special friendship.

As Anne gained in experience, environmental sounds entered her world—at first, one by one, and then by the thousands. She started to

Anne Dunn hears her husband David speak for the first time in 35 years (1985).

appreciate sounds we normally take for granted, like the rustling of paper, or the sound of a light switch being turned on or a knife being dropped on the floor.

The first year after the bionic ear operation was a busy learning period that required training exercises and interacting with people. During this period, progress and difficulties came side by side. There were, and still are, frustrations, as not all sounds make sense.

At first it wasn't easy for Anne to tolerate so much new sound, but gradually, as the background noises became less bothersome and her brain began to discriminate between them and significant sounds, she found she could stay tuned on. 'I was discovering exciting new sounds every day and felt quite proud to report I could hear a jet going over the house— only to be told it was, in fact, Joan Sutherland on the radio!'

Anne's new world was at times alarming, often difficult, but more and more rewarding. Noisy meetings weren't appealing, and music was beyond her reach. Learning a new language required a great deal of persistence, encouragement and practice. Anne was an enthusiastic user from the start and gradually her understanding of the new sounds increased, along with her confidence. On 20 May 1986, a year after her operation, she spoke of her experiences at the Better Hearing Conference.

> You may want to know—how does it sound, this new language? It can be crackly, squeaky, metallic, rumbly, jumbled, resonant, piercing and quite unlike the sounds I think I can remember. But with variations in pitch, rhythm and length the noises do have some meaning—especially with imagination and wild guesses. Being unable to hear speech clearly is the main drawback. But lip-reading is a lot easier now, so communication is better. Sometimes while talking with my husband I have been able to follow him when he covers his mouth and lets me see just the top half of his face. I can also lip-read him side-on while he is driving the car, which means a safer trip. So, perhaps I am gradually hearing with my ears and not only with my eyes. My own head noises are thankfully less troublesome. I almost forget about them while using the implant.

Anne also had to adjust to the bionic ear equipment.

> The gadgets aren't hard to manage once you get used to them. The headpiece I now wear is a vast improvement on the first over-the-head style, as it stays firmly in place at all times and isn't noticed by me or anyone else. The cord can be a problem if the speech processor is worn on a belt, as the connecting part is delicate. Twice we have had to send for a replacement, so I found a safer place to stow the processor.

She continued:

> Interactions with people came with a rush following our brief moment of fame on the Willesee program and then a photo in the newspaper. We received many warm letters, some from people with whom we have had no contact for many years. We had to answer many questions and try to explain the benefits and limitations. An increase in confidence means I can talk more comfortably with new acquaintances, as well as shop and business people. Friends seem to have become more relaxed and chatty, so conversations are more natural. This means I can manage nearly everyone in small doses. It can be tiring talking to even only one or two people for very long.
>
> Many outdoor and indoor sounds help to make life more interesting and also more safe. Some of the recognisable ones are quite surprising— on a quiet day in the country I can pick out a dog barking from across the valley about half a mile away. I really enjoy the rural noises—streams

and rivers, rain falling, waves and wind, as well as sheep, frogs, lots of birds, and even a peacock rustling his tail feathers. Traffic noises are not pleasant, but bearable. They make life safer.

Within the house, general awareness is better, especially if I stand still to listen, as my own movements can be a noisy distraction. I can now recognise doorbells, the phone ringing, the kettle boiling, a baby crying, people coughing, sneezing and laughing, and even air-conditioners, refrigerators and the dog's toe-nails clicking on the vinyl floor. There are some peculiar effects where high frequencies dominate and voices seem to disappear. This can happen when meat sizzles in a frying pan or when plastic wrap and Alfoil are rustled, or even when the crickets in the garden start up their monotonous chorus on warm nights. Then the OFF switch can be very useful.

Limitations must be much like those of any lip-reader and severely deaf hearing-aid user. I am quite out of my depth in groups or at theatres and concerts. Music holds no pleasure, nor does TV. Use of the tele-phone is restricted to mostly one-way talks with family members. To hear my own voice is strange and off-putting. It may sound soft to others, but to me it mostly seems excessively loud. People tell me it is a better modulated voice than previously, so I try to believe that and not think that I sound like a fog-horn. At no time did we expect the implant could restore much of my hearing, but rather that it would help with communication and so improve the quality of life. With the support of family and friends, I have found this to be true. It seems important to look on this learning and adapting as an enjoyment and not a worry. I can well understand the shock and disappointment that some optimists might feel when they first realise that their cochlear implant does not enable them to hear running speech. The more successful results gen-erally come to those whose hearing loss has been much shorter than mine.

In summary, this marvellous device certainly works for me—up to a point. I am still improving its value by working hard at it, and it has brought an excitement into my life that outweighs its difficulties. It has not been my nature to seek support from organised groups, but I believe now that I would be happy to be part of one—perhaps as a giver as well as a taker.

We have maintained our speech research and found ways of present-ing more information through the bionic ear. The advances were passed on to Anne and, by 1987, speech was sounding more natural and she could talk over the phone more easily. Nucleus, and by now its subsidiary, Cochlear Pty Limited, had done away with the head-band to hold the transmitting radio aerial over the implant. Paired magnets were being used instead. A special magnet was also placed over Anne's implant through a small operation that enabled her to use the bionic ear much more freely. Further advances in speech processing in 1989 and 1990 have been implemented in her bionic ear to help in hearing speech and other sounds. In 1995, Anne reflected as follows:

> In the last decade I have appreciated significant improvements in the equipment worn, especially the processor, which has almost done away with the need to lip-read. I now envy the latest breed of implantees who don't have to wear the pocket-sized processor at chest level and put up with the cord leading to the behind-the-ear microphone. And there is talk of further miniaturised marvels.

I yearned that Anne and all my patients would be able to hear speech without having to rely on lip-reading. A year after Anne's implant, she was using the telephone to have limited conversations with David. In 1999 I wanted to find out just how much improvement she had made, so I rang their number on the off-chance that she would answer. To my surprise, Anne picked up the phone, and we had a remarkably fluent conversation! She described the conversation as follows:

> My husband came home to find me sitting at the telephone chatting to one of my very special friends. (Remember, I couldn't have heard the telephone for 35 years even if it had blown up in front of me!) Professor Graeme Clark had telephoned to ask how I was progressing, and I heard the telephone, identified the voice, and had a normal—but miraculous—conversation!

2

My childhood

Creatures who feel as keenly as I do, and are
unable to change this characteristic of their
nature, have to dissimulate it at least as much
as possible.

Marie Curie, 1888

DAD'S DEAFNESS

One of my earliest childhood memories is of living with a father who was deaf, in the days before hearing aids had become readily available. It was a cause of some embarrassment. Friends would come over and Dad would seem aloof. Mum usually had to carry the conversation.

Dad first noticed difficulty hearing in 1927 when he was twenty-two and had commenced pharmacy. He went to his local doctor in Glen Innes, New South Wales, and asked to have the wax cleaned out of his ear. 'I'm sorry, Mr Clark,' said Dr Gall. 'You don't have any wax. Your hearing might get better if you hold your nose, blow up your cheeks and pop your ears.' But it made no difference.

By 1932, when he had become engaged to my mother, his hearing had deteriorated. He sought advice from a Macquarie Street specialist in Sydney who, after examining him, said: 'Mr Clark, I can't do anything to help you. Your hearing loss will worsen.' Dad was very concerned, and arranged to meet my mother to discuss their future. Dad thought Mum would be foolish to go ahead with the marriage. Neither of them knew what the future would be like, but Mum said she would stay with Dad whatever happened.

During my childhood, Dad's deafness became worse. One holiday we were staying in a hotel in Oberon, a small country town in western New

My father, Colin Clark, in his pharmacy in Camden, 1943.

South Wales, and had a room near the public bar. During the night there was a lot of shouting and banging. Mum was fearful the shearers and pea-pickers would break in and assault us, so she stacked furniture against the door. In the morning, Dad asked: 'What's all that furniture doing over there?' He hadn't heard a thing, and consequently knew nothing of Mum's mental anguish during the night. It was so easy for Dad to sleep soundly.

I was most embarrassed over Dad's hearing loss when I was in his pharmacy. I spent hours in the shop helping to dispense medicines, washing bottles and serving at the front counter to earn some money. People would come in and ask for an item. Dad would sometimes give them the wrong thing, or ask them to speak up. All the other customers would be able to hear what items had been requested. To help relieve the embarrassment, I would stand guard, signal that I knew where the item was located, and rush off and get it.

In spite of all his problems, with the help and understanding of his family and others, my father managed successfully to carry on with his work until he was fitted with one of the first hearing aids after the Second World War ended in 1945.

As a result of these experiences, I resolved I would become an ear doctor and try to help people like my father. I didn't know how I would achieve this goal, but it grew into a burning ambition.

PRE-SCHOOL

I was born on 16 August 1935 at our home in the small country town of Camden, in New South Wales. In those days, many women had their babies at the residence of a midwife. These midwives received their training through an apprenticeship, and often the knowledge was passed down from mother to daughter. My mother, who always considered her options carefully, decided it would be safer to have a trained nursing sister, who had also qualified in obstetrics, with her at a home delivery. Sister Absalom slept in the second bedroom for two weeks prior to my birth, which meant that my father was relegated to the back veranda. At that time, fathers weren't encouraged to be present at a birth, and when I was born in the early hours of the morning he was asleep. The officiating medico, a big, warmhearted man whose specialist training in obstetrics was limited, arrived too late to assist in the delivery. As there had been doubts as to how well he would cope in an emergency, it was a good thing for me that my birth was normal.

My arrival quickly changed my parents' lifestyle, as there were many interrupted nights. My father's deafness meant he couldn't hear my cries, so I was attended to mostly by my mother. Later, however, when I was a few months old, I became very active and an early riser. Dad, not one to wake up at the crack of dawn, was nevertheless called on at 5 a.m. to take me for a walk in the stroller. My high level of activity was to continue throughout my childhood.

I tested my mother to the limit in finding things for me to do. She was wonderfully patient, but in the end I had to discover ways to entertain myself. At two years of age I said I had had enough, and packed my bags to see the world. At age four, I remember using my mother's lipstick to disguise myself as a 'Red' Indian (having had my father read to me from E.S. Ellis on the exploits of Deerfoot, the noble warrior), and sitting on the front pavement waving to passers-by. When older, I would try and make money to buy 'bull's eyes' at the local sweet shop by harvesting the seeds of the vine that grew like a weed on our neighbour's fence. The seeds were packaged in the envelopes used for the church collection, and I hawked them up and down John Street.

Before attending school, my home was my source of stimulation, as were my friends, the neighbours' children, in particular Ken Whiteman.

The author aged two years, with bags packed, setting out to leave home and see the world.

Having Ken as a friend meant I had the complete run of his father's produce store. It was stacked high with bags of chaff that were excellent for somersaulting from, or burrowing between, to make secret passages. Fortunately, the bags didn't collapse on us, as we could have been suffocated.

As my sister Robin grew up she was admitted to this inner circle of friends, after tolerating dirt being rubbed in her hair, and being pushed into 'well-disguised' animal traps. My mother instilled in us children the importance of helping each other, and Robin and my brother Bruce, born ten years later, provided great family support and encouragement through the trying years spent developing the bionic ear.

PRIMARY SCHOOL

I started in kindergarten at the Camden Primary School, and had a kindly teacher, Mrs Pat Hider (now Colman). She had me tracing the shapes of numbers on the blackboard. During enforced quiet times, she asked us to lie still and let our minds go blank—something I have never been able to do. She soon realised that I needed more stimulation, and so I was moved up a grade. Right through my schooling I was a year younger than my classmates.

After a few years I formed some good friends at the primary school, and felt grown up being with them, as they were more 'worldly-wise' than I. To satisfy our desire to be mature, we decided to smoke. We weren't allowed to go into the cafes to buy cigarettes, but we succeeded in getting tobacco by picking up all the discarded cigarette butts from the gutter along the main street of Camden. When we had filleted enough tobacco from the butts, we went to Cassimatis's cafe and bought cigarette papers. They didn't suspect that we were buying them for ourselves. The next problem was to find somewhere to smoke without being detected. We picked a spot in Fred Skinner's father's vegetable garden, down by the Nepean River near the 'Little Sandy' swimming hole. When we got there, it looked ideal as the corn had grown high and we found a clear space in the middle that would be well hidden. We then lit up and began to puff away. Unfortunately, the smoke was seen rising from the middle of the field by Mr Skinner and, fearing a fire, he came down to investigate. I can remember going home with his threats ringing in my ears that he would tell my parents when he next came to sell them vegetables.

Cubs was a great outlet for my energy, and I enjoyed the fantasy of being part of the Mowgli story. I was the wolf, Grey Brother, and gained my two stars by learning to tie knots, play games and do first aid. Then came the challenge of winning badges: Collector, Artist, Toymaster, Gardener, Athlete, Homecraft, House Orderly, Guide, First Aid, Team Player, Observer, and Swimming. I found most of these easy, as I was already running a garden, painting landscapes, doing carpentry, knitting, boxing and training at athletics. I was disappointed in only winning eleven of the twelve badges. To obtain the swimming badge, I had to float for ten seconds without moving, but as my body was too heavy in the legs, I would invariably touch bottom at nine seconds.

Dad was a very good father, and I learned a lot about being a doctor through working in his dispensary. He would let me experiment with the chemicals, and taught me what they were used for. Instead of going home after school, I would rush to his shop. I became 'the Bunsen burner boy'. I watched him, too, when he tested people's sight, as he was also an optometrist. I learned about eye problems, and enjoyed being allowed to look at the back of someone's eye.

I also developed a keen interest in people and their medical problems, while assisting in the pharmacy, and discovered what doctors prescribed for different ailments. Magnesium and calcium carbonate relieved indigestion, and potassium citrate made the urine alkaline for kidney and bladder infections. Senega and ammonia loosened the secretions with a cough, and rhubarb root or senna pods made the bowels run if you were constipated. For a tonic or general pick-me-up, one of the best ingredients was liquor of strychnine. Sometimes, the doctor would even add a little brandy, without the patient knowing. People who were teetotallers would come back for more, saying what great medicine it was.

I began to learn clinical judgement by relating a person's illness to their physique, job and family background. It became a challenge to try and guess someone's ailment or what prescription they had when they came into the shop. I also discovered the idiosyncrasies of the doctors, and how this affected what they were likely to prescribe.

It dawned on me that being a pharmacist wasn't just about making up medicines, but involved relations with people. There were also ethical considerations. Although my father was in competition for customers, he taught me how important it was to stand up for what you believe to be the right course of action, even when it wouldn't bring personal gain. For example, at that time it was possible to buy antibiotics over the counter without a prescription. The medical profession was just becoming aware that antibiotics used indiscriminately could lead to resistant strains of bacteria, and so Dad refused to provide them to customers unless prescribed by a doctor, even though they could get them over the counter elsewhere.

What struck me most was my father's honesty and integrity, and the genuine, quiet interest he took in his customers, regardless of their status in Camden society, a society which, surprisingly perhaps, had a definite class structure. In those days, 'tramps' would sometimes come in asking for money for sustenance. They were always directed to the nearby cafe at Dad's expense. By his example, he also taught me to stand up against the crowd. Though not an absolute teetotaller, at the bowling club, where members were expected to drink alcohol, he only drank lemon squash.

My debt to my mother is just as great. She showed me the value of creativity, which she expressed as a gifted pianist and watercolour artist. She was generous almost to a fault. Her greatest joy was to give to her

The author with his parents, sister Robin and brother Bruce, Camden, 1949.

family. We were her life, and she would take on our concerns as though they were her own. She, too, mixed in all walks of Camden society, and after her death it was said that she was a lady in the true sense of the word. She didn't want me to go into medicine, thinking it would be stressful and difficult, and involve many late nights. She wanted me to be a pharmacist, like my father, because it was a secure and stable way of life. However, I had already decided I wanted to be a doctor and to help deaf people.

One day I asked our family medico, Dr Jim, what qualities were needed to be a doctor. 'You just need a good memory,' he said. That didn't sound too difficult. I also remember when I was ten our Methodist minister asked me what I wanted to be when I grew up, and I replied, 'an eye and ear doctor'.

My emerging interest in medicine was given a boost in my last year in primary school in 1945. When the school doctor came to check the health of all the pupils, I was given the responsibility of evaluating their hearing by holding a watch close to their ears, and asking them to tell in which hand they heard the watch. It was also war time, and as a first aid officer I carried a bag with antiseptic, safety pins, bandages and sticking plaster into the 'trenches' in the playground. If the 'enemy' scored a direct hit or there were shrapnel injuries, it was assumed that I would know what to do!

I was fortunate that Mum and Dad had surrounded themselves with good books, and I mostly read the ones about medicine and science. Two books that really impressed me were *The Life of Louis Pasteur* and *Madame Curie*. Pasteur fascinated me with his beautiful yet simple experiments that showed why wine fermented. He didn't stop at fermentation, but demonstrated how vaccination could prevent anthrax and cholera in animals. He spent many hours finding out how to immunise against rabies, a frequently fatal disease spread by the bite of an infected dog. He had to risk vaccinating a young boy before the vaccine was completely proven, and saved his life. If he could do those things, I wondered, why couldn't I?

I set up a very crude laboratory in Mum's laundry, and started to think about the biological challenges in my backyard. One of my activities was to run a vegetable garden, and I noticed that I was losing tomato plants. The leaves were all turning yellow and the tomatoes looked pretty bad. Was this due to something in the soil, or could it be one of the organisms that Pasteur had discovered? I set about conducting experiments. Playing around in Dad's shop with glass-blowing enabled me to make a crude syringe. Using a cork as a plunger, I extracted material from one plant that looked diseased and injected it into another that had a healthy appearance. I then monitored the progress of the tomato plants. I didn't discover a causal agent for the disease, so I assumed there was something wrong with the soil. This was the start of my curiosity about biology and my desire to make discoveries.

From Dale Carnegie's book *How to Win Friends and Influence People*, I learned that to be a good conversationalist, you had to be a good listener. I thought it strange that people would think someone spoke well if they just listened. So, to try it out, I paid a visit to Mrs Evans, wife of the manager of the Rural Bank, who knew our family well. I spent some time asking her about herself and her family, and she rang my mother to say what a good conversationalist I was. My experiment had worked!

I felt very fortunate to be brought up in a country town with all the freedom it provided. I was also aware of the beauty of nature. On my birthday, I would invite friends to a paddock to play games among the bushes or climb over old logs. By the Nepean River there were little sandy beaches enclosed by tea-trees. Paths could be discovered through the thickets, and they would break out into open areas bordered by majestic gum trees. I would often ride my bike along the back lanes, and sit under a gum tree in a paddock just thinking, planning and dreaming. As I got older, I thought about the meaning of life. Was there a God, or a reality beyond what I could see and hear? I later found contemplation to be of great importance in developing ideas for research.

SECONDARY SCHOOL

At the age of eleven, in 1947, I was sent to Sydney Boys High School, as there were no high schools in Camden. My father wrote to the head-master, who agreed to take me provided I stayed during the week with relations in Sydney and didn't travel all the way from Camden each day. My grandmother and grandfather Thomas put me up for a year in their flat at Brook Court in Brook Street, Coogee. I had the opportunity to get to know my grandmother especially well. Like my mother, she was a creative and intelligent person who was a wonderful role model. She was also accepting of adversity, no more so than a year or two later, when she developed inoperable cancer.

On Monday mornings I would be up at 6.30 a.m. and run to the station to catch the little steam train, 'Puffing Billy', to Campbelltown. At Campbelltown I would then board the main steam train to Sydney, unless there was ice on the track at Kenny Hill. When this occurred, 'Puffing Billy' didn't have the power to get up the steep grade, so the passengers had to get out and walk while the driver poured sand on the rails for traction. On the Goulburn Express to the city, there was always a group of us who sat together in the same 'dog box'. We formed an exclusive club. On arriving at Central Railway Station at about 8.30 a.m., I would run down to Eddy Avenue to catch the tram up Chalmers Street and through Strawberry Hills to Sydney Boys High School. Untrue to its name, Strawberry Hills was an area of overcrowded, dilapidated tenement houses that made returning to school all the more depressing.

As my grandparents could only have me stay for a year, due to the fatigue that foreshadowed my grandmother's cancer, my parents had to arrange for me to go to another school. When the summer holidays of 1948 were over, I was packed up in the Chevrolet and taken to be a boarder at the Scots College. I wouldn't see my family again until the next holidays, except for a mid-term break. I felt I was being sentenced to gaol. For the first few months at Aspinall House I was in a bed in the corridor that led to the boss's apartment. I felt very lonely, and would often cry myself to sleep at night.

On being transferred to Royle House, I discovered that I was going to have to put on a brave front if I was to survive, as the house seemed to contain the toughest boys at the school. Gradually, I learned that the way to be accepted was to try and relate to the other boys, and to participate in sports. Scholastic performance was of lesser importance. Fortunately, I wasn't too bad at athletics, and had in my primary school years been obsessed with learning how to play various cricket strokes. I also threw myself into playing rugby in the winter term. Even if you only had one leg, you could be in the Z-team.

To my surprise, I was put in the back line of the Under 13 A-rugby union team where I was expected not only to weave and swerve through the opposition, but also to deal them a bone-shattering tackle when they advanced with the ball. Before long, my performance in the Under 13 A-team was noted by the House first football team members. The team had a large number of players from the school's first team, one of whom later played A-grade for the state. They needed to distribute some of their good footballers into the seconds team so that we would win at all levels. For this reason, I (a slightly-built newcomer to the school) was promoted to the wing of the first House team at the age of twelve. My most notable experience was when a burly Aspinall House player broke loose, and there was only me between him and the try line. I thought my best option was to go through the motions of a tackle; if I missed, it would still look good. As he came steaming towards me like an express train, the idea of grabbing him around the ankles in the correct manner seemed suicidal. As he got closer I couldn't bear to look, so I shut my eyes. At the same time, instead of a low tackle, I grasped at the air at thigh level. To my great surprise, he jumped just as I lunged, and I caught him around the ankles. He thudded to the ground amid the cheers from the House. I was a hero.

Playing rugby each year would drain my physical energy, so that I would catch flu just before it was time to go home for the end-of-term holidays. This would require treatment at the school hospital, which would delay my departure. It had its compensations, however, because

I would be cared for by an attractive nursing sister. There were also endless rounds of card games to play before finally being pronounced well enough to leave.

Cricket was one of my greatest enjoyments and I remained in the A-team as the opening batsman. My self-training in playing the correct strokes, through studying Donald Bradman's book, had paid off. In my last year at school, when I was trying to find time to do my Leaving Certificate studies and didn't turn up at practice, our coach Tony Rae still kept me in the team, which went through the season undefeated.

If my last two years at boarding school weren't already busy enough, it was made compulsory to join the Army Cadet corps. As with football, there was no escape. Although I didn't relish the thought of training to kill people, I figured that as it wasn't for real I might as well do it to the best of my ability. During the holiday before my last year at school (1950), I volunteered to go to Singleton to attend the Officer Training School. After learning to fire a real Bren gun, throw hand grenades, and go on search and destroy missions at night, and memorising the training handbook, I passed my officer exams. I could now look forward to getting respect from the troops, and could even send them on disciplinary runs around the oval with their rifles held above their heads.

Boarding was a wonderful way of learning to use time efficiently for study. For a boarder, the week would unfold in the following way: formal sports practice two days a week after school; voluntary sports practice on a further two days; and cadets on Friday afternoon. Homework for the boarder in junior years was a strict two-hour session after tea. In later years, some study could be done in the House for an additional hour.

On Saturday morning, it was off to play your game of football or cricket, and that might mean going half-way across Sydney by public transport. It was also compulsory to go and watch the school first football team play in the afternoon and to barrack for them. Cheering for the school as it struggled for a place at the rowing regatta was mandatory. Then, on Saturday evening, we watched an out-of-date film in the school hall. Occasionally this might be a more memorable one, like *Arsenic and Old Lace* or *The Lavender Hill Mob*. This routine meant that we had very little chance to develop our social skills with girls.

On Sunday morning, it was off to St Stephen's Presbyterian Church in the city by bus to sit up in the stalls while the Minister, known as

'Bory Tory', gave his sermon. Apparently attentive, we were actually vying with each other to write the most creative or rude comments in the hymnbooks, which would then be passed around for replies and further comments. These books were locked away exclusively for the school's use, never to be shown to anyone. After the service we were free for five hours. I would catch the tram out to my Uncle Keith and Aunt Kathleen Thomas's place at Coogee, and have lunch and spend the afternoon with their family of three daughters, my cousins Margaret, Judith and Elizabeth. It was wonderful to feel part of a family, even if just for a few hours. During these visits I would have discussions with my uncle about my future career. He encouraged me to study medicine, as he could see how enthusiastic I was about becoming a doctor.

I had some wonderful teachers who inspired me, especially Rhys Jones and Tony Rae in English, 'Hoey' (Dr L.M. Simmons) in chemistry, and Fred Pollack in maths. I believe that Rhys Jones's methods later helped me in my medical studies. He was absolutely fanatical about summaries, and inductive and deductive thinking. While others read Shakespeare, we would have to summarise different passages and then reproduce them in our own words. This discipline helped me to organise my thoughts and keep abreast of information that I needed in my study and practice of medicine and, later, bionic ear research. I also remember with gratitude Barny Cubis, a history teacher, who would sometimes take chapel on Sunday evening. He saw the wonder of new life, and God's hand in it, and he and the chaplain, Reverend Bruce Gentle, encouraged me to join the Student Christian Movement when I went to university.

3

Becoming an ear surgeon

> For me there can be no recreation in human
> intercourse, no conversation, no exchange of
> thoughts with my fellow-men. In solitary exile
> I am compelled to live.
>
> *Ludwig van Beethoven*, The Heiligenstadt Testament, *1802*

UNDERGRADUATE MEDICINE, UNIVERSITY OF SYDNEY

The end of secondary school meant that I could start medicine, and in 1952, at the age of sixteen, I enrolled for first year studies at the University of Sydney. Zoology, botany, chemistry and physics were interesting enough subjects, but how could the intestines of the hydatid worm, the sexual reproduction of a flowering plant, the chemical structure of alcohol, or the bending of light through a prism be relevant to the real issues of being a doctor, I wondered?

The university was also a meeting ground for ideas and philosophies: theosophy, atheism, Marxism, Christianity. I threw my lot in with the Student Christian Movement, where the big issue was relating evolution and determinism to the teachings of the Bible. The debates helped me to see that science and theology were two different and complementary ways of looking at reality. That year, on a national Student Christian Movement camp at Otford in New South Wales, I committed my life in a personal way to Jesus Christ.

On the strength of the first year exam results, I was invited to spend a significant part of my summer holidays doing prescribed dissections of the human body. If they were well done, you were made a prosector in anatomy and the dissection was placed in the University of Sydney's Anatomy museum.

I was given two tasks. The first was to prepare a dissection of the front of the elbow joint so that doctors and nurses could see the structures they might injure when giving injections into the main vein. The second dissection was the hamstring muscles at the back of the thigh, commonly injured in football.

We prosectors dissected one body on our own and another with the general group. As my surname started with 'C', I was with Chinese students whose names were Chong, Cheung and Chow. Friendships are formed while dissecting, and this also meant discovering the best of the Chinese restaurants in Dixon Street.

In the summer holidays at the end of second year, the Anatomy Department provided an additional body for enthusiastic students wishing to improve their knowledge of anatomy, and George Dunea and I got stuck into it! After Christmas the family went to Avalon Beach for a holiday, and in case I became bored I took with me my weighty physiology textbook on body function. In between swims I started reading. I found it so interesting that eventually I read it from cover to cover, something I hadn't done with any of my other textbooks. Although I had always been interested in the anatomy of the body, I now began to find its function even more fascinating.

Anatomy in the third year involved understanding the structure of the brain, and to assist me in my studies I bought one from the mortuary. This practice would not be condoned today, and is now illegal under the *Human Tissue Act*. I kept it in our laundry, which doubled as my study when I was home at the weekends. Florrie Gillespie, who came to boil up the copper and help Mum do the washing, would have been shocked if she had known what was on the top shelf. Thus began an absorbing interest in brain function and neuroscience.

In the third year exam, a high distinction in physiology was my best result. One of the main questions was the function of the inner ear, and although most students didn't think examiners placed much importance on this structure, I had read a lot about it purely out of interest.

Sometimes students took a year out to do a Bachelor of Medical Science degree, and I was offered a place by Professor Peter Bishop to do research with him on vision and brain science. I knew it would have been an excellent opportunity to start my research, but I declined as it wasn't on hearing and I felt I had to train as a surgeon as soon as possible.

The August holidays in 1954 were a pause between the basic medical sciences and future clinical work with patients in hospitals. For once I forgot medicine, and I am so glad I did. My sister Robin brought one of her school friends home for the weekend. Margaret Burtenshaw, who was fifteen at the time, captivated me. This visit started a friendship that seven years later led to marriage. Without Margaret's support as a companion I could not have developed the bionic ear; it is as much her achievement as mine.

In fourth year, at long last, we launched into clinical medicine. This meant treading the wards of the Royal Prince Alfred Hospital (RPA) in Sydney—meeting patients, feeling their lumps and bumps, listening to their heart murmurs and discussing their problems.

In my summer holidays I found I could further satisfy my new-found passion for clinical medicine through Dr Crookston, one of Camden's family doctors with a strong interest in surgery. He gave me permission to use a small pathology laboratory so that I could do blood tests on some of his patients. I attended ward rounds with him, and even took blood from the same vein I had once dissected for my prosection in anatomy. The biggest thrill was when I was allowed to go into the operating theatre and watch him perform a gastrectomy—that is, removal of part of someone's stomach. To see it actually happening helped me to appreciate the training and skill needed.

In fourth year we also had to learn about the causes of disease and its pharmacological treatment. I tried hard to learn everything, but I only succeeded in getting a pass mark and even had to do a 'post'—a supplementary exam in one of the subjects. To find out the results I had joined the crowd of students who went to the printing office the night before they were published in the daily newspaper. I was shocked when my name wasn't on the list. The worst part was having to spend my summer holidays going over a subject I wasn't especially interested in.

I had obviously not learned to study properly. In medicine you have to understand the important information, and not the minutiae. I vowed that in the remaining two years, I would summarise the essential information and simply make sure that I passed. The plan worked so well that to my surprise and everyone else's, I topped my final year of medicine.

POSTGRADUATE TRAINING IN SYDNEY

As a raw resident medical officer at the RPA, I was quite unprepared for the tough routine. I have never worked so hard in all my life! There was no forty-hour week. While doing surgery I would often start at 8 a.m. on Monday, help with emergencies during the day and right through Monday night, assist at routine surgery all Tuesday, and then look after these patients until midnight—forty hours straight. I was on call for patients every second night and every second weekend. I also had to sleep at the hospital during the week, even when off-duty. I had to learn not to make mistakes although I was nearly falling asleep on my feet.

At times I felt I was simply a clerk having to fill out a myriad of requests for pathological tests that my senior resident or registrar thought might help. Then, at night, there would be piles of patient histories waiting to be summarised.

A never-ending routine of ordering tests and running blood and saline into veins would unexpectedly be interrupted by an emergency. For the doctor on the scene, it might mean a cardiac massage, putting a tube into the windpipe to assist breathing, or giving a drug to relieve an asthmatic attack.

I also had to learn the idiosyncrasies of the senior nurses and doctors and how to humour them. For example, the charge sister, nicknamed 'Leaping Lena', had served at the hospital for many years and knew all there was to know about the management of neurosurgical patients. As a lowly junior resident I arrived thinking I could tell her a thing or two, but almost invariably I found I was wrong. Another character, one of the surgeons, had a preoccupation with making sure his patients weren't con-stipated and would arrive at all hours to check that I hadn't left them in discomfort.

At the end of the year it came as a big shock not to be in the group of residents selected to stay on for a further year's resident training at RPA. I had worked hard, though I was rather immature, and it was a surprise and a blow to the ego. Not being reappointed, however, turned out for the best, as I was selected as a senior resident to the Royal North Shore Hospital, and this led me towards a surgical career.

In 1959, when I took up my duties at the Royal North Shore Hospital, it was called the 'Country Club' and certainly had a different atmosphere from RPA. It was smaller and the pace was less frenetic. I welcomed the change and was determined to do my best. After I had topped my year, I temporarily changed my ambition to be an ear, nose and throat surgeon to that of a cardiac physician, because physicians were thought of as the 'thinking doctors' and surgeons as the doers, mere craftsmen. Unfortunately, all the terms with physicians were offered to those who had been junior residents at the hospital previously, so I really had no choice but to accept the surgical ones with gratitude.

Being settled into surgical jobs, I set about teaching myself to tie knots and stitch up the skin. After work, when I had returned to stay with my elderly aunt Varley and uncle Perce Youdale in Lindfield, I would get out the needle, thread, needle-holding forceps and artery forceps and stitch up the bedspread and tie knots until I became almost expert.

The year at the Royal North Shore Hospital gave me a very good grounding in surgery, with terms in heart and lung, vascular and thyroid, trauma, and gynaecology and obstetrics. Heart surgery was fairly primitive by present-day standards. However, Dr Ian Monk, a masterly surgeon, would go regularly to the laboratory to try out new procedures on sheep, and I remembered the importance of using experimental animals when developing the bionic ear.

A term in general surgery with Drs Felix Rundle, Tom Reeve and Doug Tracey drove home later the value of creating a specialised, interdisciplinary team for the management of children and adults. Those surgeons had developed excellence in thyroid surgery through collaboration with the physicians and nuclear physicists.

I was really keen to do a good job in this unit, and I made my mark one day when assisting Felix Rundle and Tom Reeve at a thyroid operation. When cutting into the thyroid to remove part of it, Felix found a nodule that looked quite unusual. While he was thinking about it, I had the inspiration to suggest it might be a Hurthle-cell adenoma, a rare tumour. This suggestion quite impressed him, and then even more so when I told him that I had arranged for a frozen section to be carried out by pathology should that be required. With frozen sections the tissue is sent straight to pathology and sectioned on the spot. A report is then given to the surgeon within fifteen minutes, so it can influence how he or she proceeds with the surgery. The frozen section was duly done, and the result came back: Hurthle-cell adenoma. Felix thought for a moment, and then said: 'Clark, all your sins are forgiven you.' Then he revised it: 'Clark, *some* of your sins are forgiven.'

Of the other two terms at Royal North Shore, one was on second-ment to Wollongong Hospital where I had charge of the Casualty Depart-ment, which was the main one for this large industrial city and shipping port. It was here that I saw life in the raw. One might see a young girl with venereal disease after a pack rape, and next a man with 100 per cent burns from having fallen into boiling water at the BHP Steel Works. I saw medicine at its best, and its worst. But I enjoyed having the respon-sibility of being in the front line for the management of patients. I also achieved local notoriety through the Wollongong newspaper when I removed the appendix of a patient named Clark who was being operated on in the Clark Theatre, with an anaesthetist named Clark.

Having embarked on a surgical career, the only way forward was to pass an exam where I had to know all the anatomy of the body in great detail. The best way to do this was to spend a year as a tutor to medical students studying anatomy at the University of Sydney, and in return receive teaching from the senior staff of the Department. I applied to be part of this small band of tutors and was accepted.

In 1960, as a tutor in anatomy, I had a respite from the demands of a hospital residency and could not only spend time studying, but start thinking about girls again. Being a resident had put my social life on hold, and I had lost touch with Margaret. On meeting again we fell in love, and decided to get married within two years.

To increase my knowledge of anatomy, I also hit upon the idea of obtaining a human leg so that I could dissect it at home. I approached one of the surgeons at a local city hospital to ask if any amputations were being undertaken. I was in luck. I was given a leg that I preserved in formalin and kept in a drum under the house in Camden. This presented my father with a problem some years later when he was tidying up while I was overseas. What was he to do with a dissected leg? As he often did when in doubt on medical issues, he sought advice from our local doctor. The result was he took it to the incredulous attendant at the hospital incinerator!

Before the first part surgical exam to become a Fellow of the Royal Australasian College of Surgeons I knew my anatomy so well I could recite the relationships between structures while driving the car through traffic.

The group I was in became so practised that someone could throw one of the little bones in the wrist into the air, and we could identify not only what bone it was, but which side it came from, before it was caught.

After passing the exam I was invited back to RPA. My first job was as a registrar in brain surgery, as well as being responsible for surgical emergencies in a general surgical unit. The training in brain surgery was later helpful to me when developing the surgery for the bionic ear, where it became necessary to drill through the skull to the lining of the brain to make a bed deep enough for the implanted receiver-stimulator section. I also enjoyed the emergency surgical work and developed expertise in removing badly infected appendices. These were quite difficult operations, as often the patients had reached the hospital at a late stage. The appendix had to be carefully dissected from around the abscess. There was always the danger, when doing this, of pulling on the large vein at the back of the abdomen, thus causing severe bleeding. This surgical training was important in my developing the confidence to handle different situations quickly and safely.

After three months a vacancy arose as the registrar in ear, nose and throat surgery, and I knew that the time had come to start fulfilling my childhood ambition to help deaf people. It was like entering a new world. Although the work was performed down the cavities of the ear, nose and throat, where it is more difficult to see, the operating microscope was just being introduced, making it possible to see everything enlarged. This also meant using fine drills and other instruments. The speciality was being transformed into a top-flight one, and the staff were very enthusiastic about using the microscope to restore hearing by replacing one of the middle ear bones (the stirrup) with a steel strut, when it was blocked from sending sound vibrations to the inner ear. I also had the responsibility of doing the hearing tests to select people for the surgery. In 1961 I had to virtually teach myself how to do the tests, as there was no professional training available in Australia in audiology.

At the end of the year, Margaret and I planned to marry and go to Scotland and England so that I could gain more surgical experience. The trip was also a great chance to cement our relationship away from the family, and to share in a whole new set of experiences. The plan was for Margaret to teach to earn some money, while I studied to pass my exam in general surgery in Edinburgh, which some consider to be the home of

Margaret and Graeme Clark were married at the Burwood Methodist Church, 27 December 1961, by Dr R.B. Lew.

surgery. I would then look for an ear, nose and throat job in London. We wed on 27 December 1961 and sailed for the United Kingdom on 30 December on the HMS *Oriana*.

POSTGRADUATE TRAINING IN SCOTLAND AND ENGLAND

Our trip was meant to be a honeymoon, but that had to wait. We could only afford a berth way down below the waterline. As a result, in the Great Australian Bight and the Bay of Biscay we were dreadfully seasick. As newlyweds, we found it a little irksome to be reprimanded by the waiter if we were late for breakfast, and were surprised at how restricted we felt even on a large liner.

The highlights of the voyage were day tours in each of Colombo, Aden, Cairo and Naples. After three-and-a-half weeks on board ship, it was a relief to arrive. It was very exciting to be in England for the first time: this was the country of our ancestors, and about which we had read much in our literature and history books.

We weren't very organised travellers and had brought ten suitcases and trunks filled with clothes as well as all of Margaret's university notes and our wedding presents. Our luggage formed a great mound on the Southhampton docks and had to be moved in stages to the train to London and finally to Edinburgh.

We arrived in Edinburgh on a cold Sunday afternoon in winter, and found even the churches closed. The architecture was so different from Sydney's, and the city buildings had a sombre, black appearance from layers of ingrained soot. It emphasised how far we were from our families and friends. By contrast, our accommodation in the Victoria League House, which catered for students from the colonies—South Africa, Australia, India, and so on—was quite a refuge. Some Scottish women who took an interest in the students had placed a vase filled with wattle in our room. They will never know how much we appreciated their gesture. We soon adapted to the place and felt at home, as there were other compatriots from Australia, including John Leeton, who later played an important role in the in vitro fertilisation (IVF) program at Monash University.

The Edinburgh College of Surgery was ancient in appearance, but seemed to capture the great tradition of surgery in Scotland dating back to the sixteenth century. I imagined the great Lord Lister walking through its portals. I joined the throng of potential surgeons from all around the Commonwealth going to the lectures to prepare for the examination that would allow us to use the famous letters 'FRCS (Edinburgh)' after our names.

For mobility, Margaret and I bought an Austin panel van; it was to be our means of transport for the next two years. It was old, and the driver's window wouldn't close, so we had to rug up during winter outings. Driving also presented new experiences like tobogganing down a snow-covered farm road in the van.

At the end of May I passed the exam. To celebrate, we went on a belated honeymoon, touring around Scotland and Ireland. We had an indoor Aladdin heater that we thought would do for cooking, but as it blew out in the least wind we mostly resorted to dining on tins of sardines and mixed vegetables served cold. It was a carefree interlude before my next phase of work in London.

On arriving in London, the FRCS in general surgery helped me to secure a training position at the Royal National Throat, Nose and Ear Hospital. I was appointed as the senior house officer at the Golden Square Hospital near Piccadilly Circus. Golden Square was an old building with corridors and rooms more suited to the Guild Hall of Music. The hospital was steeped in history: for example, Dr Morell McKenzie, a founding figure in the surgery of the larynx, had practised there.

On Boxing Day, 1962, a patient became unconscious. As I had done neurosurgery, I was able to recognise that he had a brain abscess from chronic middle ear disease. He needed the abscess drained, and antibiotics given urgently. I rang the consultant neurosurgeon, who lived in the south of England. However, there had been a heavy snowfall and he couldn't get to London. He was much relieved to learn that I had been a neuro-surgical registrar and so he left the patient's management to me. I had a great sense of satisfaction when the operation was completed and the patient regained consciousness.

The Royal National Throat, Nose and Ear Hospital didn't offer much experience in ear surgery, so I was fortunate in 1963 to be appointed as senior registrar to Dr Jack Angel James of the Bristol Royal Infirmary. He was a well-regarded surgeon specialising in the management of giddiness due to inner ear disease. We therefore moved to Bristol in 1963, where I had the opportunity to extend my surgical experience. It was a very busy job, partly because the National Health Service had overloaded hospitals, and visitors like me had to help with the load. In an outpatient session I would have to see as many as forty patients in a morning. That meant less than five minutes for every patient. They hardly got into the cubicle before I had to think about how to get them out. If I ran over time, it would interfere with the next outpatient session and I would then arrive late for my afternoon's operations at another hospital.

I was allowed to do quite major surgery, and more or less had to do it on my own. One became a surgeon by having the fortitude or nerve to do things without a lot of guidance. My most agonising case was a teenage girl requiring a mastoid operation. I was told to start the opera-tion, as the surgeon was late in arriving. Although I had learned to use drills, the hospital provided only a set of hammer and gouges to do the operation. I wasn't experienced in the use of these, and should have said I wouldn't proceed. In performing the operation I cut through the nerve supply to the muscles of the face, which resulted in a facial weakness. I felt terrible after that experience, and resolved that I would only use a drill, practise the operation repeatedly on human temporal bones, and learn the anatomy very well. It became the motivation for me to make sure later that our approach to the facial nerve when carrying out the bionic ear operation was rehearsed ad infinitum.

Perhaps my most dramatic surgical experience while at Bristol was to help a Somerset farmer who came in so breathless he was blue. Looking into his throat with a mirror, I could see a large cancer involving the voice box and upper swallowing tube. I needed to get a biopsy and have a good look at the lesion under anaesthetic. The anaesthetist thought she would be able to induce the anaesthetic and pass a tube by the mass to the windpipe. I wasn't so sure, and before the anaesthetic was commenced I scrubbed and was poised ready to do an immediate tracheotomy (where the windpipe is opened to allow breathing). In fact, the anaesthetist found it was impossible to get the breathing tube into the windpipe. I was thus ready and poised to cut down on to the trachea and establish an airway almost immediately. Then, to my horror, the patient's heart stopped. As he had a huge barrel chest, it would have been impossible to do an external heart massage by pressing up and down on his breast-bone. I had no option but to open his chest and massage his heart. As I had assisted at many heart surgery operations, this wasn't a problem and his heart soon started again. I sent a message to the chest surgical registrar to sew up the chest and put an appropriate drain in place. The message came back from the registrar that he wouldn't be able to do it for another two hours. So again, fortunately having done thoracic surgery, I just had to do the job myself. The patient recovered from his ordeal!

At this time I decided to do the first part exam to qualify me for practice in ear, nose and throat surgery (the Diploma of Laryngology and Otology from the University of London). This required me to study up on some special anatomy of the ear that I hadn't done previously for my general surgical fellowship. I went to London after one of my busiest and most exhausting weekends and failed the exam—and it was said to be an easy exam! What's more, I failed because I didn't know enough about the structure of the inner ear!

During my time at Bristol I had an offer to enter an ear, nose and throat practice in Melbourne from a friend of my father's, Dr Russell Donald. Before returning to Australia I had to obtain a qualification in ear, nose and throat surgery, and so I sat for the College of Surgeons' exam in London, a harder exam than the Diploma from London University.

I was very relieved to receive by mail the fat envelope rather than the thin envelope telling me of my success, and requesting me to complete the enclosed papers and pay the necessary fee. However, just in case I failed the London exam, I had decided to remain in the UK to sit another College of Surgeons exam in Glasgow a few weeks later, so that I would have one specialist qualification after my name. As a result, Margaret had to take the ship, HMS *Canberra*, back to Australia without me, as she was pregnant with our first child, Sonya, and for medical safety reasons had to travel at this time. I sadly farewelled Margaret, but then proceeded to make the best use of my remaining time in Europe by visiting some of the major cities. I had arranged to return to Australia for free as the ship's surgeon on a Shaw Saville merchant ship.

After returning to London from Europe, I boarded the ship to inspect the dispensary and had to order additional antibiotics. A few nights later, we slipped quietly along the Thames and headed for Australia. While we steamed across the Bay of Biscay, I developed pain in the abdomen. Self-examination revealed the early signs suggesting appendicitis. I had no option but to wait and observe. If it's a bad case, it's necessary to operate within as little as six hours before a rupture occurs, leading to possible death. Would I have to operate on myself? I had heard of doctors doing this, but I wasn't looking forward to the experience. It would have been necessary to use mirrors, and the movements would be back-to-front. Sterility would also be a problem. I thought I might cause more complications by operating than by waiting. I informed the captain of my dilemma, and decided to sit it out. Then, after a few days of waiting, my symptoms and signs started to abate. As we approached Port Said at the top of the Suez Canal, I told the captain I was sure now that it wasn't appendicitis and that I could risk making the two-week passage across the Indian Ocean when we would be out of touch with land.

The captain shocked me by ordering me to leave the ship and see an Egyptian surgeon in a French Catholic hospital somewhere in the back streets of Port Said. I hadn't realised the captain could overrule the surgeon in medical matters; in fact, I learned that on a ship at sea the captain has a higher authority than God. As we came into Port Said harbour, the radio operator telegraphed the shore that the doctor would be the only one leaving the ship. He also sent a telegram home saying that I was about to leave the ship and was sick in Port Said. He could see how forlorn I was as I left his cabin, and advised me to contact the British Embassy if I had any trouble.

I disembarked that night, feeling lonely and dejected. As I passed all the foreign faces on the docks, I wondered what sort of unknown I was heading into. I was escorted to a small hospital run by French nuns. It had a friendlier atmosphere than the world outside, and with my school-boy French I could pick up some occasional words. I was given a bed in a large ward and told to get some sleep until the surgeon saw me the next morning. Get some sleep? How could I sleep in such a strange and unfamiliar environment?

Morning finally came, and after the normal flurry of activity that greets patients on first awakening, the sister announced the arrival of the senior surgeon. He prodded and poked me, and being a surgeon too I knew exactly what he was feeling for and that there were now no signs of acute appendicitis. After looking thoughtful for a moment, the surgeon announced that he would remove my appendix and that I would remain at the hospital until the next ship arrived in a couple of months! I knew that the shipping company would be reimbursing him for all the treat-ment, and this was probably a key factor behind his recommendations. I said I would think about his decision and let him know. I was now in a quandary. I decided that I needed to pray with someone. I asked a French nun and she took me to the chapel where we prayed fervently, she in French and I in English. I had an additional problem in that I had for-gotten to disclose my traveller's cheques on entering the country, and at the time Colonel Nasser, the power in the land, had decreed that anyone who failed to declare any cheques would go to prison.

After praying I decided I had to discharge myself from the hospital—the risk of having a surgeon I knew nothing about operate on me was greater than trying to find my way back to Australia. I knew I had to get to Cairo and find the British Embassy to arrange to exit the country. How could I do this with no money and the risk of going to prison? Then the nun who had shared my prayers offered a solution. A Norwegian sailor who had fractured his leg would be leaving hospital to return home to Cairo that afternoon, and I could get a free ride with him. I accepted the offer gladly.

It was dark when I was dropped off in the centre of Cairo on Sunday evening. After asking directions to the British Embassy, I was disappointed to find the whole building in darkness. What was I to do? Then I thought of the Hilton Hotel, where Margaret and I had eaten lunch two years previously on a sightseeing trip while our ship to England travelled up the Suez Canal. When I arrived at the hotel, it occurred to me to ask at the enquiry desk whether they knew where the Australian Consul was. If I had no success with the British Embassy, maybe the Australian Consul could be found. But why would this hotel receptionist know? To my surprise and enormous relief, I was informed that the Consul was at a party and I could be put through to him by telephone. The Consul told me how I could cash my traveller's cheques and pay for a plane flight out of Egypt. I didn't have enough for the two-day trip by Qantas to Australia, but I could afford to return to the United Kingdom. I rang the office, but Qantas was booked out. All I could get was a United Arab Airlines Comet to London. This was just after the Comets had been exploding in mid-air! When I arrived at the airport in the mist of the morning, very few Egyptians were boarding the United Arab Airlines plane for London; instead, they all filed out to catch the Qantas flight. In fact, very few people took the United Arab flight. While I was standing on the tarmac waiting to board the plane, the British pilot singled me out and came up for a chat. Shortly after, an official appeared and the pilot complained to him about the lack of service the plane had received, at the previous airport.

Despite my apprehension, we had an uneventful flight to London where I saw my good friend Geoff Shead, who was a surgeon at the London Hospital. He confirmed that I didn't have appendicitis, and kindly let me stay with him and his wife until I could get another ship. It was a time of real Christian fellowship, and Geoff and his wife helped me to grow in faith. My recent experiences had demonstrated that I couldn't rely just on my own ability, but had to learn to depend more on God. I consider myself blessed in then catching the steamship the *Willem Ruys* back to Australia on possibly its last voyage, because there I met Dr Bill Hawes, an English doctor who was going out to be a missionary in Borneo. During the voyage I had plenty of time to realise that the Bible was a book to study well.

EAR, NOSE AND THROAT PRACTICE IN MELBOURNE

In 1964, following a joyful reunion with my wife and family after a ten-week separation, I settled into an ear, nose and throat partnership in

Collins Street in Melbourne with Gwen and Russell Donald. It was primarily an allergy practice and, as a result, patients requiring potential nose and sinus surgery were often referred to us. To increase my experience in ear surgery, I also applied to some of the main teaching hospitals in Melbourne for appointment as assistant honorary surgeon. This meant that after doing three days of voluntary work, I had to cram my partnership duties into two days. Doing the surgery for the practice meant crisscrossing Melbourne from one private hospital to another, taking my instruments, often including the operating microscope, and sometimes getting a quick bite of a sandwich in a park for lunch. I will always be grateful to God for this opportunity to begin surgical practice in Melbourne with the Donalds.

My work continued in much the same way for two years. The work in the public hospitals provided opportunities to develop my surgical skills. Reconstructing deformed noses became an absorbing passion. It combined a sense of form and even artistry, which I had learned from my mother, with attention to anatomical detail. Our small rented house began to resemble a museum of people's photographs and face masks before and after operations.

However, I still wanted to do ear surgery. With this aim I experimented with ultrasound as a cure for an inner ear condition called Ménière's Disease in which there is loss of hearing and of balance. I became enthusiastic about doing the new stapedectomy operation to correct middle ear deafness. Operating at high magnifications required a new level of dexterity. To achieve this, I had to obtain human temporal bones from the mortuary and practise the surgery with a cheap Beck microscope at night in our living room. I soon became quite good at this operation, and by the end of the three years in Melbourne I had done several hundred procedures.

Nevertheless, towards the end of my third year in Melbourne I was starting to feel 'the fire in the belly'—the creative urge to do research that had been suppressed for so long. Tonsil and adenoid removal was becoming too routine. Research—going into the unknown—seemed so much more exciting.

I had a few profoundly deaf people visit my outpatient sessions at the Royal Victorian Eye and Ear Hospital, but I felt quite depressed at having to send them away, saying there was nothing that could be done.

I still remember their disappointment. The difficulties for profoundly deaf people are reflected in the following letter from an ear specialist and friend, the late Dr Les Caust, to a patient written in 1967.

4th April, 1967

Dear Mr Kearton,

Thank you very much for going along to the Acoustic Laboratory and having their somewhat more sophisticated tests . . .
It does appear that you have a complete bilateral sensori-neural hearing loss and that no surgical or any other attack would be of any avail to you. I would agree entirely with this that you rejoin the Australian Association for Better Hearing and I have enclosed a form for you to fill out to this end. It was disappointing that nothing surgical can help, but I'm sure with your perseverance and continued attack on it with the ability that you have got then you will make the most of a pretty bad lot.

One day towards the end of 1966 I stopped for lunch between operating sessions, this time in the park near the Royal Melbourne Hospital. Having more time than usual, I pulled out a journal and read an article by an American surgeon, Dr Blair Simmons, who wrote that a profoundly deaf person had heard some strange sounds when electrical currents were passed through wires placed in his hearing nerve. Although the person couldn't understand speech, that initial report was enough to fire me up. I felt this was my mission in life. It was clear from the article that there was still much to learn before profoundly deaf people might be able to understand speech by electrical stimulation of the hearing nerve. If I were to make a contribution, I had to understand more about auditory brain science so that I could lay a firm foundation of understanding and build on that. Where could I get this training?

I remembered Professor Bishop at the University of Sydney who, when I was a third year medical student, had offered me a place to do a Bachelor of Medical Science degree in vision research. He was foremost in Australia, but would he offer me a position? I wrote to him and was pleased to get a reply that encouraged me to go and discuss it with him. When he saw that I had sensible motives for doing research, he told me that Dr Colin Dunlop had been appointed to do research in hearing and brain science. I met Colin, immediately felt a rapport with him and was accepted.

It was also a great relief to be able to do research, because my neck had become so painful through operating on noses that I thought I wouldn't be able to continue and would need an alternative career. I had developed severe osteoarthritis of the neck at an early age due to a high-jumping injury, and all the craning and twisting to see into the recesses of the nose had aggravated the situation to the point where I was getting severe pain in the arms, shoulders and even the chest. I had prayed for guidance in being able to overcome my neck problem, and I felt I was being led to go to Sydney University to study hearing and brain function.

So, the die was caste. I decided to leave specialist practice for the insecurity of a research position. Just when I had a reasonable income and some security, I uprooted my wife and our young family (Sonya, nearly three years, and Cecily, sixteen months) to go to a lecturer's salary which was considerably less than I had been earning. It was very clear that I couldn't have it both ways: an academic career and an income comparable to that earned in private practice. Nor could I have a private practice and concentrate on research.

4

Learning about hearing

From the first observations of the vibrations of
the cochlear partition it was clear that they
represented a system about which physical
science provided little knowledge and that
many years would be required to understand
it clearly.

Georg von Bekesy, Nobel Laureate, 1960

I t was essential for me to understand how we hear, before I could learn
to use electrical stimulation of the hearing nerve to help overcome
sensory and nerve deafness. The Department of Physiology at the University of Sydney provided a great opportunity to do this. Margaret and
I left Melbourne with our two young girls just before Christmas 1966.

We had to look for a flat that we could afford, and were fortunate
to find an unpretentious one in Cremorne, on the lower North Shore.
Although needing repairs, including chicken wire around an upstairs
veranda to stop the children falling out, the flat was in a beautiful area
of Sydney, and I could catch the ferry across the harbour and then the
bus to the university.

When I turned up in the laboratory, Colin Dunlop asked me what I
wanted to do. I was surprised that he let me make that decision. I had
come to Sydney to learn how to study the hearing pathways in the brain,
and was looking for guidance. This was my first lesson that research
requires independent thinking. For the next two months I read everything
I could in order to learn about hearing, before deciding what my research
project would be.

I also found that scientists thought very differently from most doctors,
as they had an overwhelming commitment to discovering new knowledge.
Dr (later Professor) Liam Burke in the next laboratory confided that in

his spare time he mostly thought about solving research ideas. On the way to work he would park his car until the traffic cleared so that he would have more time to think. I started the thinking habit and found it addictive. It was like a shot of adrenalin to realise that I might be pushing back the frontiers of knowledge.

I was surprised that becoming poorer gave me relief from a 'rat race' where I felt I had to keep up with colleagues who were acquiring big houses in Toorak, expensive cars and even farms. The demise of our Vauxhall which Dad had given us in 1963 (it was now only thirteen years old) was sudden. We had decided to take the girls (now aged four and two years) to Melbourne and Bendigo where my sister Robin lived. After a wonderfully early start from Cremorne at 4.30 a.m. we made excellent progress and reached Gundagai, nearly half-way, at 9.25. As we were stopping, the car made a rattling sound and never went again. A bearing had gone in the engine. I decided the only thing to do was to send the car, with its four new tyres, to the wreckers, and hire a taxi to take us and all our bags and bundles the eleven miles to Cootamundra, where we could catch the *Daylight Express* home. The train left at 4 p.m., so we had plenty of time! On our inglorious return at 9.30 p.m., someone must have met us, for I remember one wise-after-the-event remark: 'I would no more have thought of driving that car to Melbourne than trying to swim across Sydney Harbour.' After the loss of the Vauxhall we travelled every-where by public transport or walked, and if people wanted us to go to their place at night they had to pick us up. While waiting for public transport, I had more time to think about research. Playing about with ideas in a bus queue beat driving in the traffic.

During my first two months of reading I discovered that we recognise the frequency of sound or pitch by the pattern of electrical responses in the brain cells. There are two codes used. According to the time code, we recognise the frequency of a sound when the brain cells fire in time with the sound wave. This is illustrated at the left of the diagram on p. 48. On the other hand, according to the place code, the frequency is recognised by the site of stimulation within the brain. The hearing path-ways in the brain are set out in an orderly way so that a frequency scale is preserved similar to that of the keys on a piano, as illustrated at the right of the diagram. To make this place code work, the inner ear acts as a filter for sounds, with the highest frequencies causing excitation at one

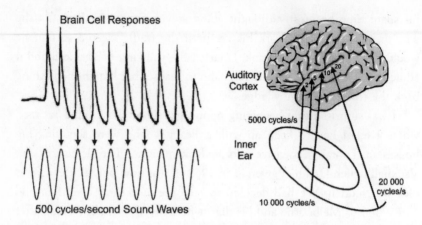

Left: *The time coding of frequency showing how the hearing nerve fibres fire in time with the sine wave of the sound.* Right: *The place coding of frequency showing how the inner ear and brain are connected so that a frequency scale is preserved according to the place of stimulation.*

end of it and the lowest frequencies at the other end. I also learned that the intensity or loudness of the sound seemed to be conveyed by the rate at which the nerves fired or the number of nerves excited. The coding of sound is discussed in more detail in Appendix 1.

THE RESEARCH STUDIES

In planning the research for my Doctorate of Philosophy degree, I found it very hard at first to think of original ideas. So many good minds had already studied how hearing takes place. Nevertheless, after some weeks I hit upon the idea of examining a particular group of cells in the brain stem that hadn't been very well studied because surgical access was difficult. With my surgical training I thought I could make a difference. It would also give me an opportunity to analyse the effects of electrical stimulation of the inner ear and hearing nerve on this brain centre.

When I started my experiments I ran into big problems. The first six animals died under anaesthetic. I even tried performing cardiac massage! Eventually I discovered the problem was toxic material in the bottle containing the anaesthetic. Research wasn't going to be as easy as I had thought!

I soon developed a liking for hearing brain cells popping away as the electronic equipment amplified their minute voltages. The experiments were long and somewhat arduous. I would start at 8 a.m. and often still be going at 4 a.m. the next day. The first time this happened, Margaret rang the police fearing that I had been involved in an accident. I knew, too, that at the end of these experiments I would have to clean up the lab until it looked spotless—Colin Dunlop was strict about that. But the excitement of learning how a hearing centre in the brain worked was worth the effort.

Part of the satisfaction in making discoveries is writing up the findings in journals for others in the field. I had written a few papers on medical subjects and came to the task full of confidence. I wrote a draft and asked one of the most critical members of the staff if he would make comments on it. I could hardly read my writing for his red ink. It was then I learned how logical, precise and incisive these scientists were. After all, it was their life and it required rather different skills from medical practice.

After a while I realised that not only could I use animal experiments to study electrical stimulation of the hearing nerve, but I could also answer many other medical and surgical questions. I started doing research to see how best to refine the technique for replacing the middle ear bones with a metal strut in the disease otosclerosis—the condition my father had. I also became absorbed in trying to record electrical activity from the brain outside the skull, and so use the technique to diagnose a hearing loss in babies and young children. These hearing research studies were to lead to a Doctorate in Philosophy degree.

I was so enthused by research I also made time to study problems in nasal surgery and to continue my interest in this area. I wanted to learn about the mechanical forces supporting the nose so that it would be easier to fix breathing problems and do cosmetic surgery at the one operation. An advantage in being in a university was the access it gave to many disciplines. For example, I was able to measure the stresses and strains on the nasal bones by using the equipment in the Mechanical Engineering Department. I wrote up that research on the side for a Master of Surgery degree.

THE FAMILY AND SUPPLEMENTING THE INCOME

In 1968 Margaret had become pregnant with our third daughter, Roslyn, and it was clear that we would need to move from our small flat in Cremorne. To add to our income I took a small job at night examining people for the Repatriation Department. Next I looked to the share market buzzing from the mining boom—to poor effect. I rushed to donate $2000 of my hard-earned money to a diamond mine—it failed and I lost the lot. So I returned to familiar territory and found a part-time position with the National Acoustics Laboratories to set up biological research. Dr George Kossoff, who was overseas at the time, wanted the effects of ultrasound on the inner ear to be studied towards the treatment of Ménière's Disease, which causes people to lose hearing, become giddy and experience a whistling noise. The Acoustic Laboratories had nothing, so I had to start from scratch; I even had to order the glassware and chemicals. I needed an animal laboratory for the experiments, and returned to the one at the Royal North Shore Hospital where I had worked many years previously with Ian Monk in cardiac surgery.

ELECTRICAL STIMULATION OF THE HEARING NERVE

At the beginning of 1969 I had finished most of my experimental work on the normal functioning of the brain centre, and was set to do what I had originally come to study—a comparison of the responses of auditory brain cells to electrical stimulation with those to sound of the same frequency. Furthermore, Colin Dunlop was taking six months' leave, so I was left in charge and could do what I liked.

At the time there was a great debate on which was more important for the coding of high frequencies by the brain—the timing code or the place code. If it were the timing code, a single-electrode implant could be used, as the important frequencies in understanding speech are as high as 3000 cycles per second.

In starting my research I discovered that electrical stimulation caused interference in the recordings from the brain cells, owing to the high resistance of the electrode wires. I would have to find a way of isolating the brain cell recordings from the stimulating voltages. Don Larnach, the Department's chief technical officer, thought that infra-red light should be used to link the brain to the recording equipment to prevent the interference. Don said he would build the unit for me, but I needed $100 and the Department didn't have the money. I would have to find it myself. I went to many hearing aid firms to see if they would make a donation for my research. The first ones I approached said they couldn't help; it was hinted that my work might eventually lead to the development of a product that would compete with theirs and so reduce their business. (In fact they were right, because the bionic ear manufactured today by Cochlear Limited resulting from the research gives better results for severely to profoundly deaf people than does a hearing aid.) Finally, the Hughes brothers, owners of Stelaid, agreed to provide the money. This was my first grant for bionic ear research! It enabled me to examine the responses of brain cells to electrical stimulation.

Although I was limited in the analyses I could do using the laboratory's old computer, I did what I could and wrote up the research. It was published in an overseas scientific journal in 1969. In this research study I found the brain cell responses were different for electrical stimulation from those for sound, and that they didn't keep in time with the high rates of stimulation needed for speech understanding.

My conclusions, outlined in my Doctorate of Philosophy thesis, were that stimulating hearing nerves with a single electrode at the same rate as the sound frequency would not be effective, and the place coding of frequency would be needed. This required inserting multiple electrodes in the inner ear to excite the separate groups of hearing nerves that convey different pitch sensations.

Writing up my thesis was the incentive to plan the future research on electrical stimulation of the hearing nerve for speech understanding (see Appendix 2). Although my studies suggested that multiple electrodes in the inner ear would provide the best chance of helping a profoundly deaf person to hear speech, the electrical currents might short-circuit through the fluid in the inner ear and not reach the nerve fibres. I would have to find a way of solving this problem. In addition, there are 10 000 to 20 000 hearing nerve fibres taking speech signals from the inner ear to the brain in normal hearing, and it would be impossible to put anything like this number of electrode wires into the inner ear. No more than ten to twenty wires would fit. In other words, electrical stimulation of the hearing nerve creates a 'bottle-neck' between the world of sound and the brain, limiting the flow of information. To achieve speech understanding, I believed it would therefore be necessary to select the important information from speech and ensure that this got through the 'bottle-neck'.

During my three years at the University of Sydney I had become committed to continuing the research on electrical stimulation of the hearing nerve, but there was little future for research of this nature in the university's Department of Physiology. Physiologists both locally and internationally thought it was outrageous to suggest that electrical stimulation of the inner ear could adequately reproduce frequency information to help profoundly deaf people understand speech. Furthermore, at age thirty-three, I was behind science and engineering graduates in basic research training and university-level maths.

In 1969 the inaugural Chair in Otolaryngology (ear, nose and throat surgery) at the University of Melbourne was advertised, and I knew that I must apply, however unlikely my chances of success might be. The selection was narrowed down, and I was asked to prepare a statement (see Appendix 2) of how I would run the Department. In the document I stated:

> I consider it is important to concentrate on an aspect of surgery that
> needs further development—such an aspect is the surgical treatment of
> perceptive deafness in which most advances in otological surgery in the
> next 10–20 years are likely to be made.

I didn't realise how prophetic this statement was at the time. I also said I would like to 'develop a clinic that would restore hearing and speech to children who had nerve deafness which is so severe that conventional hearing aids are ineffective'. I added that I would raise money for research from trusts, etc. I had, after all, raised $100 from a hearing aid firm for some basic research at the University of Sydney!

Given the attitude of the scientific community towards electrical stimulation of the inner ear as a way of restoring hearing, I was apprehensive that the university might consider my aims unrealistic. I needn't have worried, as I have come to learn how much the University of Melbourne values the pursuit of challenging research objectives.

My future in developing electrical stimulation of the hearing nerve for deafness rested very heavily on the decision of the University of Melbourne on the Chair of Otolaryngology.

5

Establishing essential research

> The true method of discovery is like the flight
> of an aeroplane. It starts from the ground of
> particular observation; it makes a flight in the
> thin air of imaginative generalisation; and it
> lands for renewed observation rendered acute
> by rational interpretation.
>
> *A.N. Whitehead, 1978*

I t was an exciting moment in October 1969 when Tom Hazell, registrar
to the University of Melbourne's Council, rang to say that I had just
been appointed the foundation professor in otolaryngology at the University of Melbourne. This meant I could now direct research into electrical stimulation of the hearing nerve as a cure for deafness, and put my
energies wholeheartedly into this work—or so I thought.

On the strength of the registrar's telephone call, I threw financial
caution to the wind and that night Margaret and I dined out at the revolv-
ing restaurant at Centrepoint in Sydney. We weren't just celebrating the
opportunity I had been given; I also wanted to thank Margaret for all her
support in the lean years up to this point. Our lives with our three young
children, Sonya, Cecily and Roslyn, now seemed less uncertain.

Eager to get on with the job, we returned to Melbourne in January
1970. It was somewhat daunting to realise the responsibilities I was taking
on. Although warmly welcomed by my ear, nose and throat, and academic
colleagues, especially in the address of the chairman of the Otolaryngological Society of Victoria, Dr George Gray (see Appendix 2), I sensed I
was nevertheless on trial. Not being a confident person, I found taking
up this new position quite stressful. There were people to meet, dinners

to attend, committees to set up, operations to do, clinics to run, staff to appoint, many meetings to convene, politics to come to terms with, people to appease and funds to raise, all while planning a new department. I hadn't realised that all these things were the lot of a professor.

I was expected to be all things to all people, including a well-rounded surgeon. On this score I had the advantage of first training as a general surgeon, which, together with the fact that I had been one of the first ear, nose and throat surgeons in Melbourne in 1964 to undertake plastic surgery of the nose, and major head and neck surgery at the Repatriation Hospital in 1965, helped to give me some credibility in a surgeon's world.

But would research be squeezed out by everything else?

The first difficulty in setting up my research program was inadequate laboratory space. Until the new department was built, we managed in makeshift quarters in the Royal Victorian Eye and Ear Hospital. My office was a room in the old Australian Medical Association building, my technical officer was housed in the old operating theatre, and across the road the experimental research laboratory was in a disused hospital mortuary.

When I looked at the mortuary my heart sank. It was dilapidated and bare. There was a stone table in the centre, but little else. The walls needed painting, and the light diffused poorly through the high windows. Anyway, I had no money to buy equipment even if the laboratory itself were satisfactory. I would have to be a fundraiser for research that most people said wouldn't succeed.

RESEARCH QUESTIONS

The fundamental objections scientists and clinicians quite reasonably raised to the development of a bionic ear were as follows:

1. The inner ear, with 20 000 hearing nerves, was too complex to be replaced by twenty or so electrodes stimulating groups of hearing nerves.
2. An implant in the inner ear would damage the very nerves it was hoped to stimulate.
3. Speech was too complex to be presented to the hearing part of the brain by electrical stimulation.
4. There were too few residual hearing nerve fibres in the inner ear after they died back due to deafness to transmit essential speech information.

(Top) *The first staff of the University of Melbourne's Department of Ear, Nose and Throat Surgery in 1970 outside the old Australian Medical Association building housing the author's office. Left to Right: Rodney Walkerden (senior technical officer), Sue Rubenstein (part-time secretary), Cynthia Kent (secretary), the author. (Bottom) The author's impression of first setting up a research department.*

5. Children born deaf would not have developed the essential nerve connections to brain cells for electrical stimulation to give adequate hearing.

To answer these and other more specific questions, priorities in research were needed to make best use of whatever funds I could obtain.

FUNDRAISING

The most urgent research would be to substantiate the findings I had made at the University of Sydney in 1968–69. This research on animal brain cells had shown that electrical stimulation couldn't reproduce the frequencies of speech sounds on the basis of the timing of the stimuli on a single electrode. If the speech frequencies could have been reproduced by electrical stimulation using rate of stimulation alone on a single electrode inserted into the inner ear, this would have made the engineering for the bionic ear easier, and therefore cheaper, than for a multiple-electrode implant. Consequently, it was essential to be sure that electrical stimulation on a single electrode wouldn't reproduce speech frequencies.

Funding of the research in the first year was helped by a fixed grant of $5000 from Professor Sir Sydney Sunderland, Dean of the Faculty of Medicine, to all departments, whatever their size. This gave me a real lift since I was in a small department that had to justify its existence. After a couple of years the rules changed, and funds were allocated according to a new funding formula on the basis of the number of students in training. A large department doing a lot of teaching was much more able to attract students for postgraduate degrees than a small one just starting. I could see it was almost hopeless to try and get involved in undergraduate as well as postgraduate teaching to attract students in order to raise research funds. If I were to do bionic ear research, I would have to find other means of support. Meanwhile, funds were needed to purchase the very basics, such as an electrical stimulator unit and consumable items like rolls of film. I therefore turned to the premier Australian medical research granting body, the National Health & Medical Research Council of Australia (NH&MRC).

How could I frame an application on electrical stimulation of the hearing nerves when I knew that my scientific and surgical colleagues who would review the application believed it wouldn't work and was a waste of time? I decided to apply primarily on the grounds that studies on electrical stimulation would contribute to our understanding of how sound was processed by the brain—that is, more basic research.

I was elated to learn in July 1970 that I had been called for an interview for an NH&MRC grant. I was at least through the first round, but would I make this one? I then had my first taste of an NH&MRC review panel. These interviews were to become almost a way of life for the next thirty years. They were like the oral exams in medical training—quite forbidding. One had to go in thoroughly prepared to answer any question, and be sharp in replying. It was also strange to meet friends across the interview table and realise that in this scenario no favours were given.

Later in the year I received the good news that this modest application had been successful; I was to receive $5214 in total for the years 1971–72 to help with starting the research. I could now approach research students and ask them to work on the project, since I at last had some equipment!

This was to be the last time the NH&MRC funded my research for the bionic ear until I had proved the concept in 1978. I learned later that my peers and colleagues had voted against funding my subsequent applications, primarily because they were on the subject of electrical stimulation of the hearing nerve. I was even advised to consider changing the title of my application and reducing the emphasis on electrical stimulation so that it could go to another review panel.

As well as a basic electrical stimulator unit, I needed a computer. At the time a basic computer with a mere 8000 bytes of random access memory cost $15 000. That seemed a huge amount of money. Where could it be found?

Service clubs were my next hope, and the Apex Club of Melbourne gave most support. The members were all young and enthusiastic, as I was, and I could relate to them best. In fact, I was delighted to be invited as guest speaker at a joint meeting of the Apex Club of Melbourne and the Lions Club of Melbourne on 10 March 1970. More meetings led to the idea to run a public appeal to which the university gave official support.

Fifteen thousand dollars was a large sum for Apex to raise, but I discovered that Melbourne had been well endowed with trusts and foundations, partly as a result of the gold rush the previous century. More

Department of Otolaryngology in 1971. Top: John Delahunty (surgeon), Don McMahon (surgeon), Sue Rubenstein (secretary), Cynthia Kent (secretary), Kim Berner (research assistant). Centre: Graeme Clark (professor). Bottom: Jo Tong (research student), Rodney Walkerden (senior technical officer), Field Rickards (research student), Howard Kranz (research student), John Nathar (research student), David Scrimgeour (research student). (Cartoon drawn by David Scrimgeour)

than any other city in Australia, Melbourne used this resource for helping medical research, and I was to rely heavily on this support for a number of years. The Felton Bequest was the first to help.

However, by early 1971 we were still short of our goal. I continued with speaking engagements at a number of Rotary and Apex dinners that raised $200 here and $300 there. Finally, about a year after the appeal had been launched, we were able to place an order for the computer.

BUILDING A RESEARCH TEAM

Early on I realised that I couldn't do all the research alone and would have to start to build up a team—again without any special research funds. Moreover, to start research the next year in 1971, I would need to attract students to come and work with me. I had learned while at the University of Sydney that medical students did excellent research even if they only took a year off their studies. What's more, they didn't cost any money!

In return, you had to give them time so that they could learn about research.

But giving them time was one of my greatest pleasures.

I wrote to the medical students who were completing their exams half-way through their course inviting them to work on this new project. I was delighted that John Nathar and David Scrimgeour were keen to do so. The next year, 1972, another medical student, Harry Minas, joined me. I was also able to persuade Howard Kranz, with a psychology background, to undertake one of the studies; and Jo Tong, a graduate in mechanical engineering referred by my friend Dr Cecil Pengilley, a senior lecturer in that department, joined the team to do research to model the working of the inner ear. In 1971 and through into 1972, I finally had a small and enthusiastic group of students actively engaged in research to establish in particular whether the rate of stimulation on a single electrode would be adequate for speech understanding.

SINGLE- VERSUS MULTIPLE-ELECTRODE STIMULATION OF THE HEARING NERVE

My initial research at the University of Sydney had shown that brain cells could only respond to the timing of electrical pulses up to about 300 pulses per second. This was much slower than the 3000 pulses per second needed to cover the important frequencies in speech, in particular those of many consonants.

Could I rely on my research at the University of Sydney, using responses from relatively small numbers of brain cells, as the answer to one of the most important questions for the development of the bionic ear? My answer to this question was no. I had to undertake similar studies on the alert experimental animal. I couldn't afford to embark on the expensive development of a multiple-electrode implant to reproduce the place coding of speech frequencies without being confident of the answer to this question. Neither was I prepared to undertake unnecessary experimental studies on humans.

So, just when I thought it would be enjoyable to study one area in depth, namely how the individual brain cells responded to electrical stimulation, it became more essential to study the effects of electrical stimulation in the intact behaving animal. I had therefore to turn around and learn about training animals to respond to sounds. All through the bionic ear research and development, I had to learn about new areas and scientific disciplines so that I could direct the next important stage of the work. Just when I became familiar with one area, and was starting to contribute to the field and publish results, it became necessary to move on to another unexplored discipline for the good of the project as a whole.

The training and testing of an experimental animal with an inner ear implant required a special test box, which I developed with my senior technical officer, Rodney Walkerden. This was then made ready for the start of the research in 1971 that commenced in the hospital's old mortuary. The aims of the experiments were to see whether the implanted animal could detect the same changes in the rate of electrical stimulation as it could for the frequencies of sound. I also planned to do further auditory brain cell studies. As I had no proper electrically-shielded laboratory (Faraday Room) until the new Ear, Nose and Throat Department was built, we constructed a box enclosed in flyscreen wire to house the animal. This was also set up in the hospital mortuary. It provided electrical isolation from the trams sparking on the overhead lines as they passed down Gisborne Street, East Melbourne, as well as isolating the recordings from the alternating current (AC) on the mains.

Thus, by 1971 some basic equipment had been purchased and developed, and a few enthusiastic students found to embark on the first research projects. We all worked closely together on these projects, and there was great communal spirit, the more so because we were starting something very new. This is reflected in the preface to John Nathar's Bachelor of Medical Science thesis written in 1971 (see Appendix 2).

John's research was important in showing that behaviourally there was a limit of only about 200 pulses per second above which it wasn't possible to reproduce the time coding of frequency with rate of electrical stimulation. It was becoming increasingly clear that it wouldn't be possible to use a single-electrode implant for speech understanding, but I decided that further behavioural studies should be done to be sure of the results. These were undertaken by Howard Kranz and Harry Minas in 1972–73. As with John Nathar in 1971, in 1972 Harry Minas completed another significant Bachelor of Medical Science research project.

This study and other research with Howard Kranz and later Aileen Williams helped to confirm the results of the previous behavioural study which indicated that the brain could not distinguish rates of stimulation high enough for speech understanding. The very upper limit detectable by the brain was 600–800 pulses per second.

In arranging for John Nathar, Howard Kranz, Harry Minas and later Aileen Williams to examine the question of whether rate of stimulation on a single electrode could code the frequencies required for speech understanding, I was determined that I would rather over-prove our results than be shown by someone else to be wrong. (This also turned out to be the best approach for the speech processing strategy on our initial patients, as people didn't believe our findings when they were first presented.)

These studies also told us to beware of using a plug and socket to connect external electrical stimulation to the hearing nerves. Infection could be passed through the skin (see Harry Minas's thesis in Appendix 2). Some overseas centres who had started by carrying out studies on patients with a plug and socket abandoned this practice because infection was indeed a problem. Thus, I decided to embark on the more expensive task of developing an electronic package that could be implanted under the intact skin—even if we lost the race to develop a successful bionic ear.

The research just referred to was published and also presented to local scientific meetings. I went with the students by car to one such meeting in Adelaide and it turned out to be largely a holiday together. It was an opportunity to get to know each other outside the work environment, and this created a good spirit. We spent only a day at the conference, and the rest of the time touring the vineyards, sampling the wine, and buying a quantity to bring home.

CRITICISMS

My concern for us to be our own stringent critics arose from the complaints I received soon after taking up my university position. The first came from my friend and mentor, now Associate Professor Colin Dunlop. In January 1970, he sent me a press cutting with the statements I was reported to have made underlined. His concern was that I was rashly claiming that I would actually bring hearing to the deaf and that it would be as exciting an advance as heart transplants. In May of the same year, a senior research scientist accused me of having, while at the Physiology

Department of Sydney University, fabricated results on nerve/brain cell connections. I was especially taken aback by this unfair accusation, but the experience prepared me for even more heat that was to come in developing the bionic ear.

Self-criticism became a dictum around our department as a result. Indeed, I took the view that with the implant research we shouldn't go looking for or expecting to find good results, as this would bias our findings and conclusions. I was impressed by the story I had heard of the true scientist who worked all his life on a discovery, and even at the end was pleased that he was able to prove himself wrong.

The next charge came from some of my ear, nose and throat colleagues. They had expected their professor to spend more time training ear, nose and throat surgeons, in the style adopted by some professors in North America and Europe. Their concern led them to meet with the vice-chancellor, Sir David Derham, to complain that I was wasting my time and that our experimental work wasn't likely to lead anywhere. Fortunately, Sir David listened to my colleague, Professor of Ophthalmology, Gerard Crock, who believed in the value of our research. So, our work went on.

In the mid-1970s the single-electrode device being developed in Los Angeles was coming into vogue, and scientists and surgeons were asserting at meetings that the more complex multiple-electrode system that I had embarked on wouldn't be needed. This attitude was due in part to a conservatism prevalent in Australia at the time, which held that innovations weren't expected to be achieved in this country. All I could do was pig-headedly press on.

Escape to Eltham

The stresses of these years were counterbalanced by, along with faith and family, living in the environment of Eltham. A bushy suburb of Melbourne near the Yarra River, Eltham had been settled early and become home to writers, painters, professors and other non-conformists. As I crossed the Diamond Creek each night, went through the arch of majestic river gums leading to the town and approached the dirt road that would take me home, I relaxed and left many of my cares behind. Our house, designed by Melbourne self-taught architect Alistair Knox, was made of mud-brick and old hand-made bricks with rough wooden exposed beams. We built it on an acre of land that had been a paddock—the cowshed still a landmark near the front gate. Some of the native vegetation had survived and Egg and Bacon, Early Nancies and Everlastings would appear each spring. When we bought the block I wanted a view for inspiration but had to be content with a glimpse through the neighbour's huge pine trees. Years later, new owners took a dislike to them and while they were being removed I rang to thank them. They thought I was about to complain.

On the weekends, Margaret and I enthusiastically planted hundreds of tiny native trees and bushes, all very fast-growing. There were enough varieties of wattles to flower the whole year, and we soon had a forest that had to be culled. The children would invite their friends over to camp. One night the screech of an owl, sounding like someone being murdered, sent them racing for the house.

Die-back disease had already spoiled some of the old eucalypts, and I spent many weekends removing dead branches with a bushman's saw. It was all part of the adventure and romance of living in Eltham, even if it was at the expense of a traumatised shoulder.

Canoeing down the nearby Yarra River with the children was an adventure made more exciting by various rapids and overhanging willows. The presence of tiger snakes occasionally created panic; several times one appeared near the house and twice inside. One was a three-footer that slithered into our bedroom. Margaret had the presence of mind to coax it out of the house with a torch.

Eltham was a place to do all kinds of things. I bought a potter's wheel and we tried our hands at that. Sonya became an excellent spinner of raw sheep's wool, and the variegated brown jumper she knitted me twenty years ago is still the warmest and the most comfortable I own. Cecily's creative urges were nurtured by wandering around Montsalvat's Artist's Colony with a camera, and by Eugenie Knox's creative dancing classes. Roslyn's chief loves at one stage were her pet ducks and the goat, Zinky, who we hoped would keep down the grass in the front 'lawn'. And Merran remembers nostalgically the carefree times spent swinging on the tyres suspended by long ropes from two trees.

We became part of the community not only at the local church, but also within our neighbourhood. We were united with our neighbours by our love of the bush and the possible need to fight bushfires. Everyone invested in knapsack sprays, but fortunately they were rarely needed. Keeping our dirt roads from being sealed by the council was also a strong community binding force, and the idea of chaining ourselves to trees to save them from bulldozers was often mentioned half-jokingly. There were always a few dissenters who didn't like their cars to look dusty in summer or muddy in winter, but to this day our road is still a narrow, winding dirt track. Long may it continue.

RETREAT TO KIAMA

The peace and beauty of Eltham helped me to cope each week, but I had to retreat to our holiday house in Kiama, in New South Wales, once a year to survive long-term. Kiama is at the centre of some of the most beautiful coastal scenery on the east coast of Australia, and our cottage had the luxury of two beaches close by. Here we could get together with my parents and brother and sister and their families. It was a time to be recreated physically and also spiritually. I bought a surfboard and for a while tried to keep up with the younger generation, but I soon turned to boogie boards and bodysurfing. There was time, too, just to sit and think about research. It might be after a walk at Minnamurra Falls, on the headland after a swim, or on the beach while the children played at the edge of the surf. I filled notebooks with research ideas and plans for their execution the following year.

For seventeen years our Peugeot station wagon made the trip, with us and our four children and then, when Jonathan arrived in 1979, five children. Towards the end of its life, one of the regulars at the caravan park nearby was heard to say: 'Here it comes again!'

Kiama was, and indeed still is, our second home. In a small three-bedroom house it scarcely seemed like work to paint a room, put up a new curtain or add a few new plants to the garden. Our most inspired idea was a small patio from which we could enjoy the now diminishing view of waves crashing on the headland below the lighthouse. It was hard to resist the temptation to poison two young Norfolk Island pines planted in the caravan park!

Each year we had to store our furniture in a loft so that the house could be let for the rest of the year. The neighbours, who are extremely

Graeme and Margaret picnicking at Minnamurra Falls near Kiama.

tolerant, must have been glad to see us go after the takeover by our growing clan with their caravans or camper trailers over the summer. My brother Bruce has always been unfailingly generous and kind in coming to our aid from Camden and helping us in innumerable ways to keep the house maintained and the holidays rolling.

From about 1972, one other vital means of rest and recreation was to spend thirty-six hours or so with Margaret somewhere quite close like the Dandenongs or Port Phillip Bay, having farmed out the girls to obliging friends, neighbours or especially to my sister Robin. More than once she minded eight young children for a weekend—her four and our four. A shot-in-the-arm for us! But for her?

OTHER RESEARCH AND RESPONSIBILITIES

Although my prime interest was research to develop electrical stimulation of the hearing nerve to help profound deafness, from 1970 to 1974 I couldn't spend the greater part of my time on it. There were other responsibilities.

I was fascinated by the idea of diagnosing communication difficulties and deafness in children by recording electrical activity in the brain from the surface of the scalp. For this reason I encouraged a Doctorate of Philosophy student, Field Rickards (now Professor of Education of the

Hearing Impaired), to study the possibility. The research also involved long experiments on animals, and we would often still be working at 3 a.m. As we were both young and enthusiastic, this didn't trouble us a great deal. It was only later that I couldn't participate fully in these all-night affairs because of the pressure of surgery and other responsibilities.

The research led some years later to the development by Field of the 'Brainwave Audiometer' for measuring hearing thresholds in very young children.

Not long after we arrived in Melbourne I became involved in deaf politics and the different methods of educating deaf children. There was a division between those who advocated educating children to use only their residual hearing supplemented with lip-reading (auditory/oral), those who recommended using Signed English with residual hearing (total communication), and those who advocated Sign Language of the Deaf (Auslan). People who held to the auditory/oral philosophy believed it was important to be able to communicate in a hearing world.

I participated in the debate well before the bionic ear came on the scene, especially when given the task of chairing a committee to establish the Deafness Foundation of Victoria. The Deafness Foundation had the aim of bringing the factions together to see if a common policy could be developed to help all deaf people. Although I preferred to support auditory/oral education, as it was consistent with my ultimate aim to help children with a bionic ear communicate in a world of sound, I appreciated the need to use other modes of communication, but believed the debate could only be resolved by carefully controlled studies.

My interest in deafness also became the focus for establishing a university-based training in audiology for professionals to diagnose a hearing loss, as well as provide for its non-surgical management. This school needed to be complemented by a course to train educators of the deaf, and was supported by a number of people, especially Mrs Janet Calvert-Jones and Mrs Nancy John.

It seemed appropriate to consolidate audiology (the non-medical management of deafness) in the Department of Otolaryngology (ear, nose and throat surgery), since they were both important in helping deaf people. Establishing the course meant time-consuming negotiations, which were all the more worthwhile when I realised later how important audiology was for the success of the bionic ear. I broke with tradition and appointed Field Rickards, who was a physicist, rather than a psychologist to head the training course. The course meant we had experience with the tests to assess the first benefits of the bionic ear. Furthermore, our trainees became essential clinical partners with surgeons in improving bionic ears and rehabilitating implant patients.

The new postgraduate course in audiology began in 1974 with ten students, so there were then lectures to be given to them, besides those in ear, nose and throat surgery for medical students.

I finished chairing the committee to coordinate postgraduate training in ear, nose and throat surgery in 1976, but for a while after that I chaired the Consultative Council for Maternal and Child Health. This committee advised the Victorian Minister of Health on issues and made recommendations. I must have been there often, for one of the doctors in the Health Department told my secretary he had a dream that I was taking over the Department. Although a large number of reports was generated, they were not acted upon soon enough for my liking. When trying to initiate legislation to have swimming pools fenced to prevent children drowning, I came against the manufacturers' lobby and learned how hard it is to achieve reform. (This has, however, been achieved since I left).

My failure caused me to ask the question: what am I doing on all these committees? I then resigned from every possible one and concentrated on the bionic ear research. It was only with this single-minded approach that real progress occurred.

6

The 'gold box'—
multiple electrode
implant

> Give an Australian a pair of pliers and a piece
> of wire and he'll invent something.
> It may be just to keep his car together, or to
> prevent his gate from falling apart.
> It may be of no benefit to anyone but him,
> but it will be something that fills a need.
>
> *Leo Port, engineer, inventor and Lord Mayor of Sydney, 1978*

B y the end of 1973 I had shown the limitations of using rate of electrical stimulation on a single electrode to convey speech frequencies.
In other words, a single-electrode implant would not be an effective bionic
ear. But would a multiple-electrode implant achieve speech understanding
anyway? It was imperative to develop a multiple-electrode cochlear
implant or bionic ear to find out.

THE CHANNEL 0 TELETHON AND NERVE DEAFNESS APPEAL

This meant expensive engineering. I didn't have anything like the necessary money for it, but in answer to my prayers, the breakthrough in
funding came when Sir Reginald Ansett, the owner of the Channel 0 (now
10) television station, contacted me to say he wanted to run a telethon
to help raise funds. His offer came after he had been watching the news
on the National ABC television network which reported that I had
received a donation of $2000 from the Apex Club of Melbourne to
develop an implant to electrically stimulate the hearing nerves in the hope

of curing sensori-neural deafness. This announcement gave him the idea for a telethon, as he considered his channel needed one in order to be competitive with the other two commercial stations which already had telethon appeals. His special interest in helping deaf children arose because his daughters had a good friend who was profoundly deaf as a result of meningitis.

Sir Reginald, always one to be thorough, then made discreet enquiries from Dr Jean Littlejohn, one of Melbourne's most respected ear, nose and throat surgeons, about whether I had my feet on the ground as well as my head in the air. At any rate, I received a telephone call from Dr Moroney, the doctor for Ansett Transport Industries, who said that he would like to discuss the possibility of a telethon. I was surprised that one of Melbourne's most senior and highly regarded businessmen would be interested in the work I was doing. I didn't realise at the time what a strong personal interest he had in helping this cause.

On 16 July 1973, I wrote to Sir Reginald about the basic biological research we had been doing and said that we were developing computer programs to present speech to a device. I stressed that the main problem was obtaining the money for engineering to develop the fully implantable section of the device. I thought that, given the money, it would take up to three years to be ready and could be developed commercially.

I was then summoned to meet him in his office. He sat behind a large desk, and during the interview he typified the successful, dynamic businessman by taking a number of phone calls and messages that obviously couldn't wait. He was encouraging, and said he would put the resources of his station behind an appeal to raise the money for our project. I soon appreciated that if Sir Reginald said the telethon would happen, it would. The channel staff respected him, and he definitely determined policy.

I knew that it would be necessary to get approval from the authorities at the University of Melbourne for something so radical as a telethon to appeal for research funds. In July 1973 I approached the vice-chancellor, Professor Sir David Derham, and the vice-principal, Mr Ray Marginson, wondering how they would view this novel and unprecedented approach to the public on behalf of a university department. I was agreeably surprised when they saw no fundamental problems. The university set up a committee on 1 August consisting of the deputy chancellor, Professor

Emeritus R.D. Wright, the acting vice-chancellor, Professor David Caro, and Ray Marginson to advise and deal with all matters relating to the telethon. The university also committed itself to managing the donations and sending out the receipts. So the scene was set.

Mr Max Stuart, station manager of Channel 0, was given the task of running an appeal for the $75 000 to start the project. However, in the latter half of 1973 there was no time to organise a major telethon, so an appeal through a mini-telethon with captioned telephone numbers for donations was planned. The appeal and telethon needed a name: I suggested the medical term 'sensori-neural deafness'. But that really got the thumbs-down from the public relations people. So, in the end, it was the Nerve Deafness Appeal and Telethon.

For the lead-up to the appeal, Mr Hector Crawford, the owner of Crawford Productions, donated the time of his staff and resources to make a documentary film, *Living in Silence*. The documentary focused on what a bionic ear might look like, and those likely to benefit, namely diverse age groups—a fact we hoped would encourage donations from a wide sector of the community. Making this documentary was a new experience for me! Again and again, I had to emerge from behind a row of potted plants to say my lines, using the right gestures and expressions. Almost invariably, I got something wrong. There was a lot of film taken those few days, and I learned why professional actors and directors have a reputation for being temperamental.

The ten-minute documentary was shown on Sunday night, 25 November 1973, to launch the appeal, and was re-screened the following Sunday night.

The big problem facing Max Stuart, with the mini-telethon set at short notice for Tuesday, 11 December, was how to present a program that would motivate viewers strongly to donate to the research. Fortunately, he was able to procure a film from Thames Television London called *Sunday and Monday in Silence*, which was about two days in the life of a family with a deaf child. It was a very moving account of the difficulty a hearing family had in communicating with a deaf family member. The film was very well received, including by parents and teachers of the Glendonald School for Deaf Children (see Appendix 2), and on the night we raised about $30 000, counting donations from the channel and Sir Reginald. This seemed like untold riches! It gave me the confidence to sit down and plan the engineering development, as well as further basic research.

The money raised was still short of the minimum $75 000 needed for each of the next three years, so the channel set out at the end of 1973 to plan for a major telethon late in 1974. The artificial ear, or 'hearing implant' as it was first called, would have to wait a little longer.

During one of the planning sessions with Max Stuart and the station staff, the name 'bionic ear' was coined. We were discussing our research while the television series 'The Six Million Dollar Man' was running, and someone suggested that we were really developing a bionic ear for such a man. The name stuck. One disadvantage of the term was that, by associating it with the 'Bionic Man', some people thought it would bring super-hearing. This misconception later created the wrong expectations by the press, and led our critics to complain that I was publicly overstating its potential benefit.

Our lack of a support group of volunteers who would go out and raise funds before the telethon was a major difficulty, as telethons only brought in large amounts of money when it was raised during the year. Most didn't come in on the night. We also needed a chairman for the appeal, and fortunately I had known a leader in the financial community, Mr David Elsum, who was happy to take on this role. He continued until 1977, when Mr John Calvert-Jones, a senior stockbroker, took over. They both had a strong personal interest in helping deaf people.

Our committee had to plan functions to raise money during the year. Max Stuart and the staff of the station had the contacts. We began with a charity concert on Sunday, 20 January 1974, by John Farnham, the popular Australian singer. As there were few people available to do the hack-work for the concert, I went around Melbourne putting up posters on lamp-posts and buildings to advertise it. The station was also able to get some press coverage. In the end, the concert, held at the Dallas Brooks Hall, was well attended, but after paying for the hire of the hall we made only a few thousand dollars. It was clear that raising money through public appeals was going to be hard work. There followed functions such as the 'Gown of the Year' award that I was to attend to explain my vision and the need for support.

Prior to the telethon in 1974, the Melbourne City Council gave us certain days on which to shake tins. The members of our university

A cartoon of the author shaking a tin on the corner of Collins and Swanston streets appealing for funds for bionic ear research.

department were enthusiastic about this, and it became a challenge to see who could raise the most money. My secretary, Miss Joan Maher, chose to stand in front of the exclusive George's store, in Collins Street, hoping that the wealthy would donate freely. This wasn't the case. I had better luck on the corner of Collins and Swanston streets with elderly female shoppers heading for Flinders Street Station. The young, well-dressed businessmen would look right through me.

The major telethon was set for 1–2 November 1974 at the studios in Nunawading, and organised to run for 26–27 hours. To an outsider it looked like chaos, with about 200 people in a frenzy of activity. Max Stuart estimated that he had three hours' sleep in three days! In the studio, people milled everywhere, large cameras with their snake-like cables moved to and fro across the studio floor, and actors came and went from one set to the next. During the day, there was a steady stream of people visiting the make-up-rooms prior to 'going on camera'. Tired workers returned from time to time, triumphant with tins full of money. They included my wife Margaret, who had succeeded in getting generous support from those at the bar of our local Eltham hotel. Food was available at any time, provided by the channel staff and volunteers. For the Saturday evening variety concert, a seemingly endless queue of people waited to get a seat in the audience. There was a sense of excitement, and the audience didn't need signs to remind them to applaud! Behind the scene,

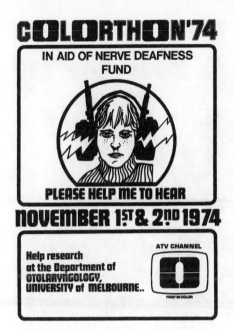

Poster advertising the first major telethon for the Nerve Deafness Fund.

visiting politicians and other dignitaries were being met and entertained in the boardroom before appearing on the set to give their support. It was marvellous the way many federal, state and local politicians, from both sides of politics, joined in for the occasion. The telethon, called a 'Colorthon' to emphasise the introduction of colour television to Channel 0, was opened by the Premier of Victoria, Mr Rupert Hamer (later Sir Rupert). Other politicians giving support were the Leader of the Federal Opposition, Mr Billy Snedden, the Federal Minister for the Media, Mr Doug McClelland, the Federal Opposition Spokesperson for the Media, Dame Margaret Guilfoyle, the past Premier of Victoria, Sir Henry Bolte, and the Mayor of Melbourne, Councillor Ron Walker. Mr Bob Hawke, the then president of the Australian Council of Trade Unions, also gave the telethon his blessing. To give a focus, I too had to speak and join in with the celebrities in reading out some of the donations. I didn't try to compete with their repartee!

Channel 0 really went out of its way to make the telethon a success. The popular actors Julie Egge from Norway and George Montgomery from Hollywood, and the British entertainer Garry Glitter, were invited. Local entertainment personalities included the 'Young Talent Time' team, Mike Walsh, Mike Preston, John Farnham and Linda George.

The president of the Lions Club of Melbourne, Fred Agar, presents a cheque for $10 000 to the author in the presence of the 1974 Nerve Deafness Telethon compere, television personality Mike Willesee. (Photograph courtesy of Fred and Anna Maria Agar)

While all these activities were going on, 160 volunteer telephonists were in Ansett House answering the calls from people promising donations. These included a $10 000 donation from the Lions Club of Melbourne for floor space which the Australian University Commission had left 'in shell' for me to complete. The cheque was presented to compere Mike Willesee by Mr Fred Agar, president of the Lions Club.

The telethon was a considerable success, raising $87 233 to further our research. Although it didn't match the amount raised by Channel 7 for the Children's Hospital, it was the largest sum I had received up to that time and I felt very grateful. The money was enough to pay for an engineer, a computer programmer, a technical officer, electronics parts and some other equipment. I kept a little money aside to ensure some continuity for staff, but I avoided telling them how uncertain their future was!

A few months later, after reviewing my budget, I could see that we would run out of money by the end of 1975. So again I had to appeal to Sir Reginald Ansett in the hope that further telethons would be held. To retain his interest, I kept him regularly informed of the advances we were making, and assured him that we were doing the best we could to produce a result in the shortest possible time. He responded to my letter of 3 February 1975, and I'm sure he was influential in arranging for us to have another mini-telethon on 16 December of that year and then a major telethon the following May.

By the end of 1975 it was time to have a break from the distractions and politics of fundraising and just think about the research questions that still needed to be answered. In particular, I had to learn more about speech science so that I could better advise our engineers on the final design for the implanted section of the bionic ear. At this stage, I still envisaged that we could do the first operation late in 1976 as I had first told Sir Reginald.

For these reasons, I arranged to take overseas study leave at the University of Keele, in England, from 1 January 1976 in order to generate ideas. The timing of the leave was awkward, but I was able to cram the trip in and be back for the major telethon on 14–15 May. While overseas, I arranged to see any publicity material about the telethon to ensure that it was accurate and sensitive.

The May telethon was also a success, again due to the efforts of the Channel 0 staff and the appeal committee. The appeal committee had wide representation: from the Glendonald School for Deaf Children, the Australian Association for Better Hearing, the State Government Visiting Teacher of the Deaf Service, and Arthur Andersen & Co. accountants. By this stage we also had regular donors, a women's auxiliary run by Mrs Margaret Douglas, and groups prepared to shake tins on the day of the telethon. These groups included Apex, Lions, the ANZ Bank, Uncle Bob's Clubs, deaf schools and the Metropolitan Fire Brigade. This telethon raised $125 588, although approximately $200 000 had been promised on the night.

By the end of 1976 we had reached a stage where the electronics for the implant receiver-stimulator had been designed and tested. They still had to be incorporated into a small silicon chip, and enclosed in a water-tight, gold-plated box for implantation in the body. This meant the operation wouldn't be carried out in 1976 as I had expected.

On 15 December, I received a letter from Sir Reginald Ansett in which he said that although he was prepared to give us first call on further funds, he thought it would be beneficial to each of us if their fundraising was 'integrated with other organisations associated with the problems of deaf people, to widen the scope of future Telethons'. Unfortunately, widening the scope, and the fact that the telethons lapsed for three years,

David Dewhurst, the University of Melbourne. (Photograph courtesy of Mike Hirshorn)

meant a reduction of funds for us from 1977 to 1980 when the Nerve Deafness Appeal was taken over as the Deafness Appeal by the Deafness Foundation of Victoria under the able chairmanship of the Honourable Peter Howson.

This marked reduction in funding ($21 051 in 1977, $49 477 in 1978, and $13 944 in 1979 from the Nerve Deafness Appeal) came at a critical time in the race to develop the bionic ear. Fifty thousand dollars was needed for the cost of converting the electronic design into a custom-made silicon chip, but our budget now only allowed $6000 for the purpose. The Australian government had no specific allocation for developing silicon chips, so we would have to find another way.

DESIGNING THE 'GOLD BOX'

As I had no background in electronic engineering, I had been pleased in 1973 to convince a colleague and friend, Dr David Dewhurst, to help with the project to develop an electrical stimulator of the inner ear. David was a physicist interested in electronics who had been transferred from the Department of Physiology to Electrical Engineering at the University of Melbourne.

Initially, a decision had to be made between using a plug and socket to allow wires to come out of the head from the inner ear, or having electronics implanted, with signals transmitted to them through intact skin. I had seen the problems with using plugs and sockets on the experimental animals in our rate coding studies in 1972 and 1973, particularly those by students John Nathar, Harry Minas and Howard Kranz (see Appendix 2 for details). The plugs and sockets often became infected around their junction with the skin, or became dislodged. Consequently, I was opposed to their use for our patients, and David Dewhurst was in agreement with me.

The alternative meant designing the complex circuitry for an implanted receiver-stimulator unit to stimulate the hearing nerves. The unit would be placed under the intact skin and receive information from outside. The concept was illustrated in the promotional film I made for the 1973 mini-telethon. The design required the equivalent of 6000 radio-valves, or transistors, and could not have been miniaturised without the silicon chip.

We next had to decide whether to have all the electronics etched on to a single custom-made silicon chip, or have some silicon chips bought off the shelf and connected together on a silicon wafer the size of a postage stamp. The latter was the best option, as we really didn't know how best to design the silicon chip; anyway, it was much less expensive. The reduced funding from the telethon meant we needed to use a cheaper new experimental technique fitted around pre-designed chip components.

To design the circuitry, we ideally needed to recruit a senior electronics engineer, but I didn't have money to do this. The alternative was to attract a postgraduate engineering student to do the research for a Doctorate of Philosophy degree. This could mean the project taking longer, as postgraduate students, however clever, need time to become familiar with the area, and their loyalties are divided between writing up their thesis and performing against the timelines for the project. On the other hand, a recent graduate would be right up to date in a rapidly changing field.

David Dewhurst had become interested in the project, which had been receiving publicity through the telethon. Like a number of engineers,

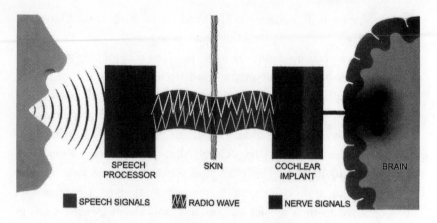

MELBOURNE UNIVERSITY HEARING PROSTHESIS

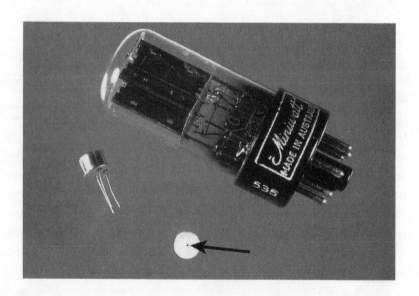

(Top) *The general concept of the bionic ear, shown in the film for the 1973 mini-telethon.* (Bottom) *A radio-valve, transistor and silicon chip with the equivalent of 400 transistors shown for comparison of size.*

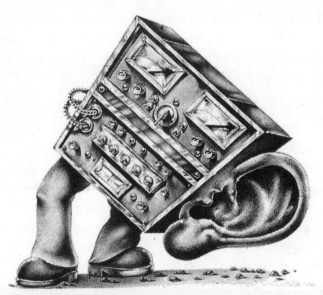

The possible size of the bionic ear if constructed from radio-valves. (Cartoon courtesy of Mr Keith Tregent, one of the first group of subjects)

he was keen to work on projects that would help people, rather than just make money for industry. He found a very able student, Ian Forster, who started his research in June 1974. Ian proved to be an excellent choice.

Ian would need to design the electronics, but additional engineering help was anticipated to develop the package. This was also likely to be very tricky, as the body is made of very corrosive fluids that can penetrate through solder and cause electronic failure.

I had to set up a major part of the Ear, Nose and Throat Department to do the electronic engineering. It was important to have all aspects of the work under the one roof. This would facilitate the rapid interchange of ideas, and people would be able to work together more effectively. I had to turn over medical areas, such as those used to wash out people's nasal sinuses and the wax from their ears, to electronics. In the end, we became the University of Melbourne's second-largest purchaser of electronic components outside the Department of Electronic Engineering!

With the funds from the first major telethon in October 1974, I was able in 1975 to advertise for an engineer. Mr Jim Patrick came out the winner—he was not only an innovative engineer and a lateral thinker, but it turned out he could apply his knowledge to other disciplines involved. Before accepting the position he asked what it would lead to in the future.

I replied that I didn't know, but maybe one day it might be developed commercially and he would then be able to work in industry. Years later he had many key roles in the firm Cochlear Pty Limited, and in 1994 he became its international research manager.

To develop the 'gold box', answers were needed for a number of questions:

1. *How should we transmit information through the skin to the implant?* It wasn't clear whether information transmitted to stimulate the hearing nerves should be by infra-red light shining through the ear-drum, by ultra-sonic vibrations to the scalp, or by radio waves through the tissues. Radio waves were, however, shown to be the most reliable, and least likely to be affected by the body. Transmission would occur via two circular matched aerials, one on the outside and the other on the implant.

2. *Should the implant have its own batteries or receive power from outside?* Power to operate the implant and provide the electricity to stimulate the hearing nerves could either be obtained from the energy in the radio signals sent through the skin, or provided by implanted batteries. Batteries were used in heart pacemakers, but they had to be replaced through a small skin incision every five years. Batteries would also increase the size of the implant. Therefore, radio signals were the better alternative.

3. *Where should the implant be placed in the body?* It was logical to site the microphone close to the ear, as we turn our heads to the direction of the sound that is receiving our attention. The electronic package would need to be small enough to place in the mastoid bone behind the ear.

4. *What would be the design of the electronics to allow us to produce a wide range of stimulus currents?* The receiver-stimulator electronics had to give us the flexibility to choose the right electrical stimuli to represent the speech signals. Fortunately, this question didn't have to be answered immediately but could wait for results from our experimental animals and the further study I did with Dr Bill Ainsworth at Keele University in 1976.

5. *How should the electronics be packaged?* This was a key issue. The body is a very corrosive environment, and salts and proteins can find their way through very fine cracks and cause electronic failure. This is especially likely where the wires leave the package to join the electrode bundle

passing to the inner ear. The sealing problem had bedevilled the heart pacemaker industry until staff from the Australian firm Telectronics discovered that ceramics could be baked to fuse with a titanium case and platinum wires.

6. *Did the implant package need a connector in case it failed and another one had to be re-attached to the electrodes in the inner ear?* As we weren't sure how often the electronics would fail, we had to consider how to replace the implanted receiver-stimulator. Neither did we know whether it would be detrimental to remove the attached electrode from the inner ear. It seemed advisable to design a connector that would allow only the packages to be changed.

LEAVE TO STUDY SPEECH SCIENCE IN ENGLAND

In 1975, considerable effort was put into the design of the electronics for the receiver-stimulator, and the transmission of information and power through the skin. The aim was first to produce an operational model on the bench that could be tested before miniaturising the circuit on to silicon chips. As the radio link restricted what we could transmit to the package, we had to choose how we would control the electrical currents. For example, would we provide lots of current amplitude steps, or fine control of the timing of the stimuli on each electrode? Finding answers to these questions was one of my aims in taking study leave to go overseas to centres in England and Europe in 1976. I also needed to obtain a good understanding of speech science so that I would know what information was important to present to the implant for speech understanding.

While planning my study leave, I had an opportunity to talk with people in London and see Professor Donald McKay's laboratories at the University of Keele when I was invited to give a presentation at the British Ear, Nose and Throat Conference in 1975. I offered to speak about our preliminary work on the bionic ear, and was listed to give one of about ten optional presentations. Five people came to mine. Why had I come half-way around the world for this level of interest, I wondered? One of those five attendees was Dr Howard House, a famous ear surgeon from Los Angeles, who mentioned that his brother, William, was developing a single-electrode device. He offered to tell him about our research.

On my return from the trip, I made plans to go back to London and work at the Imperial and University Colleges with Dr (later Professor) Adrian Fourcin. Just after I had negotiated accommodation for the family in the beautiful Sevenoaks area, I read that the Irish Republican Army had blown up a carriage on the train I could have travelled on to London. Not being conditioned to such events, I looked around for a centre in a place of less interest to the IRA. Then I remembered the University of Keele, which was situated in a quiet village. Furthermore, Donald McKay was head of the Department of Communication and Neuroscience, the field in which I was interested. He had inspired me with his logical arguments in favour of free will versus a deterministic view of life when he had been the vice-chancellor's visitor to Australia in 1972, and with his ability to relate his Christian faith to science. When I enquired about spending some time at Keele to learn about speech science, McKay was pleased to assist. He asked Dr (now Professor) Bill Ainsworth, a leading speech scientist, if he would be willing for me to do research with him. Bill agreed. It would also give me the opportunity to see the research of Dr (now Professor) Ted Evans and Dr Pat Wilson, noted for their work in hearing mechanisms and perception.

Getting the family ready for the expedition was a big ordeal. I was surprised when an acquaintance in business remarked that the trip was a university perk, or an overseas holiday at the taxpayers' expense. Just before Christmas 1975, we left Melbourne and drove to Sydney with the four children and our luggage squeezed into our small Toyota Corolla. It was a hot summer's day and on the way I had to keep the engine from overheating by wrapping ice around the manifold. A few days later, as the plane lifted off from Kingsford-Smith airport and I saw the yellow sand of the beaches lapped by the deep-blue Pacific Ocean below, I questioned the wisdom of leaving the comforts of home and the warmth of the summer, for the cold of an English winter. Two days before we left, England had been hit by one of its worst ever storms. Airports had been closed and the countryside devastated. It wasn't a promising start. As we approached London, the plane seemed to descend forever in thick fog until at last Windsor Castle, the signpost to Heathrow airport, came into view. London was grey and depressing—nothing like the children had expected. At the airport hotel we delayed going to bed, hoping to ward off the effects of jet lag. But it made no difference to the children. At 2 a.m. they were awake, and played and fought until morning. The next

The University of Keele, UK, 1975. Insert: *The author with Bill Ainsworth in the Department of Neuroscience and Communication, 1996.*

day we caught the train north to Stoke-on-Trent. The other passengers, sedate adults and their well-behaved children, didn't know what to make of our brood, who spoke with loud Australian accents and climbed all over the seats. One of the children even got up into a luggage rack!

On arrival we were met by the Anglican vicar, Rev. Graham Jones. At the last moment the university had offered us the vicarage in New-castle-under-Lyme for our accommodation. The vicar had two children with cystic fibrosis, and couldn't live at the vicarage as it was too cold and damp, and too expensive to heat. Australians were meant to be hardy, so it was thought we should be able to manage, but we did in fact heat the large, nineteenth-century building, saying simply 'Hang the cost!' for one winter.

After a week the children went to school. Merran was five and starting school for the first time. Roslyn (aged seven) and Cecily (ten) fitted in with their age groups, while Sonya (eleven) had to join children who were half-way through their first year at secondary school. The experience was traumatic for them all. To cope with the cold, they left in the morning wearing their dark-blue duffle coats, with the hoods pulled down to their eyebrows. It was very depressing leaving before the sun had risen and coming home in the dark, something they hadn't experienced in Australia.

Also, their accents set them apart as strangers. Merran asked tearfully one night, 'What's a gypsy?' However, they came to be accepted and made friends, the older two doing well in a 'swimathon' at the local heated pool.

On the weekends I had hoped to give the children an introduction to the history and culture of Britain. For the younger ones, especially, the Egyptian mummies and Elgin marbles in the British Museum weren't exactly their 'cup of tea'. 'I don't like all these old things. I want an ice-cream,' was their plea. Another time, the best part of a trip to the south-west wasn't Stonehenge or Salisbury Cathedral, but skating at Southampton. I found the answer was to explore the villages in the county of Shropshire and do brass rubbings in the little churches. Many had brass reliefs of the noblemen and women who lay beneath. Brass rubbing kept the children warm and was like colouring in a picture book.

As the weather improved and the crocuses came out, followed by the daffodils, we discovered walking. There is nothing quite as beautiful as the paths that follow the canals or a lake, pass through parks and estates, or wind up rocky outcrops such as Mow Cop.

Living in the vicarage gave me insights into the needs of people. Quite often they would knock on our door, not realising the vicar didn't live there anymore, seeking help with their personal or financial problems. It was an enriching experience to have the vicar as a friend. Graham and Heather not only had two daughters with cystic fibrosis who later died, but they had lost a son from the condition. How difficult it was for them, but they didn't blame God. They loved their children dearly and had a deep faith in God's goodness. In spite of his difficulties, Graham was always ready to guide and help others in their time of need. Years later, at the age of sixty, Graham celebrated his birthday by walking around the coastline of England and raising £20 000 for cystic fibrosis and other causes.

My time at the University of Keele proved to be very fruitful. Advised by Bill Ainsworth, I used a synthesiser driven by a computer to construct artificial speech in order to determine my own and other staff's most important speech frequencies, as well as their intensities, for understanding consonants and vowels. The synthesiser extracted the formant frequencies of speech. Formants are frequency concentrations of great importance for speech understanding. This research experience was invaluable for the later development of our first speech processing strategy with the bionic ear.

At this time, I arranged to visit Mr John Holmes at the Joint Speech Research Unit in London and see his formant synthesiser. When I arrived at the government building that housed the Unit, I walked straight past the security gate without realising, much to the consternation of the man on guard duty. I hadn't realised the importance of speech research for human communication systems in the armed forces. After this unexpected excitement, I was issued with a security badge.

Next I took the long train trip to Stockholm to visit Professor Gunnar Fant at the Speech Transmission Research Laboratories. This was one of the major speech research centres in the world. Gunnar Fant had made his name for his studies on the formant frequencies in speech. He was very courteous, and arranged for his associate, Dr (later Professor) Arne Risberg, to spend the day introducing me to the research groups. I was impressed by the variety and depth of their work. Not only were they studying how speech was perceived in hearing listeners, but also how deaf people communicate by converting speech into skin vibrations. Arne knew of my interest in developing a bionic ear, but little was said on the subject. It was only at the International Cochlear Implant Conference in Melbourne in 1995 that Arne admitted it took them some time to be convinced that an implant was feasible, and only after a careful review of the speech results from patients operated on at centres around the world.

My trip overseas made me aware of the growing international interest in cochlear implants. A group had been set up in England, work had started in Paris and Vienna, a symposium was being held in Munster, and there was strong interest in the United States, in San Francisco, Los Angeles and Salt Lake City.

CONSTRUCTING THE 'GOLD BOX'

On arriving back in Melbourne in May 1976, a lot of work was still required to complete the benchtop model of the implant. I had naively thought we might be able to package it and do the first operation in 1976. I hadn't learned that in electronics, circuits don't perform to expectations and faults develop in components.

Nevertheless, towards the end of 1976, the circuit design was completed and tested on the bench. The engineers had now to consider how to reduce the key elements to a silicon chip. Ian Forster, helped by Jim Patrick,

The engineers Jim Patrick and Ian Forster holding the circuit diagram for the Mastermos silicon chip to provide the circuitry for one of the ten stimulus channels of the first bionic ear, 1977. This chip contained the equivalent of 400 transistors.

found a way to integrate the circuit on a Mastermos silicon chip, which contained pre-designed units that had to be connected up in appropriate ways for the customer's needs. As it turned out, there were all sorts of difficulties in achieving a functioning chip this way. Several attempts were needed, with the result that we lost eighteen months in the race with other researchers in San Francisco, Paris and Vienna. But I needn't have worried.

By late in 1977 the silicon chip controlling the stimuli on each of ten stimulus channels was completed. In the process, each time a chip was fabricated in Silicon Valley it had to be sent to Melbourne and probed to determine whether it functioned according to specifications. When an error was found, a new production run was ordered.

Before the silicon chips were assembled, they also had to be tested for reliability. We didn't want them failing soon after a device had been implanted. The accepted procedure was to bake them in an oven to 60°C for some hours and then test them again. Those that passed were then set aside for later assembly. To do this meant allocating yet another area of the Ear, Nose and Throat Department for electronic engineering.

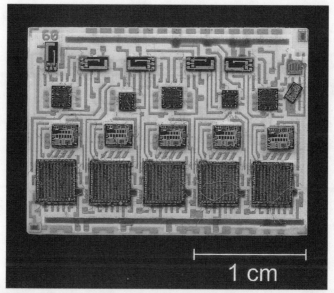

The silkscreen-printed wafers with the gold tracks connecting the silicon chips for the circuitry in the implanted receiver-stimulator unit, 1977.

The silicon chips had to be connected together using tracks of gold printed on to wafers of silica (derived from sand). To produce these tracks, we consulted Australia's only micro-electronics firm, AWA, which had experience in the development and manufacture of major components for the Australian pacemaker firm, Telectronics. However, in a letter dated 15 November 1976, it was stated that what we wanted to do was 'well beyond the state-of-the-art in normal industrial practice'. The letter continued: 'Whatever clinical risks are attached to this project, the technical risks are considerable.' If we had proceeded with AWA, it would have been costly, there would have been no assurance of a successful outcome, and it could have introduced considerable delays.

We turned for help almost immediately to the Research Laboratories of Australia's telephone company, Telecom (now Telstra), which had the latest technical facilities. I was pleased to receive a letter on 24 November 1976 from the director, Mr Ed Sandbach, informing me that they would be able to provide help free of charge, and that the job would take about four weeks. This led, in 1977, to the production of the silkscreen-printed wafers.

The silicon chips then had to be bonded to the gold tracks on the silicon wafers before they were sealed into a package. This required

The first multiple-electrode 'gold box' with connector, 1978.

welding at a microscopic level. After again casting around for help, we found a small, new firm, Hybrid Electronics, which had special expertise in this area.

The package lid and base were gold-plated ready to receive the wafers. They were joined to the wires that emerged from the package, and the steel lid was soldered into place. The wires emerging from the 'gold box' were joined to the electrode and the whole device was encased in silicone rubber, ready to be implanted in a person's head.

FUNDING FROM A LIONS CLUB FOR BIOLOGICAL SAFETY STUDIES

The telethons virtually covered the engineering costs, but not the biological safety studies. With bioengineering, there is a temptation to concentrate on the more obvious engineering issues and to neglect the equally important connection of the device to the body. In 1975, I thought a safety study should be done, but I was faced with a funding problem. At this time I had to visit my dentist, Dr Sydney Warneke, who asked me how my work was going. I managed to explain my difficulties in obtaining funds for initial safety studies just before he stood on the chair to lever out one of my long, multi-rooted teeth. He then cheered me up by saying he thought he could rally his Lions Club to support the cause. The club raised approximately $7000 for a research assistant to prepare sections for

Research Laboratory, Department of Otolaryngology. Left to Right: The author, Ray Black, Robert Shepherd.

the microscopic examination of the inner ear of the experimental animals that had been implanted. This started a long and happy association with Lions Clubs International and a number of district clubs.

BIOLOGICAL SAFETY AND EFFICACY

One of the many biological research challenges facing the development of the multiple-electrode bionic ear was to place the tiny wires in the inner ear close to the hearing nerves that convey the different speech frequencies to the brain. Could we localise the electrical current to the individual groups of nerve fibres and prevent it from short-circuiting along the fluid in the inner ear? I had convinced Jack (Ray) Black in 1974 to do a Doctorate in Philosophy degree to study this question. A computer model of the way electrical current passed through to the hearing nerves was created and tested on the experimental animal. The results showed that the electrodes were best placed in the lower tube of the inner ear (the scala tympani). They also showed we should 'push' the electrical current out one electrode and 'pull' it back through another. My initial concerns that we would get unacceptable short-circuiting of current in the fluid-filled tubes in the inner ear were unfounded.

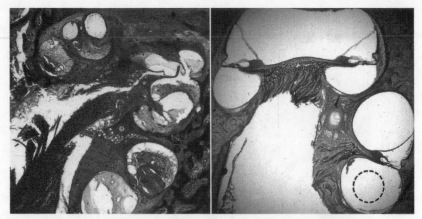

Left: *The inner ear of the experimental animal has been sectioned after drilling into it to place electrodes. This has caused considerable damage, and demonstrates that the inner ear should not have holes drilled into it in this way.* Right: *The inner ear of the experimental animal has been sectioned after the electrode bundle has been passed along the lower tube (scala tympani). No significant damage or loss of the hearing nerves has occurred (1975–76).*

The next question was, could the electrode wires be inserted into the inner ear without damaging the very hearing nerves it was hoped to stimulate? International scientists and ear surgeons were saying no. The ear surgeons had come to this view partly because, in operations to remove a small middle ear bone called the stapes and replace it with a steel strut (stapedectomy surgery), injury to the receptor for hearing in the inner ear could lead to a complete loss of hearing. However, their concerns weren't well founded, because damage to the receptor in a normal ear didn't mean that damage from a bundle of wires inserted into a deaf ear where the receptor was absent would affect the hearing nerves.

Criticisms in science are important, as they emphasise the need to do experimental work to provide data to help determine which theories are valid. In this case, we used animals for our biological safety studies. Insulated wires had to be inserted into different sites—under anaesthetic, of course. The animal was sacrificed some months later, the inner ear sectioned and the damage examined under the microscope.

New research meant learning about unfamiliar techniques, and how to interpret the findings. But in 1975 we showed that it was possible to insert a bundle of wires along the lower turn of the inner ear spiral without damage to the hearing nerves, provided key structures weren't torn or fractured, and infection didn't spread from the middle ear.

Finding where to place the electrode wires in the inner ear, and learning how to do this safely, were two important issues; producing a bundle of wires that could be threaded along the inner ear and reach the nerves transmitting speech frequencies to the brain, was another.

How do we make a bundle of ten to twenty wires small enough, when the tube in the inner ear is only 1–1.5 millimetres wide? This provided a bigger challenge than I had realised. A suitable bundle of wires couldn't be purchased. I tried all around the world. I even used my links with the Australian airline industry through Ansett Transport Industries to contact high-tech specialised firms in the United States, but to no avail.

It was another case of having to do it ourselves. Before even knowing how to pass a bundle of wires around the inner ear, I decided to adapt advanced micro-electronic procedures for putting circuits on to silicon chips so that we could have many wires on a thread-like carrier. To find a suitable student for this work, I went to Cecil Pengilley, from the Department of Mechanical Engineering at the University of Melbourne. Rick Hallworth was interested and proved to be keen. He started the research in 1975.

The only establishment that had the facilities and interest in helping with the research was the Weapons Research Laboratories in Salisbury, South Australia. In those days, governmental departments had additional resources and were keen to assist with challenging relevant projects. They didn't charge for their work, considering it good for public relations if they provided help free of charge—and it might turn out to be of benefit to the defence of Australia!

With this research, metal atoms were fired at high speed at strips of bendable materials such as teflon, thus forming a thin metal layer bonded to its surface. The outline of the electrode pads and the conducting tracks printed photographically were left after the rest was etched away with chemicals.

This research, undertaken for a Master of Engineering degree, produced in 1976 electrodes which at first seemed fine. Rick rushed a couple of these over to me to test while I was on study leave in England. To my disappointment, the metal tracks in this sophisticated electrode array cracked like a crazy pavement when I bent them so that they could pass around the inner ear spiral. This was a major, unforeseen design problem that would be difficult to rectify soon enough for the electrode to be used

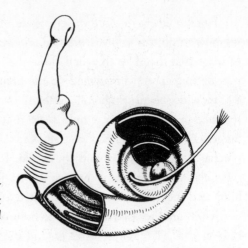

*The snail- or shell-shaped inner ear
with an opening drilled into the apex
and the electrode bundle passed
downward into a widening spiral.*

with our first patient. So, when I returned to Melbourne, I had to pursue with greater vigour the option of fabricating a multiple-electrode bundle by more conventional means.

Since 1975, I had also tried to find a way to pass a bundle of wires far enough around the human inner ear so that the terminals would lie near the nerves transmitting speech frequencies to the brain. The sites for stimulating these frequencies are some distance around the inner ear and fan out like the keys in a piano. The high frequencies are at the base and the low frequencies at the apex.

To start with, I found passing wires from below up any distance into the tightening spiral impossible. Therefore, I began a number of studies on the experimental animal and human inner ear. I also made acrylic models of the inside of the inner ear and passed wires into these, but again the wires wouldn't go the required distance.

Then I thought of inserting the electrodes back to front (that is, from top to bottom) by drilling a hole in the apex of the inner ear, and having it pass downwards into a widening spiral. However, after a number of dissections of the human temporal bone, Brian Pyman and I concluded that inserting a bundle of electrodes from the top down would be difficult and would damage some important structures.

Thus, by 1976, we still hadn't solved the problem of how to make a small bundle of wires, or of how to pass it safely along the inner ear to where the nerves for the speech frequencies lie. We had to find a way to pass the bundle of wires from below up into the tightening spiral of

The author in 1996 at Minnamurra beach, New South Wales, where in January 1977 he discovered the importance of graded stiffness in the design of an electrode for the human inner ear by inserting blades of grass and small branches into a turban-shell. Insert: A turban-shell with a blade of grass of graded stiffness having passed around the tightening spiral of the first turn.

the inner ear to minimise the surgical damage. Unless we could solve this problem, we wouldn't be able to place the electrodes correctly for multiple-electrode stimulation.

I kept mulling over the problem into the latter part of 1976. I was still obsessed by it when we went on holidays to Kiama at the end of the year. Then, one day while on the beach at Minnamurra, just north of Kiama, while the children were amusing themselves on the sand, I had a change to think about the problem once more. I had collected some large turban-shells (*Ninella torquata*), which have a similar spiral shape to that of the human inner ear, and began to experiment by inserting into them twigs from bushes, and dune grasses. I found that grass and fine twigs that increased in flexibility towards the end would pass satisfactorily. The flexible end would bend easily and follow the curve of the shell, while the stiffer part at the base allowed me to apply force to the tip so that it passed along the spiral. The finding gave me great encouragement that we could replicate a similar design with the bundle of electrodes, to be used in the human inner ear.

On returning from holidays, I was eager to get into the temporal

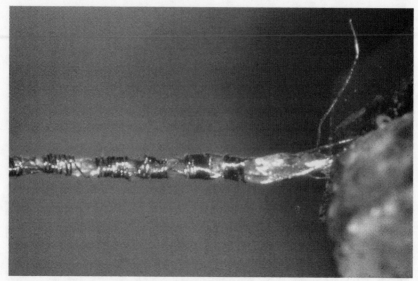

The multiple-electrode bundle with bared ends of wires wrapped around a silicone rubber tube.

bone laboratory and try experimenting with materials. It was exciting to find that tubes with graded stiffness went further into the inner ear than with our previous experiments. The preliminary results in the shells on the beach had thus been reproduced in the human inner ear, and augured well for the insertion of a bundle of electrodes at a future operation.

The final problem still remaining was how to terminate the wires on the outside of the silicone rubber tube. Back in 1970, I had experimented with soldering little steel balls on to wires, and bringing them out through holes in a silicone rubber tube. However, not knowing how to place them, and with no resources, I let the project lapse to concentrate on more pressing matters.

By 1976–77, the idea of bringing balls to the surface didn't seem so appealing, as they would cause the surface to be irregular and damage the inner ear during insertion; they could fall off; and the fact that they had a small surface area would concentrate the electrical charge and so damage the hearing nerves—a definite minus. What alternative solutions could there be? Brian Pyman remembered that a multiple-electrode bundle had been described by an overseas centre in which the terminal ends of the wires, which had the insulation removed, were wrapped around the carrier tube. We constructed an apparatus to make these bundles of wires, and proceeded to insert them along the inner ears of human temporal bones. They had the graded stiffness and could pass to the speech frequency region. One day early in 1978, as we were completing our surgical preparations for the first operation, the thought hit me: What if we needed to take this wrapped electrode bundle out at some stage and replace it with another? Could it be done easily without damage? Immediately, I set about pulling on the electrode. To my horror, it cut like a saw right through the bone in the centre of the inner ear where the hearing nerves lie. It was a disaster!

The engineers would soon be finalising the implant package and wanting to attach the bundle of electrodes. Now, at the eleventh hour, the bundle of electrodes might not be ready. I had told the Nerve Deafness Appeal Committee that we would soon be implanting our first patient. I couldn't delay the program for months to redesign a whole new array. Temporarily floored, we all sat down to try and come up with an answer. Then, Dr Quentin Bailey made a suggestion: why not wrap a band of metal around the silicone rubber tube at each site, instead of the wire strands? Why *not*?! was the immediate response and we started fabricating a banded electrode bundle. It was quite a finicky job, but we were fortunate to find Mrs Sue Derham, who was very deft with her fingers and proved just right for the task. The electrode bundle had many advantages. It could be inserted and withdrawn without injury to the inner ear; it had a large area, so that it avoided concentrating electrical current that would damage nerves; and it could be effectively rotated to allow for variations in structure and disease in the inner ear. Twenty years on, it is still the most effective and commonly used bundle of electrodes.

7

Preparing to implant
deaf adults

Deaf, giddy, helpless, left alone
To all my friends a burden grown;
No more I hear my church's bell
Than if it rang out for my knell;
At thunder now no more I start
Than at the rumbling of a cart.

Jonathan Swift, on his own deafness

I n 1976 when the engineering of the implantable receiver-stimulator for
the bionic ear was well under way, I realised I should start finding
suitable deaf recipients. I would look very silly if, having initiated this
complex and much-publicised development, I couldn't produce subjects
who needed the device. I had no one suitable on the waiting list of my
clinic at the Royal Victorian Eye and Ear Hospital. Most of my colleagues
weren't confident enough about what I was attempting to do, to send me
any potential patients. In fact, it would be many years before we received
any referrals from ear, nose and throat surgeons. It required many conference presentations, and overwhelming evidence from overseas doctors
that we had developed an effective device, before the referrals came. I
would have to cast around for people who might be profoundly deaf, and
interested in joining a small group of research subjects ('guinea pigs') to
have initial evaluations. At least I wanted to be able to say I had some
people who were being considered for the operation.

I wasn't sure yet what tests were needed to select patients or to evaluate them after surgery. It seems easy now, but it wasn't so then. If we
were to judge from the results coming from the Los Angeles single-
electrode cochlear implant, the patients wouldn't be able to understand

running speech. They had also started doing tests to determine if the patients experienced at least a psychological improvement. I maintained that we should be more positive about the multiple-electrode implant and aim for speech understanding.

I had to consider whether we should operate on one patient or a number, as was already being done in 1977 in Los Angeles for the single-electrode implant. I couldn't, however, see the logic of operating on many patients unless there were real benefits in speech perception. After all, tactile stimulation could provide the same speech understanding and awareness of sound as a single-electrode implant, without an operation. Surgeons have judged the success of an operation such as the removal of a gallbladder on large series of patients. But with our new implant, we had yet to see if it could help in understanding connected speech in just one person. Therefore, I was only prepared to operate on a small group at first, even though results might not be representative. Anyway, operating on a large number wasn't desirable in case there were any unex-pected problems. Fewer people would then suffer any ill-effects. In fact, there were some design problems with our prototype multiple-electrode implant package, and the overseas single-electrode devices failed fre-quently. These experiences only serve to emphasise the importance of testing a small group of people at the start of any new procedure.

But in 1977 the pressing problem was to find any takers at all, despite the population studies showing that about 1 per cent of deaf people were severely-to-profoundly deaf, and didn't get adequate help from a hearing aid. That translated into about 10 000 people in Australia. Their whereabouts, however, was a mystery. They didn't go to ear, nose and throat surgeons because they had long been resigned to the fact that nothing could be done to help them. They had disappeared into the woodwork.

AN INITIAL GROUP OF PATIENTS

The publicity surrounding the telethons since 1973 had heightened public awareness, and profoundly deaf people were learning that a bionic ear might one day be able to help them. Some wrote to us directly, and others approached us after being informed through the Australian Association for Better Hearing, an organisation of people who mainly had hearing before going deaf. As a result, I found four people to make an initial group. As it was such a controversial procedure, I needed initial patients with virtually no residual hearing (the smallest amount), so that they had nothing to lose through volunteering. Furthermore, if a person had residual hearing, electrical stimulation could stimulate the inner ear the same way that sound does, and so give false results.

This group helped me to learn what pre-operative tests were best for assessing suitability for the implant, and those required after the bionic ear had been implanted. Very little attention had been given to evaluating people with a severe-to-profound hearing loss, as hearing aids weren't much help to them.

A consultant advised that, after surgery, we should see if the patients could detect minimal audible cues—for example, the difference between a short vowel /i/ as in /hit/, and a long one /ee/ as in /heed/. This seemed, however, too negative an approach if that was all we were aiming to achieve, but it reflected the low expectations for a bionic ear in the scientific community. My aim was to give the patients some understanding of speech. If this were achieved, we would need standard speech tests to compare performance with hearing aids. The main ones were open sets of words, and sentences. Open-set tests are difficult, as the words and sentences haven't been practised and can be any from the language.

DEVELOPING THE SURGICAL TECHNIQUES

Reliable surgical procedures for the implant were fundamental to our success. In the early 1970s I started experimenting with methods to put electrode wires in the inner ear. It was delicate work at high magnifications. We used especially small drills and micro-instruments. In 1975, on a flight back from England when I had time to think, I realised we needed instruments that could manipulate the electrodes and direct them into the inner ear. I came up with the idea that they should be like miniature hands. Why not use a very small claw that mimicked the pincer action of the thumb and index fingers? This claw has proved to be of value in bionic ear surgery.

I had already learned from our research that a bundle of electrode wires could be inserted into the inner ear without the loss of the hearing nerves; we had also progressed in designing a bundle to pass around the

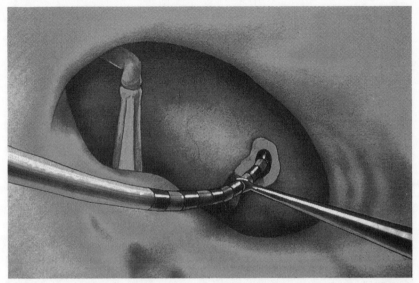

The micro-claw for directing the electrode bundle into the inner ear. (Drawn by Mr Ed Zilberts, courtesy Mr Ron West, President Cochlear Corporation US)

inner ear to lie close to the nerves transmitting the speech frequencies. But by mid-1977 I was having to think hard how best to do the whole operation, since it appeared the implantable receiver-stimulator, or 'gold box', would soon be ready! We had to decide where to place the skin incision so that it wouldn't be visible. It needed to heal well, not cut off the blood supply to the skin flap, and provide good access to the mastoid bone behind the ear. After considering all these requirements, Brian Pyman and I settled on an inverted J-shaped incision placed in the skin crease behind the ear and curling back into the scalp.

It was important to learn the best way to drill a bed in the skull to accommodate the implant package, as well as to approach the middle ear from behind so that the electrode bundle could be passed into the inner ear. The middle ear has a small window on its outer wall (the round window) that opens into the inner ear. Opening this window would allow us to view the inner ear, and direct the electrodes around the spiral without damage to the delicate structures.

Drilling through all the air cells in the mastoid would permit us to identify the key structures passing through the bone and so see our way to the middle ear. The facial nerve (nerve to the face) is one of these structures, and mustn't be damaged as one side of the face will become

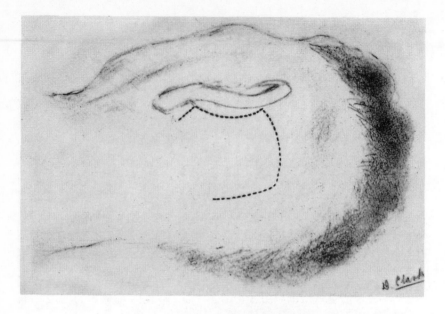

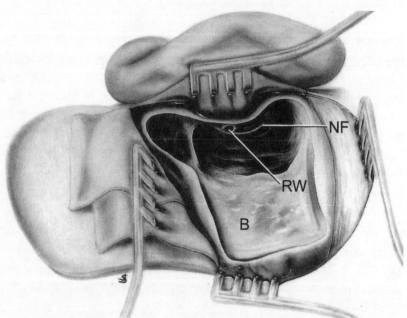

(Top) *The inverted-J skin incision and flap first used to implant the multiple-electrode bionic ear at the Royal Victorian Eye and Ear Hospital. (Drawn by my mother, Dorothy Clark)* (Bottom) *A diagram of the mastoid air cells behind the ear, drilled to expose the entry to the middle ear in front of the nerve to the face (NF), and entry to the inner ear via the round window (RW). The bed for the receiver-stimulator package in the skull is also shown (B).*

weak and droop. The entry to the middle ear lies a fraction of a millimetre above this nerve, and as it can vary in its position, a technique for safely drilling the bone away had to be established.

In addition, we had to see how to bed the package down in the skull behind the mastoid. My dissections had shown that the bone overlying the brain wouldn't be thick enough to accommodate the package without it protruding to create quite a large swelling. Although I had tried hard to get the engineers to make the package thinner, it still had a height of 13 millimetres. Therefore, I had to develop a technique to drill safely right through the skull to the lining of the brain, to make the bed as deep as possible. What worried me most was the possibility that a blow to the head could drive the package into the brain. Partly for this reason, we developed a technique for making a mould of the mastoid cavity out of silicone rubber to support the package at its front end. This would then help to absorb shocks to the region.

To ensure that we had mastered the surgical technique, Brian Pyman and I practised the operation on about fifty human temporal bones before we carried out the first surgery on a patient. Because of my concern that we also produce a reliable surgical procedure that could be followed by other surgeons, I drew up a surgical manual. That became the basis for implanting all further improved bionic ears.

Preventing infection extending into the inner ear from the surgery or after a middle ear infection was an important part of our surgical routine. I had seen infection frequently in the inner ears of implanted experimental animals, and knew the bad effect it had on the hearing nerves. I asked for a teflon felt ring to be glued on the electrode bundle so that it would fit snugly into the round window and allow scar tissue to grow in and seal the entrance against bacteria.

To further minimise the risk of infection, we adapted a method of operating in a flow of filtered air used by bone surgeons, to ensure that we wouldn't contaminate the wound with microbes shed from our bodies or circulating in the theatre. It was well known that implanting foreign bodies—for example, hip replacements—increased the risk of infection. We also carried out studies to develop a protocol for reducing bacterial contamination in the theatre generally. All this was done to ensure that the implant had the best chance of succeeding.

ETHICAL STANDARDS

Controversial research had to be done according to high ethical standards, so we set up an ethics committee in the University of Melbourne's Department of Otolaryngology. It was constituted along the lines being laid down by the National Health and Medical Research Council, which in turn followed the Declaration on biomedical research involving human subjects set out by the World Medical Assembly at Helsinki in 1969 and revised in Tokyo in 1975. The committee comprised a lawyer, Mr H. McCracken; a parent of a deaf child, Mrs J. Calvert-Jones; an external scientist, Professor G.V. Stanley; a specialist not participating in the research, Dr J.E. Delahunty; and myself as the head of the research project. We oversaw the development of a consent form that described the risks to the patient, including the fact that infection from the middle ear could spread to the inner ear with even the possibility of meningitis and loss of life. We also produced a paper outlining the proposed clinical assessment of bionic ear patients.

The Royal Victorian Eye and Ear Hospital carefully considered the research proposal at its Committee of Management, and had its solicitors and insurance brokers examine it. On 22 April 1977 I received a memorandum from the manager of the hospital, Mr C.G. Baird, that my request to undertake cochlear implant surgery in the hospital on human subjects was approved subject to a thorough assessment of patients' suitability. The memorandum concluded by wishing me 'every success with this project which may now proceed'.

The Department of Otolaryngology Ethics Committee met on 2 June 1977 to accept the memorandum. It was agreed that Dr Delahunty and Mr McCracken would interview the patients to satisfy themselves that they had signed the consent form without any coercion, that they were aware of the risks as outlined in the form, and that they understood the experimental nature of the surgery. It was agreed that patients should be informed that they might be exposed to publicity as a result of the operation, and their personal wishes should be respected.

THE PRESS AND CRITICISM

An outpouring of publicity came while we were preparing people for the implant. This really started in 1977 following publication of a feature

article by Frank Campbell entitled 'A computer in your ear' in the Melbourne *Herald* on 11 February 1977.

Press interviews were quite stressful, especially those for television. It
was essential that whenever I was interviewed, I had hard data up my
sleeve to back up what I was saying.

Press coverage was usually helpful, but there were disadvantages. The
increased public awareness, and the potential good associated with the
development, meant more people and institutions were prepared to
support our work financially. On the other hand, there was hardly an
occasion when I didn't get a telephone call from someone complaining.
Either a colleague would say I had overstated the number of people likely
to benefit, or a funding agency would say they hadn't been acknowledged.
The press didn't always see acknowledgements as essential to the story.
Incidentally, the ear, nose and throat fraternity in Australia and overseas
were of the opinion that I shouldn't be going straight to multiple-electrode
implants, but should learn to do single-electrode implants first.[1] One
surgeon frankly dismissed the idea of implants as comparable to pushing
a light bulb into the body and turning on the electricity! This comment
only illustrated the deep scepticism around at the time.

Although it might have been thought that I was deliberately using
the press, it wasn't so. Nevertheless, it was sometimes almost uncanny
how they approached me just at a critical time, or something happened
that made it appropriate to issue a press release. In any case, as a result
of publicity in 1977 and the number of requests from people for help, I
realised how desperate some parents were to provide help for their children as soon as possible.

SELECTING THE FIRST IMPLANT PATIENT

In 1977 the first implants were being packaged, and it seemed that we
might do the first operation that year. I then realised that no one in the

---

[1] It was claimed that multiple electrodes had been tried, and not found to be any
better than the single electrode. However, that wasn't correct, as little had been done
to localise the electrical currents to separate groups of nerve fibres to take advantage
of the multiple electrodes in producing appropriate speech processing strategies.
Moreover, those using single-electrode implants overlooked the importance of the
place coding of frequency which I knew, from my training in brain science, to be a
vital part of the hearing process.

original group was ideally suitable, and so I didn't have anyone for the first or second operation. I felt quite anxious, and didn't know what to do next. Not only did I need someone who had hearing before they became profoundly deaf, but he or she needed to be prepared to take risks. It was very important that the first patients were robust in temperament, as things could go wrong, and in fact did go wrong. I wasn't sure what the side-effects or complications would be. Moreover, the electronics could play up and give problems without completely failing. The first patients would actually be pioneers, as no satisfactory speech perception could be guaranteed and so, even if they received no benefit, they would need to accept the fact that the knowledge might help others in the future. I simply had to pray and trust that a suitable patient would come along.

Shortly afterwards I received a letter from Mrs Joan Keetley, who was totally deaf and searching for help. She went totally deaf at eighteen from meningitis. Her surgeon, Mr Frank Morgan, had said to her in 1943: 'I'm afraid medicine will never help, but one day science may.' Although she adjusted by learning to lip-read, Joan longed to hear again. After reading Frank Campbell's report in the *Herald*, she realised that her age (fifty-two) wasn't a barrier, and she was prepared to be a research subject.

Joan was happily married to a hearing man. They had six children, whose voices she had never heard. She drove the car, danced, and mixed freely in social circles. In 1977 she obtained a qualification in training deaf people to use residual hearing with a hearing aid, and was appointed a voluntary worker with the aged deaf. They weren't at all keen to take a deaf person, but Joan persisted and, after an interview, they agreed.

Joan had the qualities I was looking for, so I arranged to see her on 22 March. I found her to be charming and well motivated. Her background in helping to rehabilitate deaf people was ideal. I asked Ms Angela Marshall, one of the university's senior audiologists, to carry out a number of hearing tests and arranged for an X-ray of the inner ear. I wanted to know whether Joan's meningitis had caused bone to grow throughout the inner ear, making it difficult to implant. The techniques for X-raying the inner ear were only in their infancy, and when I studied the films the left side looked badly affected. Although there was some hope that an implant might be possible in the right ear, I explained to Joan that I needed to have someone where the canals of the inner ear were normal, so that I could get the electrodes far enough along to come close to the nerves conveying speech information. It was a disappointment to us both.

No one else arrived in 1977, but fortunately there were still engineering delays and it wasn't even clear if things would be ready in 1978. Then, Mr Rodney Saunders came to see me in April 1978 with a total hearing loss. He was referred by Angela Marshall, who attended the Deafness Investigation & Research Unit at the Royal Victorian Eye and Ear Hospital. When she received a call from the hospital outpatients' department that there was someone there who wanted to see Professor Clark regarding a bionic ear, she directed Rod Saunders to me. When Rod and his wife Margaret arrived, they said: 'Thank heavens we have finally got to see you. We have tried several times and no one would refer us.'

My impressions of Rod Saunders were favourable. He seemed a very stable person, albeit with a major communication difficulty. The hearing loss was so bad, he couldn't continue with his previous job as a supervisor for a grain merchant. He now stayed at home much of the time. He had tried lip-reading, but with little success. In other words, he had little to lose in the way of hearing if he proceeded with an operation.

I took a history and carried out a physical examination. Rod had received a head injury in January 1977, and his skull had to be opened to stop the bleeding. After the operation he discovered he was totally deaf.

Rod seemed an ideal candidate for the experimental procedure, especially as he had absolutely no residual hearing, which was most unusual. Later, when Rod started to get good results with the inaugural speech processing strategy, people had trouble believing our results. They thought they were due to electrical stimulation of residual hair cells in the inner ear, similar to the way a person hears normally. But Rod's hearing test was the proof that that wasn't so.

One question concerned me: could Rod's inner ear and hearing nerves recover some function, as he had had the head injury only about fifteen months before being assessed? It was just conceivable that he might regain sufficient hearing not to require a bionic ear. Should I wait longer before considering an operation on Rod? The other main question was: did the head injury cause a crack fracture to pass through the hearing nerve? If so, electrical stimulation of the inner ear wouldn't be successful as the passage of the nerve impulses from the inner ear to the auditory brain would be interrupted at the site of the fracture. The X-rays weren't clear enough for me to be sure on this score, so I started to develop a system for electrically stimulating the hearing nerve in the inner ear to see whether the nerve was intact and would transmit information.

I commenced practising on the experimental animal first. When it had been rehearsed, Rod was tested and he described some hearing sensations. This increased my confidence, and I felt I had done what was reasonable before proceeding with an operation on him.

After the tests had confirmed that Rod would be a suitable patient, I sat down with him to discuss his expectations to be sure he was prepared to go ahead. As he was a poor lip-reader, I had to write down many of my questions. Portions of the transcript of the interview are produced below.

GMC: When did you become deaf?

RS: Where do I live?

GMC: No. When—when did you become deaf?

RS: I'm sorry. January, twelve months ago—the 15th of January, I became deaf.

GMC: What happened?

RS: A car accident. I was hit on the back of the head and hit on the front of the head and that caused my deafness.

GMC: That sounds quite a blow. What was the nature of the accident? How did the accident occur?

RS: After spending three-and-a-half weeks in the hospital I realised that I couldn't hear and I thought it was due to a build-up of wax which I normally have syringed out every twelve months, so I asked the doctors to syringe my ears out and it had no effect.

GMC: Sorry, can I interrupt? How did the accident occur?

RS: I was driving home from work and I apparently swerved for some unknown reason and I finished up hitting a light-pole, knocking it to the ground, and that's virtually all I remember for about three-and-a-half weeks.

GMC: This morning I had a chat with you about the risks and the expectations of the operation. What do you expect from this operation?

RS: I would like to hear something again. It is a nightmare being deaf.

GMC: What do you miss most?

RS: Well, I miss hearing the family's voices. I miss music. I even miss the sound of the dog barking.

GMC: You understand that this isn't likely to give you the same musical sounds as you heard before?

RS: Sorry?

GMC: The implant won't give you musical sounds. What I have said is that the implant won't give you musical sounds like you heard before but may help with speech.

RS: Well, if it helps with speech so I can hear again, I will be very grateful.

GMC: You understood all the risks?

RS: Sorry?

GMC: You understand the risks of the operation? You understand the risks?

RS: Well, not completely, but what you have told me today has more or less let me know what to expect.

GMC: Are there any other things you would like to ask about the operation?

RS: The reaction, did you say?

GMC: No, any special queries, any questions?

RS: Any questions I would like to ask about the operation? I would like to think that it will be a success. I hope the after-effects aren't too great to bear. I just really want to believe that it will be a success and I will be able to hear some words again.

GMC: We hope so, too. Thank you for the interview.

RS: Thank you, Professor.

At about the same time that Rod Saunders came to see me, I was approached by another suitable person. George Watson, a returned Second World War soldier, had gradually become profoundly deaf following a bomb blast. George was referred from the Veterans Affairs Clinic by George Thermistoklis (another University of Melbourne-trained audiologist). He had progressively lost most of his hearing and been profoundly deaf for thirteen years. He was very enthusiastic and was also prepared to be a 'guinea pig'.

While Rod and George were being assessed, they came to feel part of the team. George was the better lip-reader, but communication was difficult with both of them.

As with Rod, I had a number of discussions with George about his expectations for the operation, and to answer any questions and help allay any fears he might have. Both Rod and George knew that they were free to withdraw from the study at any time.

Portions of an interview by the author with George Watson are reproduced below.

GMC: Can you tell me how long you have been deaf?

GW: When I first learned to lip-read?

GMC: No. When did you first go deaf?

GW: Oh. 1968. Yes, it would be about thirteen years ago. Oh, 1965.

GMC: When did you go completely deaf?

GW: Previous to that, I had a hearing aid. Gradually the hearing got worse and they gave me a more powerful hearing aid at the Repatriation Department.

GMC: Do you find the hearing aid helps you now at all?

GW: Yeah.

GMC: Do you get help from the hearing aid now?

GW: No use to me. They gradually increased the power until one night I just went to bed, got up in the morning to go to work, switched my hearing aid on and I couldn't hear—no pain or anything. It just went right off during the night.

GMC: What do you miss most now that you are deaf? What do you miss most?

GW: Ah. What do you do now?

GMC: No, it is awful writing. I'll print.

GW: I don't think there is any doubt about that. It is the isolation. You completely feel alone. I mean you go to a football match, people cheering and so forth, or you go to a race meeting, but it is all so very even all the time. What am I trying to think of now? I can't think of the word. But actually, it is very boring. Everything is the same, nothing seems to alter. You go to a party. It just seems the same thing.

GMC: How do your friends accept this?

GW: Naturally, I have restricted myself to a very small circle of friends because those that have known me and understood me for a long time, I don't have any problems.

GMC: In the family?

GW: I have two grown-up sons and a grown-up daughter.

GMC: Do they accept this?

GW: Yes. Probably I try their patience. It's the same at work. I was in charge of a staff and the people were very good. They knew I was deaf, but the subject is the thing. I got on all right, because I had been there. If something was wrong, they would want to know what was wrong. I knew what it was about and I could tell them. They didn't have much trouble, but if they did, they would always write it down. I got plenty of cooperation.

GMC: You understand this operation isn't going to make the sound like it used to be?

GW: Yes.

GMC: But our aim is to try to help you understand speech?

GW: Yes. It seems that possibly it is the cooperation to coordinate the sound and the lip-reading together. If you get a little bit of sound if the operation is successful, and you coordinate the sound with the lip-reading, it should be all right—put them both together.

GMC: This will depend on whether you had enough residual hearing nerves. If you have got sufficient hearing nerves, then there is a better chance than if you haven't. Do you understand?

GW: I consider myself reasonably fair at lip-reading, as a matter of fact, although when you meet a person for the first time, it's often a bit difficult. But I don't have very much trouble. I go shopping on my own. I don't depend on anyone else to do anything. I even ring up my friend on the phone.

GMC: How do you manage on the phone?

GW: As far as I know, I was the first person in the world that picked it up. I wanted to give my daughter a very important message and there was nobody at home and nobody to ring up for me, so I thought about it. It's just very simple: I picked up the telephone and dialled a number and just waited for about ten seconds, then I spoke into the phone and I said 'Katrina, it's your father speaking. I've got a message to give you.' I gave her the message, and I said: 'If you've received the message, if you're there, as soon as I hang up my phone, you ring me straight back on my number. I'll put my hand over the ear part and let it buzz, let it ring four times, and then I'll know that you've received the message.'

GMC: Very good.

GW: When I told the Better Hearing Association, they put that in their magazine and sent it overseas and everywhere. Apparently, nobody ever thought about it before.

Both Rod and George wanted to be the first patient, and I had the difficult job of choosing between them. George was quite disappointed when Rod was selected, but I considered it best for Rod to be the first subject as he had only recently been deafened, and I thought he should still have a good auditory memory. This would mean he could give us a better description of what the sensations were like with electrical stimulation and how much they differed from sound. He had also sung in the church choir, having come from a Methodist family, and I thought his knowledge of musical intervals would be an advantage. The biggest concern I had with George was that I didn't know how thirteen years of deafness would affect his auditory memory for the sounds we might produce electrically.

I set a date in June for Rod's surgery, but I had to abort the start because of unexpected engineering problems. I didn't want to have this happen again, and thus create uncertainty in Rod's mind. Consequently, I made a special appraisal of progress in completing the packaging and testing of the prototype receiver-stimulator. On a conservative estimate, I finally set the first of August as the date for the first operation. I then felt it necessary to apply maximum pressure to all staff to meet this deadline. Even in the last week before the implant operation there was much to do, and all the staff worked frantically to complete the tests and preparations in time. This included the final testing of the package, coating it with silicone rubber, and sterilisation.

Just before the surgery, I decided that I had done all that I could, so I went away with Margaret for the weekend for refreshment and time to pray. By Monday morning, the day before the operation, I felt very much at peace. I was surprised at how relaxed I felt, in contrast to the stress during the previous weeks.

8

The first operation

The three cornerstones of modern ear surgery:
Mastery of the complicated surgical anatomy of the ear
Meticulous asepsis for operations on the ear in a clean field
Magnification under the loupe and operating microscope

George E. Shambaugh Jr., 1959

As I left home early Tuesday morning, 1 August 1978, to do the first bionic ear operation, I felt as though I was about to cross over a chasm on a tightrope. I had done everything I could think of to ensure the operation was a success, including praying wholeheartedly. But so much was resting on the result! I had been appealing to the public in Melbourne and throughout Victoria for five years for funds for this invention. If I failed, my reputation would be in tatters and there would be many people whose hopes would be dashed.

I felt confident about doing the actual surgery, as my assistant, Brian Pyman, and I had rehearsed the steps in the operation many times on human temporal bones. We had learned to work together, and members of the theatre staff were well practised in their roles. But would any unexpected problems arise, and would the patient develop complications? It is no exaggeration to say that I was gambling my whole professional career on this day.

As I entered the operating theatre suite, my colleague, Gerard Crock, the Professor of Ophthalmology, greeted me: 'The moment of truth has arrived, Professor Clark.' Somehow he managed to make this declaration sound supportive.

The anaesthetist, Dr George Domaigne, had arrived, and when all was ready our patient, Rod Saunders, was sent for. I reassured him as best I could; I was very conscious that he, too, was going into the unknown.

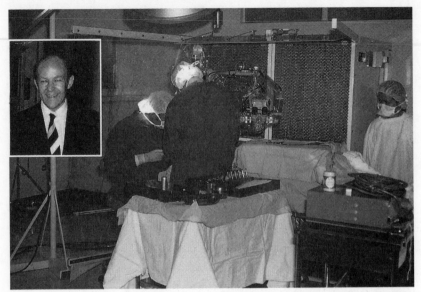

Brian Pyman preparing the skin for surgery, in the operating theatre at the Royal Victorian Eye and Ear Hospital. The unit blew specially-filtered air over the wound. (Insert) Brian Pyman.

The last thing we had to do before starting the operation was to set up the units to blow filtered sterile air across the open wound to ensure that microbes didn't contaminate it and produce a post-operative infection. Placing a foreign body like an implant under the skin can make a home for infection and prevent the body's defences attacking the microbes. We hoped that this unit, combined with a revised theatre routine, would help to ensure the best result for the patient.

I asked Sister Martin for the scalpel, took a deep breath, and pressed firmly downwards while sliding the knife along the path I had planned behind the ear. The skin gently parted, revealing the familiar anatomy of the underlying tissues. Then, carefully dissecting the lining of the ear canal from the bone, I lifted the ear-drum forward so that I could see into the middle ear. I was relieved to find a large, round window, the site for later inserting the stimulating electrodes into the inner ear. That gave me the all-clear to proceed.

I turned my attention to drilling most of the air cells out of the mastoid bone so that I could expose the round window from behind, and make a bed for the implant package. For the next hour or so, the operating theatre was filled with the screeching of the drill and the whistling of the sucker as I removed bone dust and the irrigating water used to prevent the bone from overheating with high-speed drilling.

As the anatomy unfolded, I approached the region of the facial nerve with great caution. I was relieved when I saw the nerve's unmistakable pink outline shining through a thin covering of bone. Instead of being my enemy, the nerve had now become my friend, a guide that would lead me through into the middle ear where again I would see the round window. By then, a major part of the operation had been completed.

I next had to turn my attention to the bone behind the mastoid and make a bed for the receiver-stimulator, the package that contained all the electronics to receive signals by radio waves from outside the body and stimulate the hearing nerves in the inner ear. The package, 13 millimetres at its thickest, had to be placed in the skull bone so that it didn't bulge too much under the skin. As Rod's skull was only about 8 millimetres thick, I had to drill down to the covering of the brain with the utmost care to find room for the package. Again, I felt I was walking a tightrope.

The operation to this stage had taken some four hours, and to share the load I exchanged places with Brian Pyman so that he could insert the bundle of electrode wires into the inner ear. A dummy electrode was first introduced through the window and I was greatly encouraged that it went around the tightening spiral of the inner ear for a distance of 25 millimetres, far enough to stimulate all the important frequencies of speech.

Now for the real electrode bundle with its teflon collar added to fit snugly into the window. With my little micro-claw, it was fairly easy to steer the electrode bundle into the inner ear itself. Next we placed the package in its bed so that it was supported by a mould in the mastoid cavity constructed as we went. Finally, after carefully checking that there was no bleeding, the wound was sutured. Eureka!

The operation had been successfully completed. It had taken eight to nine hours, twice as long as it now takes. After I had seen the incision well bandaged, my last concern was to see Rod wake up with normal facial movements. Yes, no sign of a deformed face, thank God.

Back in the Department of Ear, Nose and Throat Surgery, staff and family members had watched the surgery via closed-circuit television. There was a general sense of elation that all our efforts had led to a successful first operation. Many unknowns would face us tomorrow, but for now completing the operation was enough.

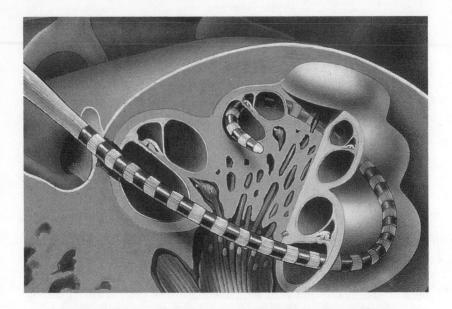

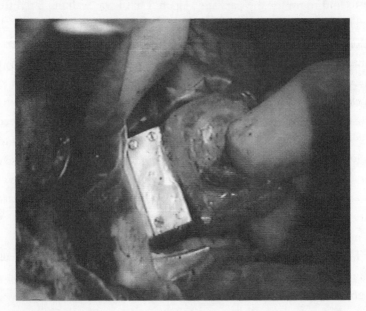

(Top) *A diagram of the inner ear with the banded electrode having passed around the first turn of the inner ear. (Drawn by Ed Zilberts, courtesy Cochlear Corporation).* (Bottom) *The receiver-stimulator electronic package in its bed in the mastoid bone at the conclusion of the operation.*

At least there was no press to face, because we hadn't told them a thing. I certainly didn't need press photographers climbing the hospital wall to try and film into the operating theatre (as was reported when Australia's first heart transplant was done at St Vincent's Hospital in Sydney).

After-care for our patient began immediately. The staff monitored Rod's vital signs, especially brain function. If there was bleeding as a result of dissecting very near the lining of the brain, action would have to be taken, but the evening wore on without any drama, so I could at last allow myself to sleep.

Rod made good progress the next day and had no temperature; surprisingly, he wasn't giddy. I had had no way of knowing whether a major operation on the inner ear would cause the same giddiness as the stapes operation in the middle ear. I started to relax, and paid little heed to suggestions that I might very probably kill my patient. That was now in God's hands, as much as mine or anybody else's; indeed, I felt His hand had been leading me on this tortuous path all along.

Then, one week after the operation when I was in my office, I heard over the hospital loudspeaker that there was a medical emergency on the floor where my patient was being nursed. Could it be Rod in trouble? As I bounded up the stairs the words, 'You could have killed your patient' came back to me. To my horror, I found that it was indeed Rod—he had collapsed while Sister Lyn Hickman was re-dressing the wound. The first on the scene was the poor young resident doctor, who, of course, had no idea what to do. Hot on his heels, I arrived to find that Rod had no pulse. Sister Hickman and I looked at each other in disbelief and laid him back on the bed. It then became obvious that he had only fainted, for his pulse had returned. My relief was immense.

When Rod went home after the surgery, I went on holiday with the family to my childhood home in Camden and spent hours walking and walking in the countryside. Going back to the place of my youth with all its memories was always refreshing, but especially so at this time. I needed a break from all the years of tension spent developing that tiny artifact. Soon enough we would be back to tackle the next phase of our mission. For now, I had the peace of mind of knowing that I had done my best and that the device had finally been made and implanted. We would wait in hope for good results.

9

Helping deaf adults
to hear

> The blind will be able to see,
> And the deaf will hear.
> The lame will leap and dance,
> And those who cannot speak
> Will shout for joy.
>
> *Isaiah 35: 5-6*

THE FIRST TEST SESSIONS

Four weeks after we had operated on Rod Saunders to implant the University of Melbourne's first bionic ear, he returned so that we could see whether it worked and how we could help him to understand speech. Everyone wanted this to happen within days, but a period of four weeks before start-up was needed to permit hearing nerve fibres to recover from injury due to the insertion of the electrode bundle into the delicate inner ear.

The team was well prepared for this moment. Jim Patrick and Ian Forster were both responsible for the equipment to transmit signals to the implant. Jo Tong managed the computer programs to control the implant and helped me to interpret the sensations Rod experienced.

When Rod arrived, I took him to the laboratory for testing. Although the staff and I tried to act as if this were routine, our voices and body language betrayed our anxiety.

Although the skin around Rod's operation site looked healthy and the wound had healed well, there was swelling over the package, which made me wonder how well I would be able to align the external transmitting aerial with the receiving aerial inside.

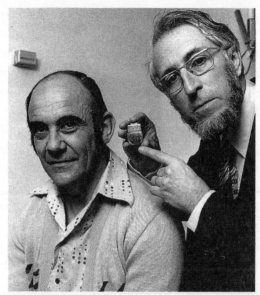

Rod Saunders with the author soon after the surgery demonstrating the receiver-stimulator section of the bionic ear implanted in Rod. (Photographer John Lamb, courtesy of The Age*)*

Calculations were made and the coil was positioned. Then the equipment was turned on and we gradually increased the strength of the electrical current, hoping that he would hear something. I asked, 'Rod, do you hear any sound?' Although he was listening intently he replied dejectedly, 'I'm sorry, I can only hear the hissing noises in my head.' (Deaf people frequently experience a hissing noise in the ear.) Even at maximum currents there were no sounds. I thought I might have placed the transmitting coil in the wrong spot, so I tried a number of sites, but he still heard nothing. This was all very disappointing. Had Rod's initial pre-operative test been faulty? Or, had the package failed in spite of positive pre-operative testing? Worse still, had the whole idea of a bionic ear been impracticable? Had eleven years of personal commitment to reach this stage been to no avail?

It was depressing having to send Rod home without any result, but we decided that he should come back in a few days when the engineers would have checked the equipment for problems. When he returned, he still couldn't hear anything. So we decided to give it a third try after a more thorough check. I had some wakeful nights trying to think of what could have gone wrong.

During the week before the third appointment, Jim Patrick discovered there was a fault in the test equipment that could explain the lack of results. What a relief! We approached the next session with anticipation. This time, Rod said he heard sounds, and he only heard them when the computer key was pressed. Each of the ten electrodes was tested, and they were all working!

I had to share the good news with Gill Martin and Mary Brennan, the operating theatre sisters who had put so much effort into getting the surgical routine right. To celebrate, Brian Pyman and I invited them out with their spouses to a banquet at a Chinese restaurant and presented them with flowers and chocolates in appreciation for all their help.

The next step was to explore the sensations Rod heard in more detail, to make sense of them. Did the sensations have pitch-like qualities? How were different frequencies and intensities perceived? How were they coded by the brain?

Rod was willing to come in many days each week for further tests for us to learn about the sounds he was hearing. His wife Margaret was a constant companion on those occasions. He was later to return that support, when she needed to go to a clinic regularly for her kidney dialysis.

At the second test session I was eager to find out whether Rod could recognise the voicing and rhythm of speech. To test for these skills, we used the computer to play tunes through the implant. The first was the then national anthem, 'God Save the Queen'. Our answer came immediately as Rod stood to attention, disconnecting some of his leads as he did so. It was good to have selected a patient with a sense of humour. Then Jo suggested, 'Why not test him with "Waltzing Matilda"?' Rod had no trouble with that one either. He could easily recognise the songs he knew, but could he hum the tune of a song that had come out after he went deaf?

We found that he could, which was very encouraging. Indeed, it was encouraging enough for us to make the first press announcement of our breakthrough on 19 September 1978. There was wide coverage in the Australian and international media, including the *New Scientist* on 28 September. The main claims were that because the patient could recognise the tune of 'Waltzing Maltida', there was hope for speech understanding.

This press coverage stimulated more interest from the companies 3M and Telectronics, who were negotiating with us over the industrial development of the bionic ear. At last we had some patient results, and not just a device. Our negotiating position was thus improved, even though we still hadn't shown that it could actually provide speech understanding.

COULD ROD RECOGNISE DIFFERENT PITCHES WITH MULTIPLE-ELECTRODE STIMULATION AND SO UNDERSTAND SPEECH?

At the next test sessions, I had another burning question I wanted answered. Did Rod experience different pitches when the electrodes along the inner ear were stimulated? If so, were the pitches scaled from high to low in an orderly way like a piano keyboard, as would be expected for normal inner ear function? Being able to experience different pitches according to the site of stimulation was the main reason I had embarked on the expensive and complicated task of developing a multiple-electrode implant.

A rather surprising answer emerged. If we kept the loudness at each electrode constant, Rod described the stimuli on the electrodes as varying from sharp at the high-frequency end of the inner ear to a dull sensation at the lower frequency end. In other words, the sensations were changing in timbre, but not in pitch. Timbre is the quality of a sound that helps us to distinguish a violin and a French horn when they are playing the same note. This was a disappointing finding. I expected there to be more clear-cut variations in pitch along the inner ear. Low stimulus rates did produce real pitch sensations, but unfortunately only at rates too low for speech intelligibility. This confirmed the inadequacy of using a single-electrode device, but the way forward with our multiple-electrode bionic ear still wasn't clear.

However, to help Rod in his daily life I needed to move on quickly. With the help of Dr Bruce Millar from the Australian National University in Canberra, we did come up with a speech processing system for speech understanding. This is described in Appendix 1 in some detail.

TESTING ROD'S SPEECH PERCEPTION

Angela Marshall, the lecturer in our new course in audiology, prepared lists of vowels and consonants to test Rod. We started with vowels embedded in the words: /heed/, /hard/, /hood/, /heard/, /had/, /hud/. Rod got

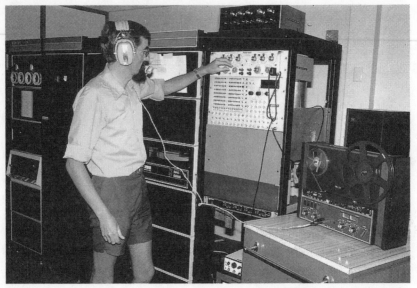

Bruce Miller doing speech research in his laboratory at the Australian National University,
1979. (Photograph courtesy of B. Miller)

about 60–70 per cent of them correct. Consonants, on the other hand, were a little more difficult. Nevertheless, at last it looked as though we were on the right track. So, if he could understand vowels and consonants, why not words and sentences?

I was keen to give Rod the ultimate test: open sets of words and sentences using electrical stimulation alone. As open sets of words and sentences are difficult, I had to agree that we should first test Rod with lists of known sentences (closed sets of words). If Rod failed to recognise the open sets, he would become discouraged.

However, when Rod became good at this closed-set sentence test, I could wait no longer. We had to give Rod the crucial test. If he could recognise open sets of words and sentences using electrical stimulation alone, then we would know for sure that our multiple-electrode system was better than the single-electrode stimulation being recommended by the centre in Los Angeles. Angela presented the material, and we all stood around waiting with bated breath. When she said 'ship', Rod replied incorrectly 'chat'. Then she said 'goat ' and Rod replied ' boat', which was nearly correct. Perhaps he would get the next word correct? Then Angela said 'rich' and Rod got it right! Although, when given the complete set, he was only able to identify 10–20 per cent of the words, it was the moment I had been waiting for. I went into the adjoining room and cried for joy.

At long last we had evidence that the bionic ear could help profoundly deaf people to communicate in their daily life. I could now say with assurance that the multiple-electrode implant justified its greater expense.

More testing and training would be required with Rod in the coming year, 1979, to see how much speech he could understand. With all her teaching duties Angela could not devote the time needed to help train Rod to understand these new speech sounds. So when I examined audiology students in their final orals, I was also appraising them for their suitability to join the team. They would need to be flexible, skilled in personal relations and have a sound scientific background, preferably strong in maths. Mrs Lois Martin fitted the bill, and after we had given her a mark, I raced across Morrison Place to offer her the position. I didn't wait for examiners meetings, selection panels and other niceties. Lois accepted the offer and commenced her duties early in 1979. Some time later I also appointed another graduate from the School of Audiology, Mr Peter Busby, to work with Lois. With his linguistics background, Peter was able to complement Lois's expertise. His help was vital when later we had to assess language development in children.

DIFFICULTIES AHEAD

At the end of 1978 our euphoria was tempered by the knowledge that I might not have sufficient funds for our group to continue. Funding had dwindled away because there were no Channel 0 telethons on the horizon, and my approaches to industry, in particular 3M, had been unsuccessful. A grant from the Ramaciotti Foundation for $15 000 for Ian Forster's salary was about to expire, and I wouldn't know until early in the new year whether the Australian government would provide funding for the next stage, through the Public Interest Grant Scheme.

There was another problem, and that was how to convert the successful speech processing strategy, developed using software commands on a large laboratory computer, into a box of electronic hardware small enough for Rod to wear. I approached David Dewhurst from the university's Electrical Engineering Department. He and two young engineers looked at the strategy and thought they could make a processor with 'whistles and bells'. Though it could be wheeled around, it would be the size of a sewing machine. I didn't consider this was satisfactory. A better solution would have to be found.

The solution was to come in 1979. It started in October 1978 when I had a phone call from Dr Peter Seligman asking if he could see me about a position. He was working for Westinghouse Brakes and wanted to change his job for one that could provide more direct help to people. I said, 'Peter, I would love to give you work, but I'm sorry, I can't fund any more staff. I'll get in touch with you if a position becomes available.' I said to Margaret that night that Peter was a Godsend, and that somehow a place would be made for him.

CHRISTMAS HOLIDAYS, 1978–79

In spite of the uncertainty, everyone joined in the Department's Christmas party with great enthusiasm. We started by taking over the oval at Wallen Road Park, by the Yarra River in Hawthorn, and played hit-and-run cricket. After the cricket and barbecue, we returned to the Eye and Ear Hospital for our traditional concert. Some of the staff spent days rehearsing their act, and I couldn't get essential research done. These concerts had nearly everyone participating, with Jo Tong acting as compere, and included such acts as Ray Black and Rob Shepherd's 'The Man from Barwon River' (a play on 'The Man from Snowy River'), with members of the department supposedly on their bicycles in hot pursuit of an escaped experimental animal through the streets of Fitzroy; Joan Maher, Barbara Weight and June Creighton doing their version of the Dance of Seven Veils; Jo's magic tricks and various musical items. The finale was to challenge surgeon Dr Don McMahon and audiologist Field Rickards, who had succeeded in leaping the length of the corridor with only one step between the black stripes on the floor.

Before leaving for my holidays by the sea at Kiama, I had to explain to the staff that I only had enough money left to cover salaries for three months, though I said I was fairly confident the government would come through with the Public Interest Grant which would fund their positions. 'Have a well-earned holiday!' was all I could add. I would have to leave the rest in God's hands.

While on holidays I had time to think. This coming year we would see how well our patient could make sense of the new sensations and understand running speech. I wanted to prove the sceptics wrong. The other big challenge was to make the computer-based speech processor portable. We would also need to demonstrate that it hadn't worked merely because of one person's idiosyncrasies, but was generally applicable. It would have to be implanted in other people and eventually tested for languages other than English before we could claim that it was suitable for commercial development.

MAKING THE SPEECH PROCESSOR PORTABLE

I returned from holiday feeling relaxed, but things soon changed when I learned that Ian Forster had resigned and was taking a job in Switzerland. The reason was apparently the uncertainty surrounding funding. It was a disappointment but I then thought of Peter Seligman, who had approached me late the previous year. I rang him to see if he was still interested. He was, and began working with us in April 1979 when the Australian government started our funding. Fortunately, Peter had been trained in industry and had learned to streamline the design of electronic circuits. Surely this would help him to find a way of miniaturising the speech processor?

There was some urgency about doing this, since the government had imposed a deadline as one of the conditions attached to the Public Interest Grant. It would be a big challenge to shrink the speech processing system on the large laboratory computer to a hard-wired unit. Peter Seligman, with help from Jim Patrick, was soon busy successfully designing circuits, and after some months it looked as though a portable unit would be available at the end of 1979 or early 1980. The next two patients wouldn't have to wait as long as Rod to be set free from their unwieldy appendage.

A THOROUGH ASSESSMENT OF ROD'S SPEECH PERCEPTION

In February 1979, when Lois Martin came on to the staff, we were able to put our main effort into training Rod to understand the new hearing sensations. I asked Lois to standardise the tests, to ensure there was no bias in our results and so that they could be reproduced by others. The words had to be pre-recorded and presented in a standard way, and were not to have been practised.

Once it was known that Rod was able to identify words and sentences from an open set, other groups started to make similar claims. However, they didn't always use the test correctly. A clinic using a single-electrode implant might have one person who did much better than the others (a 'star performer'). Therefore, it was concluded that our good results were also due to having picked a 'star performer', and that overall there would be no difference from using single-electrode stimulation. The debate between single-electrode devices and our multiple-electrode system now intensified.

THE 'GOLD BOX' WITHOUT CONNECTOR

In preparing for the second operation, which I planned to do on George Watson, I made a point of reviewing the implant package to see whether it really needed to have a connector. The connections were made with an Elastomer material, and Jim Patrick and I were concerned that the contacts wouldn't last over many years. The main point in having a connector was to replace the electronic package if it failed, without disturbing the hearing nerves by also taking out the electrode from the inner ear. However, my studies in the experimental animal had shown that the smooth, banded, electrode bundle would easily slip out—in fact, almost too easily. So I said to Jim, 'Let's have a package without the connector. It will be much easier to put in at surgery.' This was done.

THE SECOND PATIENT

George Watson, who had missed out on being the first subject, was very keen to be the second. He had been profoundly deaf for at least thirteen years, and giving him an implant would help us to answer another important question: would profound deafness over a long period affect his memory for sound so that he couldn't recognise the electrically-induced sensations as speech?

When George and I discussed the operation consent form, the mention of the risk of meningitis worried him a little. He didn't want to 'finish up a "vegetable" and be a trouble to anyone', he said. I explained that I had taken all the steps I could to prevent infection during the operation. The risk was minimal, and infection could always be treated

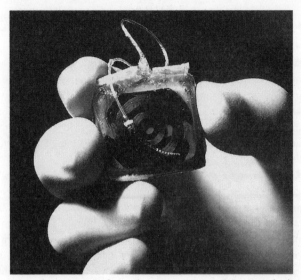

The bionic ear without connector for implantation in George Watson and other patients.

with antibiotics. George signed the form after Harold McCracken, the solicitor, questioned him independently to determine that no pressure had been put on him to have the operation.

George had further questions for me to answer. With all the prospective and implanted patients, I had promised that I would keep them regularly informed about progress. I couldn't answer all their initial questions, as there was no experience to draw upon. My written replies to George's questions were recorded on his medical history and are in the *Science Archives Project 14/9*. On 22 February 1979, I wrote:

> We don't have to repeat all the same things in such detail with you as we did with Rod as he was the first. We still cannot guarantee speech although we are doing our best to achieve it. We would need four sessions a week of testing and rehabilitation. Date of operation—if all goes to plan it should be within the next three months. Keep in regular contact.

On 31 May I had further discussions with George:

> I'm telling you what I know. This is an entirely new field; not much research has been done in the area before. Not everybody is suitable for this early research. We want people who will be patient and don't mind coming in for tests and retraining. Because it is a new field we don't know all the answers. We have recently (last two months) got

some money from the government. We have been able to employ some people and hopefully progress a bit faster! It is the cost of the people, computers, etc. We have been able to expand the staff.

We want you to come back every two weeks and meet us, and the patient who has had the operation (Rod Saunders), as well as the others preparing for it. You might like to call it a club. We now have more staff and unless something unforeseen occurs we are planning on your operation in the left ear for July. If you get a cold or an infection in the ear that would delay things. We are still designing and refining the speech processor.

Rod hears some speech sounds but not all of them so it is not as clear as it could be. It helps him with lip-reading at the moment. The testing after the operation involves trying to design the best speech processor. If the electrodes are in a slightly different place, even a millimetre, it may give different sounds when stimulating the electrodes— we won't know until we have another patient. We are testing the gold box (i.e. the implant) at the Commonwealth Scientific Industrial Research Organisation at the moment. That is to make sure it works and there are no leaks.

We are even going so far as to book theatre time. We mean business. We only want to take on as many patients as we can give time to. We hope your results will be similar to Rod's but we don't know. He can probably remember them better (i.e. sounds). I am sure you can help our understanding and by the same token we want to see how best to help you. You might have to give up a bit of golf to come in for testing. We can give you plenty of work to fill in time. Do not be despondent if we have to delay the operation a couple of weeks, for example you might get a cold. That's all from me. I want another test on your ear and we will make a time for you to come back.

All was readied for George's operation on 13 July. It went smoothly and more quickly this time, since we had fewer steps to take because of our previous experience with Rod.

The next day, I was surprised to find George standing outside my office window, having wheeled the bottle containing his drip and antibiotics down with him. He was very enthusiastic, and quite surprised that he'd had so few after-effects from the procedure.

THE THIRD PATIENT

As George's operation had gone well, I scheduled surgery for the next patient, Joan Keetley, two weeks later. Joan, aged fifty-three, had lost hearing from meningitis at the age of eighteen. She had been considered for the first operation, but I had been worried that as the X-ray had shown bone growth in the inner ear, we might not be able to insert the electrode far enough for speech understanding. Joan was still very keen to be considered and wrote to me on 20 September 1978, after reports of Rod's successful operation appeared in the press:

> Dear Professor Clark,
>
> Sincere congratulations to you and your wonderful team behind the scene for the success of the cochlear implant operation on Rod. Will be interesting to hear the progress of the interpretation of the electronic sounds now. I must admit at first the news was quite a shock that luckily I have known for five weeks, so was able to cope with all the phone calls of 'why', when you released the news to the press on Tuesday. Rod's knowledge of music and memory of sound would be a great advantage I'm sure and he should have more confidence to rehabilitate now. For you, the winter has been long and hard, but when the summer comes it will be all the more glorious—Joan.

As the X-ray had shown her right inner ear was probably normal, I agreed to operate on Joan. However, after successfully completing the first stage of the surgery, I was surprised to see how completely the inner ear was filled with a plug of bone. As we drilled along the lower canal, the bone didn't clear. How could the X-ray have shown that the canal was probably clear? Then I realised that the top tube was still open, and I confirmed this with a small drill hole. For five minutes I agonised over whether I should implant this other tube, which I hadn't studied. This was the one remaining site for an implant to give Joan hearing. I decided that we would stop the operation and preserve this remaining channel for a subsequent, improved device. I regret the decision, because of Joan's disappointment over the aborted operation. Everyone was barracking for her. When I walked into the Department I must have looked very sad, as my laboratory manager, Rodney Walkerden, came over to say how sorry he was. George Watson too expressed his sympathy in a letter dated 26 July:

> Dear Professor,
>
> I am truly sorry about Mrs. Keetley, also for yourself. It must have been nearly as bad a disappointment for you. Only last Tuesday whilst waiting

128 SOUNDS FROM SILENCE

for the Op to finish I told her husband that in my opinion Mrs. Keetley would prove to be the best one of the three of us, to really get this project working well, she was so keen. It will make me try all the harder. I couldn't sleep thinking about it, I am lucky so far.

Now please, could I get a nurse to help me wash my hair a little, we should have no problems keeping the water away from the ear etc. It is irritating me.

Could you please give me some idea, re going home. My good wife looks after me well, and we must book a Repat car in advance, and even if we did and had to cancel it, it would not matter.

Thanks
GEORGE WATSON

The operation I had hoped to do in the future, which would have given Joan some useful hearing, was never carried out because of my failure to make the decision to proceed with that operation at the time.

TESTING GEORGE WATSON

Nevertheless, the work had to go on. When George came back for his initial tests after three weeks, my greatest concern was whether he would be able to hear as well as Rod. Would his auditory memory still be functioning after thirteen years without any exposure to sound?

The first test session was straightforward: we wanted to ensure that each electrode was working, and to find which current levels could just be heard and which ones became unpleasantly loud. We needed this information to program the speech processing strategy. George was then booked to come back in a week for the crucial tests of speech understanding.

When George arrived for his next test session, I had to leave him with the team while I attended to an urgent matter. When I had finished I hastened down the corridor, and saw Lois smiling and holding the morning newspaper. She said that George heard speech; in fact, he had done so well they had rushed down to the hospital kiosk and bought the paper to see if he could understand articles read to him. He had to read the passage first, to get the general context, but then was able to understand the words even without help from lip-reading. It was important to know that the speech processing strategy worked for a second patient,

George Watson at the second test session with Lois Martin repeating the sentences from articles read from the morning newspaper.

and that after more than a decade his memory for speech sounds was still intact. The next months passed quickly for George—he was so excited at being able to hear again and communicate. He was very appreciative and I felt very pleased that, at long last, our implant had made a vital difference to his life.

SELECTING ANOTHER PATIENT

With the failure of Joan's operation I had to find a third patient to meet the demands of industry. I was fortunate that another patient was referred, and we had no difficulties in inserting the electrode into her inner ear. She returned for testing and we again found that different pitch sensations occurred when we stimulated various sites in the inner ear. But she started to experience strange sensations that were quite unpredictable. What had happened? We tested her by varying the current, and tried to pinpoint where the sensations were coming from. We checked everything we could think of and in the end came to the conclusion that the package had developed a leak and would have to be removed. Soldering the two halves of the package together therefore wasn't such a good idea. We needed to select a firm to refine this aspect of the package.

HOLIDAYS, 1979–80

I left for my holidays pleased that two patients had had successful implants, but feeling very disappointed about the other two. Our holiday at Kiama, and one some months later at Camden, gave me time to recover from another stressful year, and provided time to think and plan for the research on both Rod and George. Holidays also meant doing lots of outdoor activities with my wife and four daughters. This year it was a little different, as our fifth child, Jonathan, had arrived. Our children nearly always seemed to contract ear, nose and throat-related illnesses which I had to treat. This time our baby had a troublesome bronchitis that gave us some anxious days and broken nights. But he was already giving us all the joy and delight that a new life should always bring. And indeed, his arrival was to mean a whole change of lifestyle for me, going back to the simple pleasures of young parenthood. I read over again the old children's books and discovered new ones; and left my pottery wheel to the dust and the spiders while we went rollerskating, skiing, or mountain climbing and on cold Saturday mornings traipsed all over Melbourne with the Eltham Redbacks soccer team. But all that was a little further down the way.

COPING WITH THE FAILURE OF THE PROTOTYPE IMPLANT PACKAGE

On arriving back at the end of January 1980, as happened in the previous year, I was in for a shock. During my break, a couple of weeks into the New Year, George had experienced some odd 'bangs' and 'hissing' sounds in his ear. He dismissed them as unimportant, but they occurred intermittently until April when he went completely 'off the air' just a week after he was fitted with the portable unit. What a disappointment! I had so wanted to help George. Now I had to set about trying to find out what had caused this disaster. It wasn't just a leaky package either.

So, here I was at the beginning of 1980. We had carried out three implant operations, shown that a speech processing strategy could work, and developed a wearable speech processor, but only one patient still had a functioning device. The immediate problem was to overcome leakage around the package seals. One member of staff suggested, 'Why don't you buy some of the stimulator packages from the group that has started up in Vienna? They have a package with electrodes coming through glass

(Top) *The Clark family going on a holiday to Camden, New South Wales, 1980.*
(Bottom) *The author and Jonathan climbing Cathedral Mountain, 1985.*

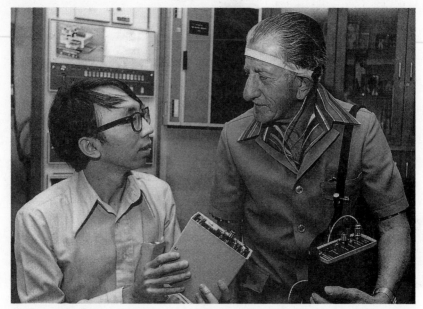

Jo Tong with George Watson in 1980 demonstrating the portable unit engineered by Peter Seligman and Jim Patrick to reproduce the University of Melbourne's speech processing strategy.

seals. This would allow you to continue the patient studies.' I was reluctant to do so, however. The thought of using someone else's technology for a project that I wanted to be totally Australian seemed like defeat. I didn't want to proceed that way, and I was pleased I didn't agree to use a package with a glass seal between the emerging metal wire and the case, as it turned out that glass seals also leaked. It had been known in the pacemaker industry that glass has very fine cracks and that the body proteins can invade these and cause them to split open.

CONVINCING THE SCEPTICS

Meanwhile, we had to convince a largely sceptical world of the validity of our results. People had to see for themselves, or at least view a film of the test being presented. I had to be scrupulous in the way the film was edited, to ensure that the number of mistakes shown was accurate. Even then, one visitor said I had fabricated the result, as he noticed there was a small time delay between Rod's lip movements and his speech sounds! Surgeons and scientists were still not convinced that our results were significantly better than the single-electrode device. At one international meeting, it was reported to me that an Australian surgeon had asked a leading American scientist: 'What is this clown Clark doing putting multiple electrodes in the inner ear?' So we still had a way to go before we would be taken seriously.

RESULTS FOR DIFFERENT LANGUAGES

With the commercial development of the bionic ear by Nucleus Limited, we were able to evaluate our speech processing discovery on more patients, to see how many people would benefit and why the results varied. After the first six patients were implanted at the Royal Victorian Eye and Ear Hospital in 1982, at the start of the worldwide clinical trial, we continued to train them and to plot their progress over the next two years. Other people came forward and were also part of the worldwide trial.

By 1984 we started to operate on people with different language backgrounds. Melbourne is a multicultural city, and we have deaf people from many different countries. I was particularly keen to see if the speech strategy we had developed for languages that had a formant structure could also work for Chinese, which is a tonal language. A tonal language conveys meaning by subtle variations in the pitch of the sound, rather than via special frequency bands. We were fortunate to have a Chinese patient from Malaysia, Mr Beng Kim Lee; at the same time, a Mandarin-speaking doctor from Shanghai, Dr Shi-ang Xu, came to work with us. We implanted Beng Kim Lee on 16 April 1985 and started testing a few weeks later. Shi-ang constructed special tests in Mandarin and the results were amazing. Beng Kim Lee was the first Chinese person to have the multiple-electrode bionic ear and I presented the results, along with a videotape of his performance, at our international meeting in Melbourne in August 1985. Dr Bob White, the Professor of Electrical Engineering from Stanford University in the US, who was also working on implants, was impressed enough to say at the end of the presentation, 'All deaf people should learn Mandarin'!

RESEARCH ADVANCES IN SPEECH UNDERSTANDING

The inaugural speech processor developed commercially by Nucleus Limited was approved by the US Food and Drug Administration (FDA)

Peter Blamey engaged in speech research using the laboratory computer.

in October 1985. Although the studies of patients in the clinical trial showed that our initial discovery helped deaf adults with lip-reading and gave them some assistance with electrical stimulation alone, I couldn't accept that the work was finished, as some people believed. We had to press on with the more basic research to see if it were possible to make the device function more effectively. Nuleus needed a good reason to redesign it. What reason could we give them?

In 1983, as we could not test new strategies on the implant patients (their speech processors not being flexible enough), I hit upon the idea of using volunteers from around our department, that is hearing subjects, to listen to speech sounds like those heard by the patients. The hearing subjects could then compare these sounds with the new sounds we wanted to try. Some bionic ear patients had said that speech sounded as though people were hoarse. It was harsh and noisy. That was the clue to the type of sounds we needed to select in order to recreate the best speech patterns.

Dr Peter Blamey, who had joined the team as a computer programmer, accepted the challenge, and before long we had good evidence that better speech processing systems could be achieved. (This was the beginning of Peter's excellent work as a speech scientist.)

The Bionic Ear Institute, East Melbourne.

Nucleus Limited modified the design of the system, and the bionic ear now allowed increased amounts of speech information to be transmitted to deaf people, thus helping them to understand speech more clearly, especially against background noise. The improved bionic ear was clinically trialled and approved in 1986 by the US FDA.

FUNDING FURTHER RESEARCH

Each advance in performance became the spur to do better. But each advance required more effort and more money. In early 1984 the idea came up in conversation with Mr John McNicol, public relations officer of the Royal Victorian Eye and Ear Hospital, to form a Bionic Ear Institute to raise funds as well as manage research. John, in turn, introduced me to Mrs Eve Sher, who had great experience in fundraising for charities. She kindly invited us to dinner at her penthouse to meet Sir MacFarlane Burnet, Australian Nobel Laureate for his research on immunology, Sir Rupert Hamer, former Premier of Victoria, and others, to discuss the possibility of forming such an Institute.

A steering committee was set up in August 1984, and it was decided to hold an inaugural dinner on 29 August to launch the Australian Bionic Ear Institute. Eve gave generously of her time and energies to organise the dinner, and enlisted the support of her friends.

The new Institute had to become formalised with a board, memorandum and articles of association, and tax exemption for donations. In this area, Sir Peter Looker, former chairman of the Melbourne Stock Exchange and now a member of the board, took much of the responsibility. Thus, an identity for the Institute was emerging as notable people added to its credibility. Sir MacFarlane Burnet agreed to be the first patron; Dr Jim McBride White, a senior eye surgeon, became the first president; and Mr Jim King, a businessman, was the vice-president.

Fund-raising commenced in earnest for our fundamental innovative research, and has continued under presidents Messrs David Brydon, John Calvert-Jones and presently Michael Robinson.

My first application for a major government grant was in 1981. Years passed, then suddenly three grants materialised in close succession—a National Health and Medical Research Council (NHMRC) of Australia program grant, extending over nine years from 1985, and in the same year a research grant and contract from the US National Institutes of Health (NIH). We were actually the first overseas centre to receive a research contract from the latter. Then in 1987, the Australian Research Council (ARC) made the award to establish the Human Communication Research Centre.

Over the next nine years, two important advances in speech processing resulted, as well as a new electrode bundle to coil around the inner ear. I had, however, to find funds of $250 000 per year to accommodate this new centre, and fortunately the State government came to our aid. Providing permanent space became a real cause for the Institute, and led to our purchase in 1990 of the property on the corner of Albert and Lansdowne Streets—'Mollison House'—as the headquarters of the Institute.

Applying for all these grants, and preparing for the various reviews they required, wouldn't have been possible without the tremendous administrative support of my super-secretaries, Miss Joan Maher and Mrs Margaret Gilmour, both of whom had trained in the Prime Minister's Department. Equally indispensable was a unified and committed team of outstanding scientists.

To elaborate on the two major advances in speech processing made possible by the grants, I should explain that consonants had not been easily recognised. Mr Richard Dowell, then a PhD student supervised by

Peter Blamey and me, was encouraged to work at the problem. He saw the need to present more high frequencies to patients. So, working with Peter Seligman, he trialled a further advance that served to keep Cochlear Pty Limited ahead in the international marketplace. This alteration was approved by the FDA in 1989.

We didn't rest there. It was still a race to provide the best system, and our international competitors were catching up. The other major advance was to further increase the number of frequencies extracted and the way they were selected to stimulate the hearing nerves.

We were continually generating new ideas, but only a small proportion produced real advances. Then, two alternative propositions were put to me by Drs Jo Tong and Hugh McDermott. Jo's idea was to extract six frequency peaks from speech, while Hugh's was to extract the six maximal outputs of a bank of filters. We didn't have the resources to investigate both proposals, so I chose Hugh's as the more novel. Fortunately, with engineering help from Mr Andrew Vandali and audiological support from Dr Colette McKay, Hugh's suggestion produced the next step up in performance and it was approved by the FDA in 1990. This came just in time to compete effectively with an alternative advance by Drs Blake Wilson and Charles Finley at the Research Triangle Park, USA. (Our improvements in speech understanding from 1978 to 1990 are set out in Appendix 1.)

The point had been reached where the speech perception of the average profoundly deaf adult was comparable to that of a severely deaf person who had residual hearing and used a hearing aid.

In 1988 I could see improved results would also require electrodes being placed close to the nerves at the centre of the inner ear. I experimented with Drs Jin and Shi-ang Xu on ways to make the electrodes curl after insertion. The techniques were to need much refinement before application to patients ten years later. In fact, this was the forerunner of the Cochlear Limited 'Contour' electrode array which won the Australian design award for the year 2000.

COMMERCIALISATION OF RESEARCH ADVANCES

These important research advances required collaboration between the university team and Nucleus (later Cochlear Limited) for their commercial

The author with implant recipients at the Bionic Ear Institute celebrating 21 years since the first operation.

development. It was a complex task and was later facilitated by an enlightened scheme, the Cooperative Research Centres (CRCs), introduced by the Australian Government. In 1992 we received a CRC grant for a Cochlear Implant, Speech, and Hearing Research Centre for a term of seven years to do industrially relevant research to improve the bionic ear and also hearing aids. With a governing board chaired by a leader in industry, Sir Leslie Froggatt, the key parties were Cochlear Limited, Australian Hearing Services, The Bionic Ear Institute and The University of Melbourne. Then in 1999 we received funding for a new CRC for Cochlear Implant and Hearing Aid Innovation under the directorship of Dr Robert Cowan.

FUTURE RESEARCH

The year 1999 was special as we celebrated the 21st anniversary of our first operation in 1978. At least one person operated on from most of the 21 years was present. The festivities coincided with a press announcement by Dr Ziggy Switkowski, Head of Telstra, of our collaborative research project in which we hope to teach machines to copy the human brain in recognising speech.

The success of the bionic ear has opened up many other vistas for the next millennium. Not only might high-fidelity sound be possible, but the whole bionic ear system could be made totally implantable or invisible. Furthermore, the inner ear and hearing nerves might be returned to normal function using recently discovered nerve growth factors (proteins) alone.

10

Commercial development

> The things that will destroy us:
> Politics without principle,
> Pleasure without conscience,
> Wealth without work,
> Knowledge without character,
> Science without humanity,
> Worship without sacrifice,
> and
> Business without morality.
>
> *Gandhi*

INITIAL COMMERCIAL INTEREST

Ultimately we would depend on industry to get our implant out to the public in any great quantities, but in 1977 I hoped for help from a firm, whichever it might be, to keep our research and development going. As the publicity surrounding the development of the 'gold box' (or implanted receiver-stimulator section of the bionic ear) had generated commercial interest, we realised it was prudent to lodge patents for both it and the electrode bundle before discussions took place.

I was quite inexperienced in patenting, and although we hadn't proved that the implant would work, we were sufficiently ahead with the design of the receiver-stimulator to lodge a patent. The design of the bundle of electrodes inserted into the inner ear was especially innovative.

The first interest by industry came from Mr Paul Trainor, owner of the Australian heart pacemaker firm, Telectronics. I wrote to him on 13 September 1977 encouraging him to come and talk more about it.

In mid-October (see Appendix 2) I also received a letter from the large American firm 3M wanting to learn more. I didn't know that 3M were also having discussions with the House Clinic in Los Angeles to develop their single-electrode device, as well as with other centres in the United States and Europe.

I replied to 3M in the hope that a working relationship would develop. Two years later, after exchanging further letters and sending them prototypes, I concluded that they wanted to keep their options open, while at the same time proceeding with the commercialisation of the single-electrode system developed in Los Angeles. In April 1978 a representative of 3M, Dr Coyne, met with us in Australia and I learned that the firm had definitely decided to enter the health-care field with one or other type of cochlear implant. It occurred to me that if they took on ours, they could then easily 'kill it' in favour of the cheaper but less effective single-electrode device.

3M were still comparing our device with the American and European ones in June when they asked for someone from our team to visit them. When Jim Patrick went over in September, they rejected our device but approached him about a job. Fortunately, Jim's allegiances were with Melbourne. I realised then that entering the world of big business could be tough!

At the same time if we didn't move quickly to get an industrial partner, further funding would be a problem. I was aware that increasing overseas competition was taking away our lead, for I had received news that both the European Economic Community headquartered in Brussels and the US government through the National Institutes of Health were about to provide major funding for a cochlear implant development in their own countries.

SEEKING FUNDING FROM THE AUSTRALIAN GOVERNMENT

I had already begun to seek funding for commercial development from the Australian government in July 1977. I now redoubled my efforts, contacting the Department of Productivity and then the Prime Minister, Malcolm Fraser (Appendix 2). I was elated to receive a reply!

The government had set up a scheme to fund projects of benefit to the community and industry. Our prototype bionic ear fitted these criteria, but it was still being developed and the concept wasn't yet shown to be effective. Surprisingly, the government showed further interest.

So I made a formal submission in 1978. This was my first application for a grant to develop an invention industrially, and it took some time to prepare. I had to set out the major problem to be solved and the engineering difficulties expected, and provide a timetable with milestones—all quite foreign to my experience. Then there were the details of how the project was to be managed, together with a budget. Finally, I had to do a preliminary market survey, and show on what basis it was calculated.

After submitting the application, I received a call from Mr Paul Schultz, the assistant secretary at the federal Department of Productivity. He came to Melbourne and we had dinner at University House. The prime purpose of his visit, I learned later, was to meet me and assess my leadership qualities, including my marital situation! Would I fit the government's 'profile'? I didn't even know they had one.

Meanwhile, I continued with the approaches to industry. Telectronics was slow to respond, but on 4 April 1978 the university received correspondence from them saying they wished to evaluate the device further. The vice-principal replied and let them know officially that 3M was also a competitor.

In June 1978, Dr Mike Hirshorn from Telectronics visited Melbourne to determine, as he later admitted, how genuine our research was. Mike had been responsible for the biological issues for the pacemaker electrode, and later for the development of a bone growth stimulator. It was the start of a friendship that extended right through the industrial development of the bionic ear. In his report for Telectronics, he wrote: 'They have not proven anything but it seems like it could work.'

On 6 December, there was an historic meeting in the office of the vice-principal of the University of Melbourne of senior members of Telectronics, the university and the Australian Department of Productivity. Paul Trainor seemed to be interested, but he wanted us to have implanted three patients with equally good results before he would commit himself to putting funds towards the project. I was rather discouraged by this reply, as I was excited by Rod Saunders' initial ability to understand speech. It was agreed that we could operate on three post-lingually deaf adults (those who had become deaf after developing language). Even finding two additional patients at this stage seemed a problem. I knew that we had George Watson, but I didn't know who the other one would be.

By late 1978 I still had the problem of finding the finances to continue our work. Before leaving for the Christmas holidays I wrote to Paul

Schultz, stressing the urgency of funding from the first phase of the Public Interest Grant. I was running out of money to continue the program.

PUBLIC INTEREST GRANT—PHASE 1

On 31 January 1979 the Minister for Productivity, Ian McPhee, announced the Public Interest Grant to achieve commercial development of our implant. The grant was for $1 million over two years for engineering, medical research and development, and for a market survey to see how profitable it would be. The potential world market was deemed to be $500 million. A board set up under the *Australian Industrial Research and Development Incentives Act* (AIR&DIB) would invite Australian firms to register interest in participating in the project.

The aim of the first stage of the Implantable Hearing Prosthesis Program would be to implant two more patients, perfect the design of the implanted receiver-stimulator and make the speech processor portable. The budget was for engineers, programmers, technical officers, audiologists and part-time surgeons. The government then moved quickly, advertising on 1 February for companies to register their interest.

The tender from Telectronics submitted by Paul Trainor on 3 May to the AIR&DIB was successful. This firm was chosen partly because it had the expertise in sealing electronics packages against corrosive body fluids.

A steering committee was set up to coordinate the activities of the University of Melbourne and Telectronics. I made a point of taking a videotape along to each meeting so that the government and Telectronics could see the human benefits of our work and not be put off by costs or engineering difficulties.

This was our first experience of an R&D (Research and Development) program. Jim Patrick became project manager. Fortunately, I was able to convince the university that Jim should be paid a higher salary to reflect his increased responsibilities and lack of job security.

Now we would have to meet our deadlines and 'milestones' to ensure further funding; either that, or I would need a very good excuse! Then there was the need to prepare a chart outlining each step of our research and specifying the time taken. Previously, like most scientists, I had enjoyed the freedom of making discoveries in my own time. I now had to learn to work under this pressure, and encourage, even demand, the staff to do the same. But everyone accepted the challenge, as well as the uncertainty of the funding. Youth was on our side, and we worked very hard to achieve the goals. The staff of the Department of Productivity also did all they could to reduce our administrative load. When I look back, I consider the bureaucrats to have been outstanding in the way they handled this project. I think in particular of Paul Schultz, Frank Montgomery, Geoff Tunaley, Nick Sterling and Ed Crowcher, as well as members of the University of Melbourne, Ray Marginson, Jim Thomas, Jim Blaney, John Newman, Brian Adams and Max Ferguson.

Having received funding for the first stage of the bionic ear's industrial development, I was shocked in July 1979 to get a letter from Paul Schultz asking me to answer criticisms from an Australian professor of physics who had written to the government saying that our work was on exactly the same lines as that of the Stanford University Research Institute (considered possibly the best engineering department in the world) and that theirs had progressed to such a stage that, in his view, there was little point in our duplicating that work in Australia. This letter was embarrassing to the Minister of Productivity, who had cited the bionic ear as a prime example of his Department's support for innovative R&D. Thus, it was essential to explain why I thought ours was the better approach. My reasons were as follows: (1) The Stanford group inserted a bayonet-shaped electrode into the hearing nerve near where it entered the brain. This could be more damaging than our flexible bundle passing around the turns of the inner ear. (2) They used four electrodes compared with our ten. (3) Their link between the external and internal components was an ultrasonic one that we had shown was less reliable than the radio frequencies which we were using. (4) Initial results with our speech processing strategy were better. These arguments were enough to clinch the matter.

During Phase 1, we worked hard at the university and the hospital preparing patients to be implanted. We used our computer to better understand what they were hearing and how to train them in interpreting the new sensations. Their stories are told in Chapter 9.

A major task was to make the speech processor portable. The Public Interest Grant had enabled me to appoint Peter Seligman in April 1979 to commence work on shrinking the computer-based speech processor to a wearable unit that was more practical in everyday life.

On 5 July, Ms Maria Yetton was appointed by Telectronics to undertake a market survey with Mike Hirshorn to assess the market size for the device, particularly in the United States but also in Europe and Australia. (The US was just becoming a large consumer of medical technology, and so a development such as the bionic ear wouldn't be economically viable without this market.) The survey also aimed to determine the proportion of pre-linguistically and post-linguistically deaf people; the distribution of deaf people (to ensure they could be managed from a central clinic in a major city, because the amount of special training required would mean a lot of travel); the number of patients a clinic could handle; and whether governments were prepared to fund the device.

There were few answers to these questions, and I had to sift through a large number of papers and books to provide some help. Being new to the field, Maria needed guidance on who were the senior ear, nose and throat specialists and audiologists in Australia, as well as overseas.

Finally, a few days before the 22 December 1979 deadline, I could report to Paul Schultz that the university had successfully accomplished all the tasks required. Telectronics had also completed their survey.

PUBLIC INTEREST GRANT—PHASE 2

As we had passed all the milestones for Phase 1, the government awarded the grant for Phase 2. Nucleus Limited, the holding company for Telectronics, would have to engineer the bionic ear to make it smaller and more reliable. They would also need to organise a trial centred in the US to gain FDA approval for its commercial use. The University of Melbourne would be responsible for further developing speech processing strategies, as well as surgical and training programs for the US clinics, and biological safety studies. There were no guidelines from the FDA for the latter, so we had to make our own. Mike Hirshorn vividly remembers sharing my sandwiches while we had a lunch time meeting to plan studies on the toxicity of materials, damage to the inner ear from insertion, the effect of radio waves on tissue, and possible complications from middle ear infection.

When the grant was awarded, I quickly arranged a press conference to announce the funding and thank the government. In itself it wouldn't attract great interest, but fortunately I could unveil the new portable speech processors developed in Phase 1 and have Rod and George, our first two patients, demonstrate how good they were—at least, so I thought. Although the speech processors had only been reduced to the size of a binoculars case, they could be used in a person's daily life and were the first to allow an understanding of running speech.

The date of the press conference had been set and people invited. To my dismay, just one week before the conference I discovered that George Watson's implant had failed completely. I would still have to go on with the conference with both Rod and George appearing, even though George was 'off the air'. Both Rod and George turned up wearing the speech processors, and I hoped against hope that the press wouldn't ask George how his implant was performing. Fortunately, the question wasn't raised and the press conference went off smoothly, demonstrating the significant progress that we had been making! Clearly we were holding on by a thread

The failure of George's package and that of the third patient emphasised the problem of sealing the implant. Telectronics had pioneered a ceramic seal for a single electrode coming out from a titanium heart pacemaker. The ceramic aluminium oxide was heated to a high temperature which caused it to bond with the metals. However, engineers from Telectronics thought that bringing the twenty wires out from a smaller package would be much more difficult. Again, extra funding was needed.

Minister McPhee had changed his portfolio and I would have to develop a relationship with the new Minister, Senator Kevin Newman, with whom I happened to have been at school. I sought an interview with him in his Melbourne office. A few days later I had just arrived in Adelaide to have discussions with the Defence Research Laboratories when I received an urgent message that the Minister was visiting Melbourne on his way home to Tasmania and would see me. Immediately I had to catch the return flight to explain how important it was for the whole project that the Commonwealth government give Nucleus Limited the extra funds to develop a reliable package. The Minister was receptive to the need and authorised the grant.

When Nucleus received both grants, Paul Trainor set about building an expert team to complete the very difficult bioengineering task. It was certainly more formidable than producing a cardiac pacemaker, their main product. The implanted electronics were more complicated, and the package had to be smaller to fit into the mastoid bone behind the ear.

Paul and Marie Trainor with Graeme and Margaret Clark at the Clunies Ross medal presentations for excellence in science and technology, Melbourne, 1992.

Moreover, twenty electrode wires, rather than one, had to be brought out from the package through a seal that would prevent the body fluids entering the box and damaging the electronics. I was relying very much on their expertise in sealing packages, as I had considered sealing was the key area to be conquered, rather than communications technology.

In developing his 'tiger team', Paul Trainor asked if he could take some of my key staff since they already had expertise, and the transfer would be good for relations between the industry group and the research team. I was taken aback by the thought of losing some of our special people, though I appreciated the fact that Paul had consulted me and discussed the abilities of members of my staff and how they would fit into the project. Paul was always courteous and warm in his approach to us and this was to be of immeasurable value in the success of our joint venture.

Indeed, I was to find that Paul strove hard to ensure that the commercial effort dove-tailed with our research, and as time went on, together we developed such a rapport in explaining our work at symposia that it seemed to me we performed like a 'Punch and Judy Show'. Above all, I was impressed by Paul's high ethical standards—he would not make exaggerated claims, regardless of the effect on the share market, and he didn't trade innuendo for innuendo when dealing with competitors.

Although I had really wanted the industrial development to be done in Melbourne so that it would be close to our research group, collaboration was effective with staff at Nucleus in Sydney in spite of the distance. It was also important that initially development be done in close association with Telectronics which had expertise in implanting microelectronics into people. Jim Patrick and electrode technician Mr Geoff Lavery left us. Peter Seligman, who had strong personal reasons for remaining in Melbourne, stayed close to the Melbourne clinic and research team. This turned out overall to be a satisfactory compromise.

Paul Trainor had his senior engineer, Mr David Money, who had experience in designing circuits for pacemakers, take charge of this new engineering task; Jim Patrick, Mr Peter Crosby and Mr Chris Daly became part of the team. To take responsibility for the construction of the package, Nucleus advertised for a mechanical or materials engineer and appointed Mr Januz Kuzma who had fairly recently arrived in Australia. At first I thought he was slow in coming forward with a solution. So, being impatient, I tried to find a way myself. I arranged to get clays (ceramics) and metal and went to work with my pottery kiln at home— to little effect, of course! Next, Jim Patrick and I visited the Commonwealth Scientific Industrial Research Organisation (CSIRO) Laboratories at Port Melbourne and met Dr Mike Murray. He had experience with zirconium, a ceramic being used in engine components, and he agreed to carry out experiments for us. Our search also took us to the University of New South Wales to get advice on a completely ceramic package. Here we learned that a ceramic package would be prone to cracking at the joins, so we put this idea on ice. It was wonderful how readily scientists in a variety of fields were willing to share their knowledge. Meanwhile, Januz Kuzma, after settling into Nucleus, did a very good job in finding a practical way to bring twenty-two electrodes out of the package through a ceramic seal.

Biological safety studies needed to be very thorough, as the multiple electrode would pass further into the inner ear than the single-electrode device and so run the risk of causing more damage. Rob Shepherd had previously shown a strong interest in the biological effects of implantation when he was seconded from teaching to complete his bachelor's degree a few years before. I begged him to come and do research on biological safety for a PhD degree. To my delight, he agreed. It was

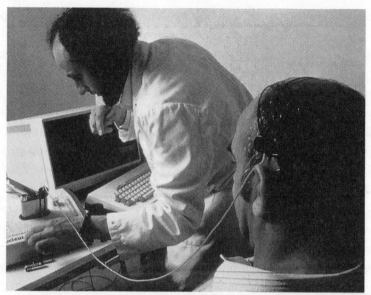

Peter Seligman with the Nucleus wearable speech processor and programming unit.

gratifying, too, when the multiple electrode wasn't found to damage the inner ear.

PUBLIC INTEREST GRANT—PHASE 3

In 1981 our hopes were raised that the Nucleus 'tiger team' would be able to design a small, reliable implant and speech processor that would repeat the results we had obtained on our first patients with the prototype bionic ear. Moreover, the task was completed on time—a tribute to the leadership of David Money and his team in achieving this complex task so quickly and effectively.

The funding for the work through Phase 3 was conditional on a licensing agreement between the Commonwealth of Australia, Nucleus and the University of Melbourne. When further approval for the next phase of the Public Interest Grant was required, we had a Labor government. Mr Barry Jones was Minister for Science and responsible for our project. Would I have to begin all over again and convince another Minister to support the new industry? I needn't have worried. Barry Jones was very encouraging and held our bionic ear up as a symbol of the 'sunrise industries' that could save our economy! Shortly after, the portfolio of

Science was amalgamated with Industry and became the responsibility of Senator John Button. He was equally ready to support our work. In fact, some time later he was able to get the government to waive its share of the royalties up to $500 000 to help essential research of the Bionic Ear Institute. But try as I might in subsequent years, I couldn't persuade the Commonwealth government to agree that their royalty payments (which were going into general revenue) should be used to further our fundamental bionic ear research. We might be a good example of the government helping out industry, but the purse-strings were still tight. Funding for Phase 3 commenced in September 1981 to run till December 1982.

During this phase we also needed to be sure that the new device would work for a larger sample of people, in order to be economically viable. So, now I had to look around for at least six suitable patients to be implanted some time towards the end of 1982. Would I have the same trouble finding suitable people as I had before the first implants in 1978 and 1979?

THE FIRST CLINICAL TRIAL

Fortunately, the press had attracted several profoundly deaf people. Mr Graham Carrick came to see me early in 1982. He had normal hearing as a young child. At the age of five he fell into a fire and suffered multiple burns, requiring the antibiotic Streptomycin which is toxic to the inner ear. It caused him to go profoundly deaf in the right ear and left him with only a small amount of residual hearing on the left side. It, too, deteriorated, and by the time Graham was twenty-one, he had been plunged into silence. He learned to speak well and could lip-read, but really missed being able to hear. He felt inhibited in his role of a father in relating to and disciplining his children.

Lorna Lewis, another suitable patient, was referred to me by an ear, nose and throat surgeon in 1980. I was really pleased that one of my colleagues now had confidence to refer a patient. Lorna was sixty-one and had been deaf for at least thirty-five years. Her hearing problem started when she was a young child and had repeated ear infections. By about thirty she was profoundly deaf and tried a hearing aid, but it offered no real help. A hole in the right ear-drum and scarring on the left side didn't rule her out for an operation on the left side.

Lionel Robinson, a local seventy-three-year-old man, was another candidate being assessed by our staff. In 1945, at the age of thirty-seven, he lost hearing suddenly in both ears for no apparent reason, and was left with just a third of his normal hearing. At sixty, he had another sudden loss, which left him with only 10 per cent hearing. Within six years he had become stone deaf. When I saw Lionel in 1981, he was also greatly troubled by noises in his ears that were sometimes so loud he couldn't sleep. He described them as 'bells ringing' and 'wooshing' noises, or like a crow cawing or wine glasses clinking. He was also very dizzy and unsteady when walking. By using the X-rays of the time, we found that he had marked degenerative changes in the bone around the inner ear, which is seen in the condition of otosclerosis.

Jennifer Dawson came to be considered for a bionic ear on 29 June 1981. We found her to be profoundly deaf. She had a long history of middle ear infections and attempts to heal holes in her ear-drums by ear surgeons, beginning when she was three or four. She progressively lost her hearing until by 1972, when she was fourteen, she found it difficult to socialise. She had become profoundly deaf. Hearing aids gave little help. For two years after leaving school, Jennifer couldn't get a job. When she managed to obtain a clerical position, it didn't reflect her true potential.

Cheryl Sheehan was being considered for a single-electrode implant in Sydney, even though she had known about our multiple-electrode bionic ear research since 1980 when her mother sent for information after she saw a TV series called 'The Work that Was'. In 1982, Cheryl heard that our bionic ear would soon be ready to implant. As there were delays in starting the US single-electrode program in Sydney, and as it seemed better to have a multiple-electrode system anyway, she became interested in participating in our trial.

Cheryl had been in good health until one morning in 1978 when, at age eighteen, she awoke with a fever and a splitting headache. Meningitis was diagnosed, and in spite of antibiotics she lapsed into a coma. When she recovered, she couldn't hear. Damage to the inner ear is a common complication of a severe bout of meningitis. When Cheryl left hospital, the audiologist found that she was virtually stone deaf. This added to the worries of her mother, who wrote in a letter to me in 1980: 'I have suffered untold anxiety due to her illness.'

Although Cheryl got on with her life, the world of silence was only two-dimensional. To be able to talk with friends, she needed to hear again. We had kept Cheryl on our waiting list since hearing about her from her mother in 1980. On 17 March 1982, when we went looking for patients, we wrote explaining how we would need to spend four to six months assessing Cheryl before and after the operation. We said that living interstate could make it difficult for her to participate, but asked if she were interested. Mrs Sheehan and Cheryl jumped at the chance to have the operation. They would find accommodation and live in Melbourne for however long it took, they said.

I especially wanted to include George Watson in the trial group of six. It would be nearly three years since George had gone 'off the air' when his prototype failed at the beginning of 1980. He had been so disappointed after having a taste of hearing. He was also a great supporter of the program, having been willing to be the first patient not only to help himself, but to benefit others as well. There were a number of problems to resolve before George would be ready.

In April 1982, he presented me with the first problem. He had been falling asleep with his glasses on, and the arm of the glasses had rubbed through the skin overlying a prominent edge of the bionic ear package. This infection got worse and needed antibiotic treatment. It was yet another disappointment for George. He wrote to me on 25 May. Was he still in the running for another operation, he pleaded? I could see that the only answer was to remove the bionic ear, because it was just acting as a home for the infection. We would still leave the electrode in the inner ear to keep the way open for another implant should that be possible. However, I couldn't run the risk of putting a bionic ear on that side, at least for a year or so. I had felt I needed a medical reason for taking his implant out so that the cause of its failure could be studied, though perhaps I should have simply asked him to let us do this soon after it failed. However, now the decision was forced on me. To control the infection the bionic ear was removed on 1 June.

The package was treated like a piece of moon rock. For the good of the project as a whole, we had to find out what the problem was. The package was X-rayed, dissected, analysed by protein chemists from St Vincent's Hospital and checked electronically. I even had Professor Lovering from the Department of Geology at the University of

Melbourne, one of the world's leading geologists selected by NASA to analyse moon rock, studying the materials around the surface of the electrode and the package.

The studies revealed that we had made a fundamental mistake in the mechanical design of the package. The wires had fractured where they emerged from the 'gold box'. Small movements from chewing and rubbing the skin back and forth had caused the wires to flex and be subject to metal fatigue. This occurred where they emerged from the box at a point of stress concentration between a rigid and flexible object. It was a similar problem to the one that caused the Comet jets to explode in the air, many years ago, when square windows had been designed, rather than more oval ones. We would thus have to allow for this problem, and make sure there was no sudden break between the rigid package and the movable electrode, while taking precautions to bury the electrodes to protect them from rubbing movements.

We obtained this information while the clinical trial device being manufactured by Nucleus Limited was going through its final design stages for implantation in September 1982. As a result, the lead coming from the package was coiled to withstand these stresses and was flipped backwards and forwards a million times to make sure that it was robust.

With George, the problem then was whether to put the bionic ear in the right ear. He had a hole in the ear-drum on this side and this had to be closed so that infection wouldn't enter. George consented to an operation on 17 August to graft the hole, which then healed well. As the ear remained clean, we set down the time for his operation at the end of the trial.

By the end of August we had the six patients ready. Nucleus, too, was completing the final testing of the implants. Some were going into the gas sterilisation units ready for final packaging. They had to be manufactured and tested for failures even more rigorously than the University of Melbourne prototype. Tests included making them part of the car crash tests undertaken by the Department of Mechanical Engineering at the University of Melbourne. You could be killed in a car accident, but the implant would remain intact!

The plan with the clinical trial was to operate on two patients and start their evaluation to ensure there were no problems. The others would follow in groups of two.

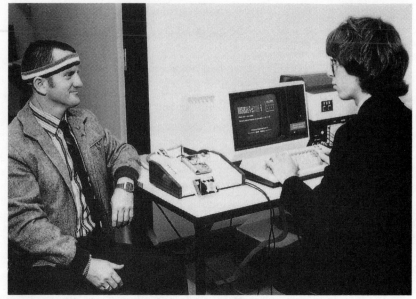

Richard Dowell at one of the early test sessions with Graham Carrick, the first patient to have the Nucleus implant.

Graham Carrick was the first to have the Nucleus bionic ear. Brian Pyman, Robert Webb and I implanted it at the Royal Victorian Eye and Ear Hospital on 12 September. Any concern I had about bone in the inner ear was dispelled when the electrode bundle went in the whole distance. Three weeks later, at his first test session, Graham was overcome with emotion when he first heard sounds, exclaiming: 'I didn't realise how much I missed hearing until this moment!'

From then on, Graham made good progress, and began to relate more easily to his family. He said he was able to discipline his children if they misbehaved, because he could now hear them and tell which one was the troublemaker. He was also able to get his licence to drive. When he was tested for hearing, the directional microphone allowed him to detect sounds at a distance that weren't audible for the examiner, who thought Graham's hearing must be extraordinary! As Graham became more confident, he came with Peter Howson and me to speak at Lions Club conventions to raise money for our research. The drives back to Melbourne gave us an opportunity to experience at first hand how the bionic ear helped him to communicate. As the light faded and he could no longer read our lips, Graham was still able to join in the conversation. Soon after, he gained promotion in his job.

The surgical team operated on Lorna Lewis on 21 September. The electrode bundle went easily into the inner ear. By now we were becoming quite skilled at the operation, and it only took five hours rather than the eight hours on Rod Saunders four years before. When Lorna had her first test sessions, she found the sensations difficult to describe. It was hard for her to remember what sounds were like after thirty-five years, but with patience and assistance from a skilful group of audiologists, she made steady improvement. The bionic ear became a real help as a lip-reading aid and was useful even when relied on alone. I remember the time she was my hope for a National Health and Medical Research Council grant. She was questioned by Professor Jim McLeod who stood behind her in my treatment room and asked her to identify the words that he had spoken. I held my breath, hoping that Lorna would give the right answer. She did!

The operations on Graham and Lorna demonstrated that the Nucleus implant was working, so we operated on Lionel Robinson's left ear on 13 October. The diseased inner ear appeared not to be a problem, as the electrode bundle went in easily for the full distance. But when the electrodes were switched on three weeks after surgery, we became aware of a problem. Eleven of the twenty-two electrodes stimulated the nerve to the face, making the muscles twitch, so we had to work around this difficulty by only using the wires that were found to be producing hearing. Lionel received significant help with lip-reading and was very grateful, but he didn't do as well as the others. Four years later he developed weakness of the face. By then we had more sophisticated X-rays, and found he also had a tumour on the nerve to the face. It produced total loss of hearing. He was helped along then by stimulation of the skin, but this wasn't as beneficial to him as the bionic ear had been. It served to remind me that, however hard we try, we cannot overcome all medical problems.

On 9 November, Jennifer Dawson had a bionic ear inserted into her right ear and the bundle of electrodes went 80 per cent of the optimal distance. Jennifer came back at the beginning of December and the device was turned on. We could tell at the first session that she would do well. Speech sounded as she had remembered. She was very enthusiastic and continued to improve week by week. She had the best results of all the patients to date. It became a great benefit to her. She even declared it was a wonderful experience to be able to hear her child crying during the night. She did so by strapping the bionic ear headband in place before going to sleep. Her work also improved—her supervisor in the Department of Social Security reported that it was immeasurably better since the implant surgery.

I was keen to give Cheryl Sheehan a bionic ear, as I believed it would also make a big difference to her life. There was only one niggling doubt. Would the inner ear, where the X-ray had shown no bone, be filled with scar tissue? At the operation on 12 November the inner ear was clear, and the electrode bundle passed the whole distance without any resistance. Cheryl was soon hearing sounds that were speech-like, and before long she had made a remarkable improvement in her ability to understand running speech when compared to lip-reading alone. In fact, there was a 98 per cent improvement. She could also hear quite well without help from lip-reading. Cheryl continued to improve over the months ahead, was soon back in Sydney and was promoted to a much more demanding position.

I left George's operation until the last to ensure that his middle ear had healed from the graft to his ear-drum. The electrode went well into the right ear, and when George returned for post-operative testing we waited with bated breath for the implant to be switched on. What a joy it was to us when he heard again! However, the result wasn't as good as the first time, owing to loss of more nerves on this side. Nevertheless, he was happy to hear and he willingly came back to participate in research studies to help others.

Two years later, on 21 August 1984, we re-operated on his left ear because that had given better results. He was now the first person to have an implant in both ears. At last we were on the road to providing George with the hearing he had fought so hard to achieve. George had an indomitable spirit. His history isn't a typical one, but it underlines his determination to hear and his wonderful support of the team. Sadly, George died of unrelated causes on 11 October 1997 and is missed by us all.

PUBLIC INTEREST GRANT—PHASE 4—AND THE WORLDWIDE CLINICAL TRIAL

The Australian government continued to oversee and help fund the industrial development of the bionic ear until approval was received from the

Mike Hirshorn is shown presenting the author with a gift commemorating the 1000 implant at the Shea Clinic on 28 June 1988.

US FDA that it was safe and effective to be marketed. Our successful trial in 1982 gave Nucleus the green light to start the clinical trial in the US and Europe. In 1983 and 1984, we continued in Melbourne implanting profoundly deaf adults of different ages as part of the worldwide study. Incidently, Rod Saunders participated in this trial when his prototype like George's had eventually failed.

From early in 1982, I had meetings with David Money and Mike Hirshorn from Nucleus to work out where the trials should be carried out in the US and Europe, and who would be appropriate ear surgeons to conduct these trials. (Mike's role in Nucleus was to establish and manage worldwide clinical trials, to gain FDA and other governmental approvals and eventually to launch the Melbourne/Nucleus implant through creating subsidiaries which would also market in the US, Europe and Japan.) We also had to decide whether we should have the centres in cities where there would be a larger population of deaf people, or in special centres in smaller cities. Would teams be able to manage people for lengthy rehabilitation sessions when they came from other parts of the US? It was audiologist Dr Diane Mecklenberg and Mike Hirshorn's contacts, as well as mine, that finally determined some of the centres.

During the week of 15–20 March 1981, Dr Brian McCabe, Professor of Otolaryngology at the University of Iowa and one of the invited speakers for the annual ear, nose and throat conference in Melbourne, heard me present our initial bionic ear results. He was very enthusiastic and wanted to do a study to compare our implant with the Vienna and Los Angeles single-electrode and Salt Lake City (Utah) multiple-electrode devices for a trial he was organising in the US for the National Institutes of Health. I passed on this information to Mike and Dianne, who began negotiations with Brian McCabe.

I had formed a friendship with Dr Jim Jerger from Baylor Medical College who had been the guest of honour at our first audiology workshop in May 1977. Jim was one of the pioneers in audiology, and I felt this would make Baylor a very good choice. Furthermore, it had two outstanding ear surgeons in Dr Bob Alford and Dr Herman Jenkins.

Once we had trialled the Nucleus implant in 1982, Dr Bruce Gantz from Iowa and Bob Alford and Herman Jenkins from Baylor were keen to learn all they could about our device and the surgery. They made special visits to Melbourne, which allowed them to see the device. Once the FDA gave the green light, Iowa and Baylor were the first centres in the US to implant our bionic ear. The operations were done on 16 May 1983, in Iowa, and one week later at Baylor. Operations on patients at other US trial centres soon followed later. The surgeons were Dr Charlie Mangam from the Mason Clinic in Seattle; Dr Noel Cohen at New York University; Dr George Lyons from the Louisiana State University, New Orleans; Dr Owen Black from the Good Samaritan Hospital in Portland and Dr Julian Nedzelski from the University of Toronto.

Europe presented a problem. I knew some of the famous ear surgeons, but they mainly operated on the middle ear. But then Dr Burkhard Franz, a visiting Fellow from Germany at our Department, told us that not only was Professor Dr Ernst Lehnhardt a good surgeon, but he had also written a textbook on audiology. That seemed the right combination. Could we get him involved in the trial?

Professor Lehnhardt had been visiting various centres to make up his mind which implant to use. After representations from Mike Hirshorn and David Money he visited us with his engineer, Dr Rolf Battmer, to see what was happening in Melbourne. He arrived in the Department on 6 February 1984, and two days later I had him watching an implant operation on Mr Jim Jewell. He also had the opportunity to see patients who had previously had the implant, to evaluate our surgical techniques, and to see the depth of research underpinning the industrial development. He must have been satisfied, as he commenced performing the surgery in

Hannover on 26 July 1984. Within a year or two he had created the largest implant centre in Europe through using our device. Before long, he had operated on more patients than we had, and was also called on to set up centres in other countries.

EARLY MARKETING

The clinical trial in 1982 heightened competition with 3M, and the relative merits of their single-electrode device and our multiple-electrode system were much debated. Was our more expensive multiple-electrode system (three times the price) really better than the 3M single-electrode device? The 3M single-electrode device was also under trial for use in adults by the US Food and Drug Administration, and was being marketed aggressively.

Then, in November 1984, the FDA approved the 3M device for use in deafened adults only on the grounds that it brought awareness of sound and not speech understanding. Nevertheless, it put the onus on us to demonstrate that our implant *was* better in providing speech understanding. Other competitors were appearing: the University of Vienna's single-electrode device (developed by Professor Kurt Burian, and Drs Erwin Hochmair and Ingeborg Hochmair-Desoyer); the London University College Hospital with Dr Graham Fraser's single-electrode device; the University of Utah with Symbion's Ineraid multiple-electrode system (implementing the research of Dr Don Eddington); the University of California at San Francisco with the Storz multiple-electrode system (derived from the research of Drs Robin Michelson, Mike Merzenich, and Robert Schindler); the University of Paris (research of Professors Pialoux, Chouard and McLeod); Zurich University Hospital (research by Drs Dillier and Spillmann); Düren Hospital with Hortmann's Implex extra-cochlear system (research of Professor Banfai); and Antwerp with the Laura device (research headed by Professor Marquet and Drs Offeciers and Peeters).

However, these implants did not prove to be commercial threats. For example, the Ineraid system had a socket (implanted in the skull) that passed through the skin to connect with a plug. This resulted in many side-effects, such as breakage and infection, and was aesthetically unacceptable. The Storz device had four separate circular aerials making it too bulky to be practicable. Some years later, in the late 1980s, when the

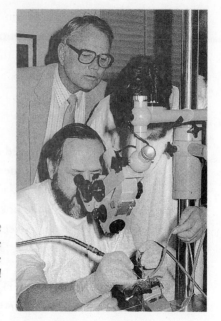

Dr Blair Simmons at the Cochlear implant surgical workshop examining how the Nucleus bionic ear is implanted. The workshop was part of our first International Cochlear Implant Symposium, Melbourne, 1985.

Cochlear Pty Limited's share of the US market had risen to 90 per cent, it bought the interests of 3M and Symbion (now Richards) and recently Laura and, with them, the responsibility of looking after their patients.

It became clear in the formative days that we would need to cooperate with Nucleus to increase international awareness of our results. We couldn't quietly get on with research alone and leave the rest to industry. Marketing this biomedical product was a new experience for us all. We soon realised the opinion makers were the surgeons and the audiologists. This meant getting the results out to conferences. Writing papers and monographs was a personal preoccupation, but it had a slow effect.

I organised a National Cochlear Implant Symposium in Melbourne for 4 October 1984 at the Royal Australasian College of Surgeons. This would enable surgeons and audiologists to participate and ask questions. Then, in August 1985, we held our first International Cochlear Implant Meeting which provided an opportunity for many leading scientists and clinicians to see the depth of research in Melbourne underpinning the Nucleus implant. Scientific credibility was vital to establish the position of Nucleus at the international level.

APPROVAL FROM THE US FOOD AND DRUG ADMINISTRATION

By 1985 the results coming in from the trial centres showed that not only did the Nucleus multiple-electrode bionic ear provide most people with considerable help with lip-reading, but it also gave them some understanding of speech using electrical stimulation alone—a result which hadn't been achieved with the 3M single-electrode device.

In 1984 and 1985 the mammoth task of presenting the information to the FDA for regulatory approval commenced. The findings had to be analysed and the histories of eighty-seven patients collected. There were forty from North America, thirty-six from Australia and eleven in Germany. The engineering details of the device and its electrical safety were presented in full. Extensive biological safety information was expected, including the effect of the electrical current on nerve survival, the toxicity of the materials used, and the reliability of the bundle of electrodes to go into the inner ear. Then there were the manuals on the surgery and its side-effects, such as the infection rate.

In 1985 as the FDA submission approached, I became aware of a spate of scientific articles that were appearing pointing out the damage from electrodes inserted into the inner ear. The implication was that the 3M single electrode was safer than our multiple-electrode bundle because it only had one electrode and didn't go as far.

Fortunately, I had taken study leave some months before to examine under the microscope the effects of our electrode on the inner ears of experimental animals, and had found no adverse effects. To be even more certain, Jim Patrick and Mr John MacFarlane from the CSIRO compared the 3M single and Nucleus multiple electrodes for stiffness and flexibility. The study showed that our array was ten to twenty times better, as it had much thinner wires. Thus, the claims being made weren't valid.

Finally, approval came through in October 1985 that the Nucleus implant could be used widely in adults who had hearing before going deaf. It was the first multiple-electrode cochlear implant to be approved as safe and effective for clinical use by any health regulatory body. Furthermore, the US subsidiary Cochlear Corporation took the initiative in encouraging certain centres in the US to set up special training courses so that surgeons not familiar with the operation could perform it with minimum risk.

PENETRATING WORLD MARKETS

After the approval from the US, other world regulatory bodies followed suit. Another milestone was approval in Japan, a country traditionally cautious in implanting devices into the body. The first bionic ear operation was on a forty-one-year-old adult on 7 December 1985 and was undertaken by Professor S. Funasaka from the Tokyo Medical School. Dr Richard (now Professor) Ramsden did the first operation using the Nucleus device in the UK in Manchester on 21 June, 1988. But first he had to raise the money to buy the implant. As it turned out, this came as a result of a parachute jump. The jump was a raffle prize won by his friend, Mr Laurie Cleary, who not only took the chance to jump, but also to ask on the spot for sponsors to donate. Thus £2000 was raised for a cochlear implant!

The successful results and good corporate management by Paul Trainor, David Money and other members of Cochlear Pty Limited (a subsidiary of Nucleus Limited) and collaboration with the University of Melbourne saw the company grow, and in the late 1980s to early 1990s it had 90 per cent of the US market and approximately 80% of the world market. Further speech processing research advances made by the University of Melbourne's Ear, Nose and Throat Department helped the company to maintain its dominant position internationally. An office of Cochlear Corporation was established in the United States in 1984 with Mr Ron West as president; Cochlear AG was established in Europe in 1987 with Dr Monika Lehnhardt in charge. In 1988, Nucleus Limited was sold to the Australian company Pacific Dunlop. Together with the pace-making company Teletronics, Cochlear Pty Limited was part of its medical division.

In 1995, Cochlear Limited was listed on the Australian Stock Exchange as a separate company, with Professor David Penington AC as chairman of the board and Ms Catherine Livingstone as the chief executive officer. Cochlear Limited has continued in the successful vein of its predecessor Nucleus (Cochlear Pty Limited).

VISITS BY ROYALTY AND HEADS OF STATE

The bionic ear has been marketed by Cochlear in fifteen years in over fifty countries and it helps thousands of deaf adults and children. Her

Majesty Queen Beatrix and His Royal Highness Prince Claus of the Neth-
erlands visited our centre at the University of Melbourne in 1988 as part
of the Australian Bicentenary celebrations. Long before she was a law
graduate, Queen Beatrix showed a concern for social welfare and for
people with disabilities: she and Prince Claus had even given some of
their wedding present money to four national associations for parents of
disabled children. To have sniffer dogs running through the centre was a
unique experience. So was lecturing to a queen!

Some years later, in 1995, Their Imperial Highnesses Prince Akishino
and Princess Akishino of Japan expressed a wish to see the bionic ear
research when on an official visit to Australia. The Prince and Princess
had a specific interest in the disabled, founded upon their broader training
in Zoology and Psychology, respectively. We were learning there were
different protocols associated with a royal visit. The Prince and Princess
saw at first hand the benefits of our work through conversations with one
of our bionic ear children.

In 1999 there was an official visit from the President of China, His
Excellency Jiang Zemin. He arrived on 7 September while making the
first visit to Australia by a Chinese head of state. As an engineer, he was
specially interested in how we had connected the electronics to the ear.
We were able to demonstrate the great benefits that the bionic ear
brought to deaf Chinese adults and children with their tonal language.
Three children with bionic ears made speeches and asked him to pass on
their best wishes to the deaf children in China.

These visits from royalty and heads of state kept reminding me of an
old English nursery rhyme:

> I had a little nut tree
> Nothing would it bear
> But a silver nutmeg
> And a golden pear.
> The king of Spain's daughter
> Came to visit me
> And all was because
> of my little nut tree.

11

Helping deaf children to hear

No deaf child who has earnestly tried to speak
the words which he has never heard—to come
out of the prison of silence, where no tone of
love, no song of bird, no strain of music ever
pierces the stillness—can forget the thrill of
surprise, the joy of discovery which came over
him when he uttered his first word.

Helen Keller, The Story of My Life

The road to helping deaf children was a circuitous one. First the
bionic ear had to be proven safe and effective for adults. Then
the storm of criticism of an understandably defensive signing deaf community had to be weathered and answered. Some of the early criticism
arose because the single-electrode implant being used in the United
States, when applied to children in 1980, didn't give them significant
benefit in understanding speech. The fears, however, were more fundamental. The signing deaf had developed a view that deafness was accept-
able, and hearing by any means could be a threat.

As explained in an earlier chapter, there have been three approaches
to the education of profoundly deaf children: auditory/oral; total communication; and Sign Language of the Deaf. In auditory/oral education,
if children have a little residual hearing they are taught to communicate
in English by using a hearing aid and lip-reading. In total communication,
hand signs can be added, especially if lip-reading is difficult or impossible
for them. These signs are really signed English. By contrast, Sign
Language of the Deaf is a unique system with its own language structure.
The signs represent thoughts, just as sounds do for English, French or

other languages, but they vary from country to country. In Australia the system is called Auslan. Sign Language of the Deaf was developed 200 years ago by l'Abbé de l'Epée at the Paris Deaf School. It has done much to help profoundly deaf people to live in a hearing world, but the disability remains. As a result, it is harder for them to compete and to obtain jobs in a community which is essentially geared to those who can hear and speak the language of the country.

When I first started my bionic ear research, I couldn't understand why deafness wasn't considered the same as other disabilities, and thus in need of help. If a child had spina bifida, or blindness, for instance, there was a need for assistance. Why did the signing deaf community not feel the same?

Some scientists were hopeful that patterns of skin stimulation could be understood as speech. The idea was that children, in particular, could discern the meaning of words through their tactile senses, thus avoiding an operation. To keep the option of tactile stimulation open, I had also pursued multiple-electrode stimulation of the skin as a parallel research development in our own department along with Peter Blamey and Bob Cowan. Nevertheless by the mid-1980s the results being achieved with the multiple-electrode bionic ear on deaf adults who had hearing before going deaf, were so encouraging that the view that tactile stimulation was the only alternative was waning. This was reflected in a letter to me in December 1986 from Dr Adele Proctor, a leading American scientist in the tactile field. She wrote:

> Professor Clark, again, I thank you for the time and energy that you and all of the members of the department devoted to my visit. As I continued my travels to Sydney and three different areas of Japan, based on comments made by colleagues, I felt quite the privileged person, that I had visited your laboratory first. Most memorable among the comments were the anecdotes that colleagues in Sydney warmly related about attending meetings in years past where your ideas were challenged, but in the 'Australian daring do', so to speak, you rose far above those negative challenges. In one small gathering, we decided that there was a considerable amount that each of us could learn from you in how to accept and manage challenges to some of our long-held beliefs.

The debate on whether a multiple- or single-electrode system was better didn't lessen until a controlled comparative study was undertaken on deaf adults at Iowa City of the Los Angeles and Vienna single-electrode devices, and of the Salt Lake City and our Nucleus multiple-electrode systems. The data on those people who had hearing before going deaf were unwrapped by Bruce Gantz on the last presentation of the International Cochlear Implant Conference, which I had organised in Melbourne in August 1985. They showed that the multiple-electrode systems gave statistically significantly better results than both of the single-electrode devices.

ISSUES FOR IMPLANTING CHILDREN

It was only after I became confident of the benefit of our multiple-electrode system for adults who could hear before deafness set in, that I really became hopeful that the same system would work for children born deaf, who had never been exposed to sound. Had we developed a system that would only work if the fine connections in the brain for handling speech had been established through prior exposure to sound? Furthermore, would the device be reliable for use in children? A fault in an adult could be explained to them as part of the risk to be accepted. But children are not mature enough to make decisions that will affect their whole lives, and a failure could have a serious psychological effect.

I had to wait until we had tested the device, developed industrially by Nucleus Limited in the latter half of 1982, on six adults, to prove that speech understanding was as good as that from the University of Melbourne's prototype. It also had to be trialled on adults for the US FDA. Furthermore, the thickness of the device meant it could only be implanted in the skull of a teenager or adult. Another problem in using the bionic ear was that the transmitting radio aerial had to be aligned accurately over the receiving coil on the package using a headband—a finicky procedure which children would have difficulty in adjusting to. Besides, it would almost certainly be dislodged when they played games.

All along, the question of whether the bionic ear would benefit children born deaf was burning away, but I decided that I would start on adults born deaf and work back in age. If some benefits occurred in older people, then the results should be better in younger children whose brains are more 'plastic', which means the connections in the brain can be altered to better process sounds such as speech.

After the airing given by the press over a number of years, there was strong interest from some adult users of Auslan in whether the bionic ear would make a radical difference. So, as soon as we had finished operating on the first patients for the clinical trial in 1982, I prepared two adults, Mr Greg Westbury (deafened early in life) and Miss Beverley Keam, now Mrs Westbury, who was born deaf, to have surgery. Studying them in depth would give me clues as to whether an auditory input could be used by an adult when the main method of communication was Auslan. Greg, who was twenty-four, had had meningitis at the age of fifteen months; he had his operation in September 1983. Beverley, who was twenty-three, was operated on two months later.

Soon after starting the tests, we found that they weren't hearing sounds the same way as adults who had hearing before going deaf. They couldn't hear a different pitch or timbre when each electrode was stimulated. Differences in timbre were one of the main advantages of the multiple-electrode system over the single-electrode device. So, this finding didn't augur well for helping them to understand speech. Try as we might, it wasn't even possible to teach them to combine the signal with lip-reading. It was as though the auditory centre in their brain could no longer use new information. They continued to use Sign Language of the Deaf for communication, but did find the device was useful as an alerting signal. Their results were disappointing and I half-doubted whether we should pursue the bionic ear for younger children deafened early in life or born deaf.

One important issue in operating on young children was being sure they didn't have enough residual hearing to benefit from a hearing aid. An implant could destroy this remnant. It was generally accepted by audiologists in the 1970s and 1980s that a hearing loss couldn't even be diagnosed accurately under four years of age. It was only in the late 1980s that we developed a precise method of recording brain waves in response to sound even in children soon after birth. Only then was it possible to responsibly think of implanting young children.

THE FIRST BIONIC EAR IMPLANT IN A CHILD

The press reports on the benefits of the bionic ear for adults who had hearing before going deaf led to a growing interest from parents wanting to give hearing to their deaf children. To explain our progress, members of the team spoke at a number of functions. After one meeting, a parent,

Mr Charles Searle, approached me and said that his son Peter, who was now thirteen, had been brought up in an educational system that emphasised the use of cues to complement lip-reading. He had lost hearing at the age of sixteen months due to meningitis. Would he be a suitable patient? I believed that the critical period for implanting Peter had nearly passed, but if we were going to help it would have to be done as soon as possible.

At the time, we hadn't been able to get insurance companies to fund the bionic ear, but Charles was prepared to pay for the device himself ($10 000). After the normal pre-operative evaluation, I operated on Peter in 1985 when he was fourteen.

We were very keen to learn how Peter would respond to the electrical stimuli, and I was pleased that he showed much greater improvements than the two earlier adults. He took to his lessons with enthusiasm, and received strong support from the teachers at St Mary's School for Children with Impaired Hearing in Knox, a suburb of Melbourne. They and the principal, Sister Francis, in particular, had faith in our work, and this gave us great encouragement. Over the next months, Peter made slow but steady progress. The device provided significant help as a lip-reading aid, but it still didn't give a great deal of useful hearing with electrical stimulation alone.

THE FIRST CHILD TO RECEIVE THE BIONIC EAR ESPECIALLY DESIGNED FOR CHILDREN

Peter was helped, but we needed to do better. I would have to operate on a younger child. This would require a smaller bionic ear, and we needed a better method than the headband of holding the transmitting aerial in place. A smaller device required dispensing with the connector on the underside of the Nucleus package. Our studies had shown that a connector wasn't really necessary. If ever we had to replace the package, it could be removed in total as the electrodes slipped out easily. It was agreed with Cochlear Pty Limited that this first design alteration was required. A better method for holding the aerial in place was the use of magnets at the centres of the internal and external aerials. It was later to be a means of showing off to the child's peer group, who would gape at the sight of pins and other metal objects sticking to a playmate's skull!

In 1985, as Cochlear Pty Limited worked to get the new implant

The bionic ear with magnet suitable for children. This bionic ear was produced by Cochlear Limited in association with the Department of Ear, Nose and Throat Surgery at the University of Melbourne. The postage stamp was issued in 1987 to commemorate Australian technological achievements. (Courtesy of the National Philatelic Collection, Australia Post)

system ready, we prepared a younger child for an implant operation. The child considered was ten-year-old Scott Smith who had become profoundly deaf at three-and-a-half, again owing to meningitis. When Scott recovered from his illness he wasn't his normal, boisterous self, but seemed somehow 'lost'—a change quickly noted by his mother, Betty, who sought professional help. A diagnosis of a profound-to-total hearing loss came as a shock. It was to be a frustrating time for Scott and his parents. He received little help from his hearing aids, and when he tired of wearing them he hid them around the house. Betty and her husband, Alan, received conflicting advice on how to manage Scott. They opted for total communication, though it meant driving long distances to attend school. Betty was determined to give Scott the best chance to communicate with hearing people, but he was still not making the progress Betty would have liked. When she came to see us, I explained to her that we would like to carry out a number of hearing and other tests to see whether Scott would be suitable for an implant. I also wanted to trial some tactile aids first to see whether they would give him the help needed.

We had been experimenting with tactile stimulation for some years and I discovered that if I stimulated my forearm in places where I knew nerve bundles to be, less electric current was needed and the sensation was more pleasant and less prickly than on other areas of the skin. Applying this principle, Peter Blamey and I sent speech frequencies ranging from low to high through bands placed around the fingers. The bands with a speech processor formed a device we called the 'Tickle Talker'. Betty Smith signed the consent form for us to electrically stimulate Scott's fingers using the 'Tickle Talker' on 7 May, 1985. But Scott's understanding of speech didn't greatly improve, so we asked Betty to consider a bionic ear operation. I hoped the new device would be ready by July or August.

Alan's greatest worry for his son was that it would stop him from playing sport. Scott loved both cricket and football and was captain of the football team. I had to disappoint him—sports with body contact, like cricket and football, were risky. If all went well, though, I might agree to his playing football while wearing a special helmet. In any case, the operation date (6 August 1985) was arranged so that Scott could play his last important game for the season.

Scott arrived at the hospital two days before the operation, but had signs that he could be developing an inflammation of the middle ear. We had to postpone the surgery. Finally, Robert Webb and I performed the operation, at the Royal Victorian Eye and Ear Hospital, on 20 August. The electrode bundle went the whole distance into the inner ear. After a two-week recovery period, we were all set to test Scott. It was timed for just after the International Conference on Cochlear Implants held at the University of Melbourne. A few visitors remained to watch the first test session. We were ready to go, and turned on the electrical current. Scott became very distressed, and said he didn't like it. He refused to have anything to do with it until audiologist Dianne Mecklenburg coaxed him to use it by placing a vibrator on his chest, neck and ear while our senior audiologist, Richard Dowell, turned the current up very carefully. Later Scott explained that he thought he would immediately hear speech. He didn't realise that all the electrodes would sound strange and that the current levels had to be set first. The next day he returned with a completely different attitude and began his training to hear speech. After some faults in the wearable speech processor were rectified the training sessions continued over the next nine months, enabling Scott to understand speech sounds, especially with lip-reading. His overall performance was better than that of our teenager Peter Searle, perhaps because he was younger and his hearing pathways more plastic.

As children born deaf or deafened early in life had to learn the meaning of sound, I knew it would take longer than for adults who previously had hearing, to demonstrate how good the device actually was. Though not wanting to go to the press prematurely, I had allowed a television documentary to be produced for 'Quantum', which showed us training a child.

CRITICISM FROM THE SIGNING DEAF COMMUNITY

The signing deaf community was quick to notice this report and a member wrote in October 1985 to the Deafness Foundation of Victoria (the organisation representing primarily all deaf people who did *not* use signing), complaining that the child should not have undergone such an operation. He enclosed a copy of an editorial in a US newspaper for the signing deaf called *Silent News*, published in September 1985, which outlined a number of arguments against the cochlear implant in the United States.

The Deafness Foundation of Victoria responded on 21 November, largely by quoting me. My first point was that there was a generally accepted principle that sound was important in a child's language development and should be heard as early as possible by whatever means. People with a total hearing loss wouldn't get any help with a hearing aid, but we would be giving them that sound with a bionic ear. I emphasised that the Nucleus Limited device had been approved for use by the US FDA as safe and effective in adults. To assure him that no coercion was used, I explained that three independent ethics committees were involved, and an assurance was required from a lawyer who interviewed the parents and child. The initial studies were planned on a small group of children who would be carefully monitored. Independent studies had shown it to be better than the 3M single-electrode implant from Los Angeles for adults who had previously had hearing. Besides, it didn't connect the person up with a plug and socket through the skin as did the Ineraid multiple-electrode system. The Deafness Foundation concluded by inviting the author of the editorial to the Department of Ear, Nose and Throat Surgery to learn more about the bionic ear.

I gained a better understanding of the signing point of view when the hearing impaired journalist Michael Uniacke wrote, in a publication called *In Future*, 'The signing deaf community views the cochlear implant with anger.' One reason for their anger was 'the bionic ear implies that deaf people are sick', and 'Professor Clark has the habit of referring to deaf people as patients'. He also quoted Breda Carty, who claimed: 'Implanted children cannot hear.' The depth of their feelings is clear from this quote from the same article: 'So many of these deaf people find their greatest satisfaction, enjoyment and support through their identity as deaf people. They feel as though others want to take away their identity and there is a lot of anger about that.'

When a Deafness Appeal Telethon was advertised in November, reaction to its theme, 'Let them hear how much you care', was forthright: 'Has anyone ever asked deaf people whether they *want* to hear?' Talk like this could have led to the television telethon being cancelled. A letter by Philip Harper published in *The Age* said that there were other more important issues to address than a bionic ear, such as interpreters, subtitling on television, and access to primary and secondary education. And of course I agreed that these were important needs, but did that mean longer term goals were to be forgotten?

The feelings against the cochlear implant were very intense in Europe and the United States. In Britain it was reported in *The Guardian* that the members of two leading British organisations representing the deaf were asked to boycott an international conference on deaf education in Manchester. They were angry because the main conference session would be devoted to the discussion of experimental cochlear implants. Mr Paddy Ladd, secretary of the National Union of the Deaf, said: 'It is quite wrong to make a medical matter, concerning something which should only be used upon adults, as the main topic in an education conference.' He went on to say: 'The education of deaf children in this country is quite appalling. The average deaf school leaver can only read as well as the average eight and a half year old. That's what the conference should be discussing. Implants are a red herring.' Needless to say, to me the very difficulty of educating deaf children was one good reason to persist with bionic ears.

An article entitled 'Cochlear Implants—the final put down', published in *The Disability Rag* in February 1986 in the United States, complained: 'Hearing people almost always believe that deaf people need to be "cured".' It went on to say: 'A majority culture has no understanding of how deaf people live day to day. It doesn't fit in with their culture. So they try to do something to change it.' The view of another from the same publication was that:

> The problem is really not about deafness, but people. It is important for them [people with normal hearing] to give thought to fixing their attitudes, to fixing their insensitivity to communicating with deaf people, to increasing their knowledge of deafness. What if I'm happy as I am? What if I prefer that they accept me as the individual that I am? To many deaf people, the reliance on implants and other cures as solutions to their problems is society's way of getting off the hook when it comes to accepting deaf people.

I could understand some of the points so eloquently made. I knew from my own experience with my father how unaware the average person is of the predicament of deaf people in trying to communicate. I also knew the dignity which sign language had given. On the other hand, if we could give deaf people the ability to hear speech and to communicate in a world of sound, they would have more scope.

Nevertheless, this climate within the signing deaf community before and just after we had carried out the first multiple-electrode implant on a child was hardly one of encouragement! We felt it was ironic that we were now confronted by the very people to whom we wanted to give an opportunity to hear. The criticisms affected all members of the team and couldn't help but weigh heavily upon us.

THE FIRST YOUNG CHILD TO RECEIVE THE BIONIC EAR

In spite of everything, once our first child, Scott, had settled down and was making progress, Nucleus Limited sought approval from the US FDA for a worldwide trial to begin. It was also the signal for me to plan surgery on a younger child to see if we could achieve even better results. Approval for the trial came late in 1986.

Five-year-old Bryn Davies was to be our next patient, the term 'patient' being used according to the dictionary meaning of someone undergoing medical treatment. He had lost his ability to speak soon after meningitis at the age of three years, in spite of wearing hearing aids after his illness in May 1984. His parents had approached me six months later, but I had to say that we weren't ready with an implant small enough for

Scott Smith (10 years) and Bryn Davies (5 years) in 1985, with the author holding the bionic ear implant. (Photograph by Neale Duckworth, courtesy of The Age)

a child of his age. We also needed more experience on older children. In the meantime, towards the latter part of 1984, Sister Joan Winter, principal of the John Pierce Centre Early Education Program for Hearing Impaired Children, prepared a videotape of someone reading five of Bryn's favourite story books along with cued speech (signs to clarify lip-reading). He watched these videotapes over and over again, so increasing his understanding of the English language.

Before the implant operation, Bryn was given a six-month trial with a device to present speech as skin vibrations. He preferred this to his hearing aid, but still had trouble communicating and his speech reception age was that of a two-year-old. The decision to go ahead with an operation was tough for his parents, Anne-Marie and Philip. They had to take quite a risk, as we still didn't know what the benefits would be. But realising that they had little to lose if they wanted Bryn to be able to hear, they consented to the operation which Robert Webb and I carried out in April 1986. Before the operation the X-rays had shown that meningitis had resulted in one inner ear being filled with bone, but there was evidence that the other side could be implanted. At surgery only fifteen of the twenty electrodes on the bundle could be eased into place, but I was hopeful that we had enough for a good result.

With children of Bryn's age, it was thought difficult to set thresholds and comfortable levels of loudness for the electrodes, as they wouldn't have the speech and language skills to tell us what they were experiencing. By having them arrange blocks from large to small, they learned the concepts of loud or soft which they could transfer to the sensations experienced with the bionic ear.

After the stimulus levels for the implant were set, Bryn was soon using his speech processor with even better success than Scott. It was particularly encouraging that he could hear some speech using electrical stimulation alone and not have to rely on lip-reading.

This was the first strong evidence that the multiple-electrode implant was going to do more to help children than a single-electrode device, and would provide speech understanding. Bryn's speech perception results came just as I was leaving for Houston to represent medical research in Australia at a Festival Honouring Australia. It was an opportunity to share the news with Professor Bob Alford and staff at the Baylor College of Medicine. In Los Angeles I met with Dr Howard House, founder of the House Institute, and his brother Dr William House, who together with engineer Mr Jack Urban had produced the single-electrode device. The group in Los Angeles, in particular Dr Bill Luxford, formerly a New Zealander, were actually using our multiple-electrode implant in adults and, to my surprise, were considering running surgical training courses in its use. They had already inserted a number of single-electrode devices in children, beginning in 1980, but these did not give them worthwhile help in understanding speech. So they were now keen to know how we programmed our device for children too young to speak.

On arriving back in Australia I had to let the public know about progress with the children. A press conference was held in the University of Melbourne's Department of Ear, Nose and Throat Surgery on 10 June. It was well attended, as we were reporting on the first child in the world to receive the miniaturised Australian bionic ear. It was covered widely in the papers, radio and television, both nationally and internationally.

Clinical trial of the bionic ear in children for the US Food and Drug Administration

By the end of 1986, Cochlear Pty Limited had approval from the US FDA to commence a trial in the United States, Europe and Australia on children from two to eighteen years of age. Approval to trial the Nucleus implant for the FDA required volumes of information, such as speech perception results on adults with hearing before going deaf, experimental animal safety data, details of the engineering, and a protocol for evaluating its performance in children. As the children often had poor language, the tests in the protocol had to be appropriate to their age and development. We produced a battery of tests with help from Dr Terry Nienhuys, lecturer in charge of the Education of the Hearing Impaired course at the University of Melbourne, and Dr Gay Nichols, an experienced educator who had arrived from Canada. We had much to learn about these tests on the children. This test battery was then adapted for the US trial by Dianne Mecklenburg.

As it turned out, when the trial began Bill House became the first to implant our device, into a five year eight month old child in the US on 6 February 1987 at the mother's request. The next two operations were done by Dr Jack Hough in Oklahoma and Dr John Kemink at the University of Michigan Hospital. Soon others followed and the trial gradually gained momentum. However, teachers of the deaf, audiologists and surgeons remained reluctant for some time to refer children. Cochlear Corporation, the US subsidiary of the Australian firm, had a very dedicated staff of audiologists and engineers, including Drs Steve Staller, Dianne Mecklenburg, Judy Brimacombe and Anne Beiter, who helped each centre set up their program. They would fly at short notice anywhere to help with a problem with a child or equipment. It was a taxing time for them, considering as well the prevailing opposition.

The first children born deaf to receive the bionic ear

The children we had operated on had become deaf early in life. Would our multiple-electrode system be effective for children born deaf? That was the next most crucial question. I set about finding young children who would fit this category. Our first child was Colleen Tarrant, who was not only born deaf but was also gradually going blind. In 1984 her mother had been told we weren't yet ready to operate. Then, having heard in 1986 about our first two children, she contacted us in October 1986 to see if anything could now be done. Colleen could soon be both deaf and blind. In that case, she wouldn't even be able to read Sign Language of the Deaf and so would be left with only touch and vibration as means of communicating.

We had to operate soon, before the critical stage in brain plasticity had passed—at fourteen years of age, it was nearly too late. Finally, the surgery was carried out in April 1987.

Afterwards, with encouragement, Colleen began to discriminate speech sounds. It was a slow process, but we could see it was going to be a big help with lip-reading and could even be useful if she became completely blind.

The second Australian bionic ear to be implanted in a child born deaf was carried out by Professor William Gibson and Dr Barrie Scrivener in Sydney. The child, Pia Jeffrey, had very little residual hearing, but the family and doctors still hesitated, as even that residual hearing could be lost. After going from doctor to doctor and group to group, they finally made up their mind to proceed with surgery. When the device was switched on two weeks later and Pia's face suddenly lit up on camera, new hope was indeed given that the bionic ear would help children who were born deaf.

In time there would be children joining Bill Gibson's group, 'CICADA', an acronym for Cochlear Implant Club & Advisory Associ-ation, and also the name of a shrill-voiced insect heard in summer in Australia. This was the first implant support group in the world and was begun by Bill in response to a double need—that of his first two adults operated on in 1984 who wanted to get together and talk, and that of prospective patients whom Bill wanted to learn what an implant was like from previous patients. They met for several years in the Gibson's garden, where their Christmas parties were also held, Mrs Alex Gibson playing a vital part in the Association. So Bill became Santa Claus for the children. When they began to see through his disguise, his twin brother took the part, while Bill mingled with the crowd—just to add to their confusion, perhaps!

With time, progress in our children and those at other centres was very noticeable. When teachers of the deaf from around the world began

MADE IN AUSTRALIA
world famous "bionic ear" - the new miracle in sound

Pia Jeffrey, the second child in Australia born deaf to receive a bionic ear, featured on the back cover of the Sydney telephone directory, 1992. (Photograph by Rick Stevens, courtesy of the Sydney Morning Herald)

saying they had never seen such improvements, we gained confidence. Their experience, coming after an initial sceptical attitude, spoke as loudly as the carefully collected data now arriving. I also discovered that as the staff really began to believe in the bionic ear, the results improved.

THE CONTROVERSY CONTINUES

By 1988 we thought that the controversy surrounding implanting children would have started to abate, but it was still a hot issue. This was partly because the full benefits were slow to appear and the results varied. Then, if there was one unsuccessful outcome, it was seized upon as typical, and adversely affected the climate. The first operation in Europe wasn't carried out until January 1988 in Oslo by Dr Henrik Lindeman; the first British operation was on 20 March 1989 in Nottingham. The British government funded a centre which included surgeons Dr Gerry O'Donoghue and Dr Kevin Gibbins, and audiologists Professor Barry McCormick, Dr Sue Archbold and Dr Mark Lutman. In Japan we had to wait until 1991, and in China 1997.

On the home front, people were still questioning our procedures and our results. I was amazed how long it took to convince them. For example, there was a panel and workshop for various organisations involved in deafness in Melbourne in May 1988. The discussion centred on cochlear implants for children and, at times, became vigorous. The Australian Deafness Council was given the task of looking for some common ground. As a result, I had a letter from the president, Dr Victor Bear, asking for information first on the form of our ethics committee, its constitution and how it approached implanting children. Second, they wanted to know what we did for the pre- and post-operative counselling of parents and, when applicable, the child. Third, were we making any efforts to disseminate information on the cochlear implant within the deaf and wider communities? I hoped our response would deal with some of the concerns people had.

The debate was still intense in the United States, and to provide objectivity the Central Institute for the Deaf in St Louis commenced a well-controlled comparison of the bionic ear with hearing aids and tactile aids. Children with similar ages and profound hearing losses were divided into three groups. Each group used a different sensory aid, but was given the same education and training. The study continued into 1993. Near the end, it became clear that the children with the bionic ear were doing better than those with the hearing aid or tactile aid. Those with bionic ears had shifted from being profoundly deaf to being equivalent to severely deaf children with some useful hearing. It became an ethical dilemma whether the children using hearing aids and tactile aids should still continue to do so, as they were being deprived of the benefits of the bionic ear.

SAFETY STUDIES FOR VERY YOUNG CHILDREN (UNDER TWO YEARS)

With the world trial the US FDA had laid down that children could only be operated on from the age of two years and above. The data coming in suggested that the younger a child was when we operated, the better.

If we were to operate on children younger than two years, there were special biological safety issues that needed to be resolved first. The head is smaller in children, and growth changes could cause the electrodes to be pulled out of the inner ear. The operation itself might even cause some deformity in skull growth. Furthermore, children under two years

frequently get middle ear infections, which could extend around the electrode going into the inner ear and even lead to dangerous meningitis. We
also had to be concerned about the effects of electrical stimulation in an
immature nervous system.

In 1987 we were successful in obtaining one of the two contracts
awarded by the US National Institutes of Health to answer these questions. The studies undertaken over the next five years were crucial for
operating on very young children. At their completion in 1992, we knew
where to fix the electrodes to avoid the effects of skull growth. We demonstrated that middle ear infections led to no greater risk in the implanted
than the normal ear. It was only then that I felt confident that we could
operate on the youngest group of children.

APPROVAL FROM THE US FOOD AND DRUG ADMINISTRATION

By 1989, results on children were coming in fast from the various centres.
The data had to be analysed to see whether they would stand up to
scrutiny by the statisticians of the FDA. Were the improvements with the
bionic ear, compared to a hearing aid, real or due simply to experience
and growing older? The study design helped to show the difference.
Richard Dowell from our clinic was seconded to the staff of Cochlear
Corporation in Denver to go through the results before the presentation
to the FDA. There were twenty volumes of data submitted, many more
than with the initial application to conduct the trial. The volumes covered
biological safety, the electronic design, the manufacturing processes,
speech and language results from each of the forty-four children, training
of surgeons, and the claims to be made for marketing. The findings were
then lodged and the staff from Cochlear waited to be summoned to a
special review panel to answer questions. Then, on 27 June 1990, the FDA
wrote to Steve Staller of Cochlear Corporation in the US announcing that
they had awarded the pre-market approval subject to certain conditions
concerning the labelling and claims. Although couched in dispassionate
language, it was the exciting news that we had all been hoping for. Ron
West, the president of Cochlear Corporation, rang to tell me. Now, for
the first time, this most important health regulatory body had formally
approved the device. No health authority from any country had sanctioned
a bionic ear for children before. The bionic ear was now being called the

first major advance in 200 years to help profoundly deaf children communicate. The previous breakthrough had been the development of Sign Language of the Deaf by l'Abbé de l'Epée at the Paris Deaf School.

Parents could now be told with authority that their deaf children could benefit from the bionic ear. It could be used in other centres throughout the country. This stamp of approval also helped its acceptance in other countries. But, as with our own experience, it would take many months before its benefits would be seen to advantage.

Publicity still sparked criticism. Even as late as October 1993, Dr Harlan Lane, an American professor of psychology, contradicted me on our results for the bionic ear in children on an Australian radio program hosted by Philip Adams. He said: 'The figures Professor Clark cited are out of the ball-park and just not like the results of scientific studies.' Nevertheless, hearing parents with deaf children were seeking help with the bionic ear, as they wanted their children to be able to communicate in the world of sound. They were very grateful and more than happy to rise to our defence, as is evident in the following letter from Mrs June Hilliar, of Berry in New South Wales.

7.6.90

Dear Professor Clark

Yesterday, in the Herald, I read what I felt was unfair, ill-informed, criticism of the cochlear implant programme, criticism tantamount to sacrilege in this household. I hope this letter reaches you, because I wanted so much to thank you for the priceless gift you made possible for our small grandson, Edward.

Edward will be three next week, and helping teach him to hear and speak has been pure joy—a miracle that seemed impossible when he lost his hearing following meningitis in May last year. Cerebral ataxia added to his woes. Though the latter gradually came good, we had finally to accept that his hearing was zilch. All members of the family, bar me, are medical, so fortunately we were aware of the implants being started in the very young. After consultations with Professor Gibson, and the requisite tests were satisfactory, Edward received his implant last September and was switched on in October. His reaction was beautiful. He was lucky enough to receive the first of the new word processors in Sydney. When the sound came on he dived down behind his father's knee. The sound went off, and he surfaced, and sat back down. The sound came on and down he went again, but this time not quite so quickly. Sat back up, looked around, then threw out his hands, palm upwards, like a Frenchman saying 'pouff', his face saying plainly: 'where did it go?' By the end of the session his smile was so wide you could tie it in a bow at the back of his head. He hasn't looked back. His map has not changed since it was first fixed, and he now comprehends about 200 words, about 100 of which are spontaneous. The vowels and diphthongs all are perfect, as are 'p', 'b', 'm', with 'w' and 'h' getting there. I can't wait to get the go ahead for the rest. My study was languages so I find his progress fascinating.

His mother, Pam, is a born teacher, and she and my son, Ian, alternate each fortnight taking him up to Sydney. They video the lesson at the Centre, then we take it from there with the homework.

Teddy loves his lessons, learning is all a big game to him, thanks largely to the great fun and commitment that his teacher, Rosalie, puts into the session. That Edward can distinguish between 'pig' and 'peg', 'house' and 'horse', 'bird' and 'bed', between 's' and 'sh', fills me with unbounded admiration for the man who conceived the operation, and the team behind him, for the technicians who made such fine distinctions possible.

Seeing Edward go off to pre-school once a week, all his old confidence restored, fitting in so well with all the other small ones, seeing Pam and Ian's joy, and their confidence in the future, I have no way to thank you adequately, but perhaps Teddy has.

In those early weeks post op. he had been aware of sound, but not yet of speech. We were sitting on the sofa having a lesson, practising 'a', when suddenly it came out loud and clear. Then, hardly daring, I said 'I'. He followed, very softly. I went on: 'e', 'o', 'u' and each time Teddy followed. I felt awed, so filled with emotion I couldn't speak. Teddy was shining, as if a light had been switched on. Then, very slowly, he leaned over and kissed me gently on the mouth. That kiss belongs to you.

Sincerely
JUNE HILLIAR

By 1994 the improved speech processing strategies first demonstrated on adults were being used for children, who were now having their operations at younger ages. This meant that they obtained better speech perception, and many could function in the hearing world without the need for signing and with minimal help from lip-reading. Word of this was filtering through to the clinics, audiologists, surgeons, educators and parents. As a result, there was an increased demand from parents for the operation.

DISCUSSING THE ETHICS OF THE BIONIC EAR IN CHILDREN

Doubts about the ethics of the procedure still needed to be laid to rest through open discussion. Some people felt that doctors were only in it for the money. Others thought that children should be allowed to wait until they reached an age when they could decide for themselves, such as eighteen. Parents, it was insisted, didn't have the right to decide for their young children.

When I organised our second International Cochlear Implant Symposium in Melbourne in 1994, I made a point of making ethics an important part of the proceedings. The debate had to be brought into the open so that both sides could air their concerns. This was to be the first major discussion of ethics at an international meeting.

As we came closer to the time for the conference, I learned there would be demonstrations against the implant. I hoped there wouldn't be the same disruption that occurred the previous year in Paris when members of the signing community in France went to an official reception in Notre Dame Cathedral and blew whistles so loudly the gathering was broken up. We took security precautions but allowed demonstrations to take place in the entrance to the Regent Hotel. We wanted to avoid involving the police.

Since the ethics session needed to be balanced and have representatives from different professional groups, I invited the Reverend Professor Davis McCaughey, theologian, ethicist and Governor of Victoria, to be the first speaker, and to present a general ethical framework. He emphasised that as the benefits of the bionic ear had been clearly demonstrated, one issue might be to decide who might receive one if there were financial or other limitations on providing an implant. Would it be on the basis of potential benefit, and how would that be decided? He assumed the importance of the family in our society and the responsibilities given to parents in deciding whether their child should have medical interventions such as an implant. This view was at odds with that of some members of the signing deaf community who had even been claiming that the management of the child would need to be governed by the wishes of the signing community. Davis also stressed that although it is the prime concern of the medical profession to promote health—in this case, the restoration of hearing—this shouldn't in any way denigrate 'the immense achievements

Demonstration by the signing deaf community against the use of the bionic ear at the International Cochlear Implant Conference, Melbourne, 1995.

and riches of those who have had to live within narrower parameters'. He also stressed the Judaic-Christian and Arabic traditions, where total health is a future hope. He said, quoting from Isaiah 35: 5–7, 'Then the eyes of the blind shall be opened and the ears of the deaf unstopped', but stressed that this doesn't mean that we shouldn't try to overcome impairments and disabilities in the present. He concluded by saying, 'It would be a thousand pities if the great advances in medical science and therapy were ever seen to be in conflict with the best interests of the deaf community. I cannot see that they are or why they should be.'

Dr Noel Cohen, a senior surgeon from New York, emphasised the complexity of the decisions on whether a child should have an implant and the help needed by the families, who may feel devastated, guilty and anxious about the future of their deaf child. He said that as physicians we have an obligation to serve our patients, and since the bionic ear has been approved by responsible government agencies, it doesn't seem fair to be accused of unethical conduct in recommending it. He, too, stressed the rights of the parents in making decisions for their children. He especially disclaimed that the bionic ear was 'a form of genocide' and pointed out that the deaf child of hearing parents is not initially a member of the deaf community until the parents made that decision. Anyway, the benefits have been established to the point where it is hard not to recommend the bionic ear for many children. Therefore, when ear surgeons and audiologists do so, it is unfair to accuse them of a mistaken sense of paternalism and arrogance, or of motives of financial gain. Surgeons don't make any unreasonable financial gain from the procedure, he said. He pointed out that although the deaf community believes that deafness isn't a disability, or even a handicap, it has been defined as a handicap and disability for funding benefits in the United States. He concluded by saying that we should all respect the achievements of the signing community in helping profoundly deaf people to communicate, and encourage open discussion through mutual respect.

Further ethical issues about implanting the bionic ear were discussed by Dr Merve Hyde from the Faculty of Education, Griffith University. He pointed out that some people advocate that deaf children should be brought up to be bilingual, with Sign Language of the Deaf as their first language and English as their second. He considered this would disadvantage those children with some residual hearing, who could benefit from being able to learn to speak English—not easily achieved if Sign Language of the Deaf is the first language. He emphasised, too, that deafness is a different type of disability from other medical conditions, as it affects language, and so it is important that we recognise the status and pride that has been achieved by signing people over a long period of time.

Finally, I invited Dr Anne Geers to make the closing points, as she had just completed the US National Institutes of Health study comparing the bionic ear with hearing aids and tactile aids in control groups of children. She was thus in the best position to speak at first hand about the benefits of the bionic ear, an important matter in any debate on ethics. She also emphasised that we simply cannot wait for a deaf child to be old enough to decide whether to have a bionic ear, as it is essential to carry out the procedure at an early age. Therefore, the responsibility for the decision must lie with the parents.

In 1996 I decided to edit a textbook entitled *Cochlear Implantation for Infants and Children* with colleagues Robert Cowan and Richard Dowell. I wrote the chapter on ethics and examined the issues on the bionic ear in the light of generally accepted ethical principles of the World Medical Assembly and those laid down on the Rights of the Child by the General

Assembly of the United Nations. In both cases, our use of the bionic ear was in line with all the recommendations. For example, Article 29:1 says, 'State Parties agree that the education of the child shall be directed to: the development of the child's personality, talents and mental and physical abilities to their fullest potential; and the development of respect for the child's parents, his or her own cultural identity, language and values.'

CHANGES IN THE CLIMATE

In 1998 I gained a deeper appreciation of the achievements of the signing deaf community over the last 200 years when I took an opportunity to visit the Paris Deaf School. I felt a sense of awe as I went around their historic library and saw some of the works about l'Abbé de l'Epée and other pioneers in the field. One of these, l'Abbé Sicard was put in jail in August 1792 for not signing an oath of allegiance to the French Revolution.

As he was about to be burned alive, a clockmaker recognized him, tried to protect him and told the crowd:

> This man is l'Abbé Sicard, one of the most useful men in the country, the teacher of deaf-mutes.
> Crowd: It doesn't matter, he is an aristocrat.
> Clockmaker: You'll have to kill me first.
> L'Abbé Sicard, very calm as usual, asks for some quiet in the crowd and says: My friends, I'm innocent. Are you going to kill me without listening?
> Crowd: You were with the other people we just killed. You are therefore as guilty as they were.
> Sicard: Listen, and then if you still want to kill me I won't complain. Let me tell you who I am and what I do, and then you will decide what to do with me. I am l'Abbé Sicard, I teach deaf-mutes. As they are more poor than rich, I am more useful to you than to the rich.
> Crowd: l'Abbé Sicard has to be saved. This man is too honest to be killed. His life is devoted to great tasks. He doesn't have time to be a conspirator.
> Hearing that, the torturers hug him with their bloody arms and protect him.
>
> (Translated from the book *L'Abbé Sicard* by Ferdinand Berthiet, 1873 and provided courtesy of Michelle Balle-Stinckwich, Paris Deaf School)

Since my visit, I have become even more aware of how useful Sign Language of the Deaf has been, and that some children, for various

Craig Miller, of the Youth Forum of the VSDC Services for Deaf Children, with the author in 1998. Craig Miller was profoundly deaf, communicated principally with sign language, and strove hard to build bridges with other approaches to deafness. He was tragically killed in a car accident in 1999. (Courtesy of the VSDC Services for Deaf Children and Mrs Miller)

reasons, will still need to acquire this skill. For example, having the implant at an early age does not preclude children from learning to sign in order to supplement their new-found auditory skills and to communicate with signing family and friends.

I was touched by the warm reception I received from members of the Youth Forum of VSDC Services for Deaf Children and the evening's chairperson, Mr Craig Miller, when I was invited to talk and answer questions in 1998 about the bionic ear. Their *joie de vivre* was also very noticeable. Dialogue like this will help resolve misunderstandings between the Signing Deaf Community and those in the Cochlear Implant field.

One of the unexpected sources of help in gaining acceptance for the bionic ear came in 1998 when the telephone company Telstra, in their publicity on the contributions they made as Telecom to the early development of the prototype bionic ear, showed the children who were recipients talking in such a natural and moving way that it demonstrated better than any argument what our implant has meant.

Our research has also demonstrated that it costs a lot less money to educate a deaf child in a mainstream school than in a special school. For

The Hon. John Howard MP, Prime Minister of Australia, with Ellen O'Connell (age five) and Shruti Gokhale (age eight), both recipients of the bionic ear, when he opened the Child Deafness Research Laboratories at the Department of Otolaryngology, The University of Melbourne on 11 February 2000.

example, in Victoria it costs about $70 000 to educate a deaf child in a mainstream school over twelve years, and about $300 000 in a special school for deaf children. As many children with a bionic ear can attend a mainstream school with or without a special unit, the cost benefits to the community are also considerable. There are longer-term gains as well, as these children will have more opportunities to get jobs and to compete in a world of sound.

New directions

Perfecting the ability of deaf children to communicate through hearing, goes on. Our two part-time Lions International research fellows, Pam Dawson and Peter Busby, have shown that children understand speech better if they perceive different pitches from low to high when electrodes are stimulated in sequence along the inner ear. In other words, the brain cells need to be connected up so that a frequency scale is achieved like that in a piano keyboard. In order to obtain this result, exposure to correct electrical stimuli is needed at an early age when the brain is still plastic.

Bryn Davies being presented to Her Majesty the Queen by the author during her official visit to The Bionic Ear Institute on the 23 March 2000. Rod Saunders is behind and to the left.

Pam and Peter's work is being extended in the Child Deafness Research Laboratories in The University of Melbourne's Ear, Nose and Throat Department situated at the Royal Victorian Eye and Ear Hospital. Additional laboratories were opened by the Prime Minister of Australia, the Hon. John Howard MP, on 11 February 2000—a very special honour for us since he was the first prime minister in office to visit this old and venerable hospital.

On 23 March 2000, Her Majesty Queen Elizabeth and His Royal Highness the Duke of Edinburgh visited The Bionic Ear Institute to learn of our work particularly with children. Because of their genuine interest in all endeavours to improve life for a great range of people, they came to us on the same day that they visited the Australian Children's Television Foundation and the Immigration Museum.

Her Majesty showed special interest in how space was found in Rod Saunders' skull for the original implant, and by contrast, how the Nucleus device was made small enough to implant in a child under one year with no need to replace it as the child grew. Queen Elizabeth herself is patron of the Great Ormond Street Hospital for Children in London, which has currently performed 120 of our cochlear implants, the Duke is closely involved with the Royal National Institute for Deaf People in the United Kingdom, and the Queen mother is the patron of the National Deaf Children's Society. These associations might have been the reason for the Queen's choice to visit us.

The occasion was a very happy one for staff and patients alike, with some patients coming hundreds of kilometres to be in the same room with the royal visitors, and it was a delight to see our gifts being presented in the natural charming way of children by Sian Neame (12 years), Ari Fisher (7 years) and Claudia Danese (4 years), all of whom have bionic ears.

At the end I was excited to be able to show the royal couple evidence gained from guinea pigs only days before of the possibility of regrowing hearing nerves through injecting nerve growth factors into deaf inner ears.

When all deaf children can have the opportunity of hearing and learning to speak, my dream will have come true. In 1970, when I was in a makeshift laboratory in the disused hospital mortuary, I couldn't have imagined that, within thirty years, 14 000 children from more than fifty countries would have benefited from this tiny artefact, our bionic ear.

Our Father in Heaven
Hallowed be Your Name

Appendix 1

The principles of the bionic ear

I have been very impressed by the emergence of the bionic ear as a practical proposition, but even more by the promise for the future that it seems to embody. It makes use of the arrangement in the cochlea for pitch recognition to bring electronic technology into direct functional relationship with the nervous system and the human consciousness. Maybe that unique relationship has no other parallel in the nervous system, and thus that direct link between electronics and physiology will find no other application to medicine. Nevertheless, I feel it may represent a new benchmark in the understanding of neural and mental function in terms of their physical components. Perhaps the work will not reach such a climax for centuries, but whatever may eventuate special credit will be made to Professor Clark and his colleagues for their pioneering and successful work.

Testimonial in 1985 from Professor Emeritus Sir Macfarlane Burnett, AK, OM, KBE, MD, PhD (Lond), FAA, FRS, Nobel Laureate (Physiology & Medicine)—the first patron of the Bionic Ear Institute

DEFINITION

The bionic ear is a device that restores useful hearing in severely-to-profoundly deaf people when the organ of hearing situated in the inner ear has not developed, or is destroyed by disease or injury. It bypasses the inner ear and provides information to the hearing centres through direct stimulation of the hearing nerve.

NORMAL HEARING

Hearing occurs when sound is transmitted down the ear canal, through the middle ear to the inner ear. The inner ear or the sense organ of hearing (organ of Corti) is

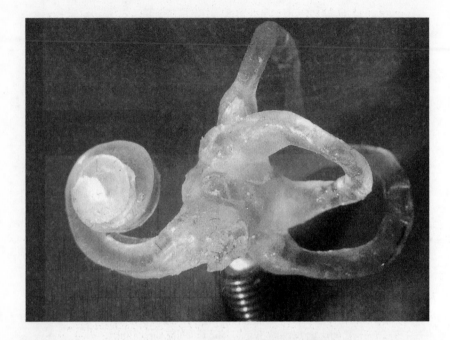

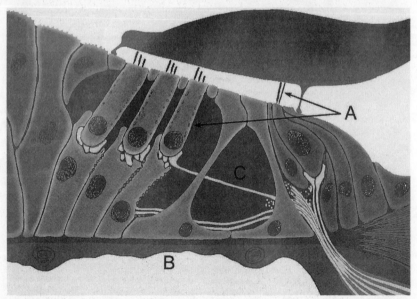

(Top) *Figure A1: Cast of the human inner ear showing the 2¾ spirals of the cochlea (the organ of hearing) at the front half.* (Bottom) *Figure A2: A diagram of the inner ear showing the sensory hair cells (A) on the vibrating membrane (B). The hairs on the cells protrude into a gelatinous membrane; when the hairs move to and fro, sound vibrations are converted into electrical currents which then excite the nerve fibres (C) in the inner ear leading to the brain.*

a very small coiled snail-like structure (Figure A1) embedded in bone. The organ of hearing rests on a membrane (basilar membrane) lying across the coil (Figure A2). This membrane vibrates selectively to different sound frequencies, so that it acts as a sound filter. High frequencies produce maximal vibrations at the beginning of the coil near an opening from the middle ear called the oval window. Low frequencies produce maximal vibrations at the other end of the coil.

The sense organ of hearing in the inner ear consists of cells with hairs that protrude into a gelatinous membrane. When these hairs move back and forth in response to sound, their vibrations are converted into electrical currents. This results from chemical and physical changes in these hair cells. These electrical currents stimulate the hearing nerves and produce patterns of excitation or stimulus codes which are transmitted to the higher brain centres where they are interpreted or perceived as sound.

The patterns of electrical responses are interpreted as pitch and loudness, as well as meaningful signals such as speech. The temporal and spatial patterns for the coding of frequency are illustrated in the picture in Chapter 4. On the left, the brain cells fire in time with the sound wave for the temporal coding of frequency or pitch. On the right as shown, the inner ear and central auditory pathways are also organised so that a frequency scale is preserved for the place coding of frequency or pitch.

Deafness

When someone has a progressive sensori-neural deafness they lose the hair cells. As a result, the hearing becomes faint and distorted and the sound has to be amplified for enough cells to respond. When most of the hair cells are absent, no amount of amplification with a hearing aid will help the person to hear speech as there is no hearing organ to excite the remaining hearing nerves leading to the brain centres. At best they will hear muffled sounds. These people are profoundly deaf and were the first who stood to benefit from the bionic ear.

Overall Concept of the Bionic Ear

My research, commenced in 1967, led to a multiple-electrode cochlear implant or bionic ear, which was developed commercially by Nucleus Limited in 1982 and refined over the following years. As illustrated in Figure A3, it consists of a directional microphone [a] that converts sound into electrical voltages that are sent to a small speech processor worn behind the ear [b] or a larger more versatile one attached to a belt [c]. The speech processor filters this waveform into frequency bands. The output of the filters is referred to a map of the patient's electric current thresholds and comfortable listening levels for the individual electrodes. A code is produced for the stimulus parameters (electrode site, and current level) to represent the speech signal at each instant in time. This code, together with power, is transmitted by radio waves via a circular aerial [d] through the intact skin to the receiver-stimulator [e] implanted in the mastoid bone.

The receiver-stimulator decodes the signal and produces a pattern of electrical currents in a bundle of electrodes [g] inserted around the first turn of the inner ear [f] to stimulate the auditory nerve fibres [h]. A pattern of hearing nerve activity in response to sound is produced, and provides a meaningful representation of speech and environmental sounds. The electrode bundle, shown in the top illustration on

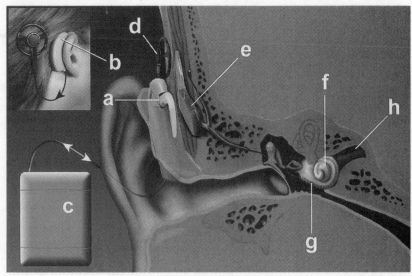

Figure A3: Diagram of the cochlear implant resulting from the research at the Department of Otolaryngology at the University of Melbourne and the Special Centre for Human Communication Research. It was developed commercially by Nucleus and then Cochlear Limited, in collaboration with the Cooperative Research Centre for Cochlear Implant Speech and Hearing Research. [a] directional microphone, [b] speech processor worn behind the ear, [c] wearable speech processor, [d] transmitting radio aerial, [e] receiver-stimulator, [f] inner ear, [g] bundle of electrodes, [h] auditory nerve fibres.

p. 114, lies close to, but not attached to, the spiral ganglion cells in the inner ear and their hearing nerve fibres.

TRAINING IN THE USE OF THE BIONIC EAR

After recovery from the bionic ear operation, the patient comes for training sessions in how to understand the sensations created by electrical simulation. The first task is to establish thresholds and maximum comfortable levels for loudness on each electrode pair. Measurements are programmed into the map of the patient's speech processor. Auditory training exercises involve listening to speech and repeating what is heard. The speech material may be sentences, words, or vowels and consonants. The exercises allow the audiologist to assess the performance of the person and at the same time provide training. The task must not be too difficult or the person will be discouraged. He or she is also counselled on how to use the device—for example, what to expect if the batteries become flat. Later, training is given in the use of the telephone. Auditory training for children will not only concentrate on improving their ability to perceive and understand speech and environmental sounds, but also their speech production, receptive and expressive language, and communication. The speech material used for the training is age appropriate. The training is integrated into the child's educational program at either a pre-school or school level. The children need to be taught by auditory/oral or auditory/verbal methods to take advantage of the new auditory information they are receiving. In certain situations the use of total communication, where signed English is combined with an auditory stimulus, will be required. Sign Language for the Deaf may also be used in certain children after individual assessment of their communication needs.

FUNDAMENTAL OBJECTIONS AND QUESTIONS

It is hard to believe that as recently as the 1960s and 1970s, the prevailing view was that successful electrical stimulation of the hearing nerve to help people understand speech would not be possible in the foreseeable future. The fundamental objections, which were reasonable, were, first, that the inner ear hair cells and their nerve connections were too complex and numerous to reproduce the temporal and spatial pattern of responses in the hearing nerve by electrical stimulation with just a small number of electrodes. Twenty thousand inner and outer hair cells and auditory nerve fibres are required for normal hearing.

The second objection was that a bionic ear would destroy the very hearing nerves in the inner ear it was hoped to stimulate. Figure A4 shows that a teflon strip with sharp edges can cut through the inner ear basilar membrane, and lead to near total loss of the inner ear nerve cells in the vicinity of the injury.

The third objection was that speech was too complex to be presented to the nervous system by electrical stimulation for speech understanding. Figure A5 shows a portion of the complex speech wave for the word 'Otolaryngology'.

The fourth objection was that there wouldn't be enough residual hearing nerves in the inner ear after they died back through deafness to transmit essential speech information. There can be an 80 per cent loss of the hearing nerve ganglion cells and their fibres after the destruction of inner ear hair cells in deafness.

The fifth objection was that children born deaf wouldn't develop appropriate nerve-to-brain cell connections, through lack of exposure to sound during the early critical phase of development, for electrical stimulation to give adequate hearing. The findings from our laboratory show that in a young bilaterally deaf animal, the number of nerve connections on brain cells is significantly reduced when compared to the norm.

Other important questions were: (1) Would the electrical stimulus currents damage the hearing nerves? (2) Were the candidate materials for the implantable electrodes and receiver-stimulator toxic to tissue? (3) Would middle ear infection spread along the electrode bundle to produce infection in the inner ear with possible life-threatening infection around the linings of the brain (meningitis)? (4) Could electrodes be inserted into the inner ear far enough so that the hearing nerves responsible for the place coding of speech frequencies could be stimulated? (5) What type of patients should be selected? (6) How should the operation be performed? (7) Would the perception of pitch on a multiple-electrode or place coding basis be possible? (8) Would the perception of pitch on a time coding basis be possible? (9) What electrical currents would produce loudness? (10) Would patients have memory for sounds and speech after prolonged deafness? (11) Could speech be processed so that patients could understand conversations? (12) Would speech and music sound natural? (13) If a speech processing scheme was achieved for English, would it be effective in other languages? (14) How important was age of implantation in helping children to learn to understand speech?

ANSWERS TO THE FUNDAMENTAL OBJECTIONS

The first fundamental objection was that the inner ear hair cells and their nerve connections were too complex and numerous to reproduce the temporal and spatial

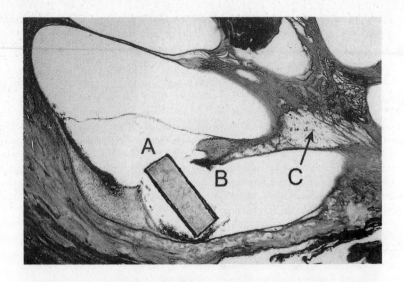

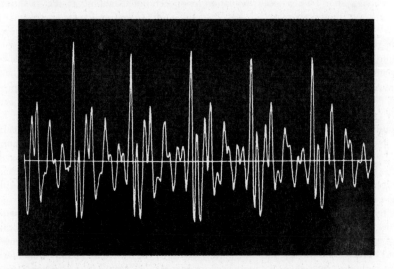

(Top) *Figure A4: Photograph of a section of the inner ear from an experimental animal showing how a strip of teflon [A] with sharp edges can tear the basilar membrane [B] and lead to near total loss of the hearing nerve cells [C].* (Bottom) *Figure A5: Part of the speech wave for the word 'Otolaryngology'.*

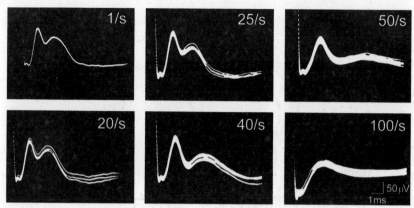

Figure A6: The voltages from groups of brain cells (brain-stem field potentials) at increasing rates of stimulation. The voltages are markedly suppressed by stimulus rates at 100 pulses/second. (Clark, PhD 1969)

pattern of responses in the hearing nerve by electrical stimulation with just a small number of electrodes. This was studied by seeing how well electrical stimulation could reproduce the coding of sound. The temporal coding of frequency was examined in the experimental animal by finding out how well groups of brain cells could respond at increasing rates of stimulation. The voltages from brain cells (brain-stem field potentials) at increasing rates of stimulation are shown in Figure A6. The electrical activity is markedly suppressed by stimulus rates at 100 pulses/second. Behavioural studies in the experimental animal showed that rates of stimulation in excess of 200 to 600 pulses/second couldn't be discriminated.

The experimental animal findings thus indicated that the reproduction of the temporal coding of frequency by electrical stimulation with a single-electrode cochlear implant could only reproduce speech frequencies from 200 to 600 cycles/second, which is much less than the 4000 cycles/second needed for speech intelligibility. Therefore, the best chance of helping deaf people to understand speech was to use multiple-electrode stimulation to provide more information.

To achieve the place coding of frequency through multiple-electrode stimulation required finding where to place the electrodes in the inner ear so that the current would pass most easily through separate groups of hearing nerve fibres connected to the different frequency regions of the brain. Our research showed that the compartment below the sense organ of hearing (scala tympani) and close to the ganglion cells at the centre of the inner ear spiral was the correct location (Figure A2). Research also demonstrated that electrical currents could be partly localised to groups of nerve fibres within the inner ear without its short-circuiting away through fluid, by pushing electrical current out one electrode and pulling it back from another (bipolar stimulation) (Figure A7).

The animal experiments referred to above demonstrated that both temporal and place frequency coding or pitch perception could only be partially reproduced by electrical stimulation. In other words, a bionic ear is like a 'bottle-neck' between the world of sound and the central hearing pathways of the brain (Figure A8).

The second fundamental objection was that if an electrode was implanted in the inner ear, which was particularly important for multiple-electrode stimulation, it would damage the very nerves it was hoped to stimulate. It was found, however, in the

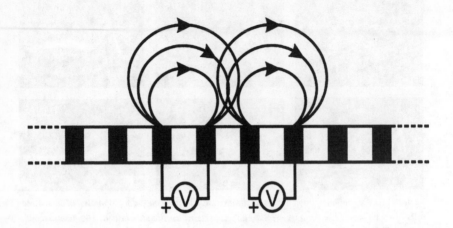

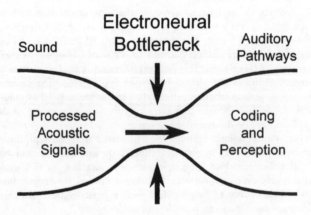

(Top) *Figure A7: Bipolar stimulation with electrical current pushed out one electrode and pulled back through another to produce the localised electrical stimulation required for the place coding of frequency.* (Bottom) *Figure A8: The bionic ear represented as a 'bottle-neck' between the world of sound and the central hearing pathways of the brain.*

experimental animal, that if no excessive force was used with its insertion, and infection wasn't introduced, the hearing nerves were preserved. The chance of injury was reduced to a minimum if the electrode bundle had the right mechanical properties. It needed to be smooth, tapered, flexible at the tip and stiffer towards the proximal end.

A high density of electrons passing through electrodes with electrical stimulation was known to damage nerve fibres. We weren't sure what the safe limits were for a bionic ear. This had to be tested, too. It was found to be safe if the current had a positive and negative phase to reduce the build up of DC current, and the charge density was below approximately 32 micro Coulombs/square centimetre/phase.

The third objection was that speech was too complex to be presented to the nervous system by electrical stimulation for speech understanding. This would have to be answered by multiple-electrode stimulation to transmit as much information as possible through the 'bottle-neck'. This required studies on patients to see how effective multiple-electrode stimulation would be, as speech perception is an especially human skill and couldn't be evaluated on the experimental animal.

Studies on patients required developing a fully implantable receiver-stimulator to receive information transmitted through the intact skin, rather than a plug and socket, which was more likely to get broken and infected.

A prototype receiver-stimulator to use on initial patients was produced by the University of Melbourne from 1974 to 1978 using hybrid technology. This meant connecting a number of silicon chips together on a silicon substrate or wafer. The wafers were placed in a watertight or hermetically-sealed container. The prototype receiver-stimulator was implanted in our first profoundly deaf adult patient on 1 August 1978 with the banded electrode array passing around the inner ear to lie near, but not in direct contact with, the nerves relaying speech frequency to the brain.

Perceptual studies were then undertaken on the first and subsequent patients to see if the findings on the temporal and place coding of frequency in the experimental animal were applicable to humans. The patient studies confirmed that rate of stimulation was not effective in transmitting frequency or pitch information over the range required for speech understanding. In Figure A9, pitch ratios are plotted against repetition rate; the figure shows that when the pitch of a stimulus is compared with a reference rate of 100 pulses/second, the pitch ratios increase linearly up to 300 pulses/second, and then plateau. Three hundred pulses/second is much less than the 4000 pulses/second needed for speech understanding.

The studies on the place coding of frequency (Figure A10) showed that with localised electrical stimulation the patients could only perceive timbre, but not true pitch. In the high-frequency areas of the inner ear, the sensation was sharp (S), and in the lower frequency side it was dull (D). They could, however, rank the timbre according to the site of stimulation. In the figure the electrodes are numbered from low to high according to their placement in the lower or higher frequency areas of the cochlea. The figure shows the sensation for the comparison electrode on the vertical axis as opposed to the standard or reference electrode on the horizontal axis. For example, when electrode 1 was compared with the higher-frequency electrodes 2–8, it was duller. In general, the sharp and dull sensations lie on either side of the diagonal, indicating that there was good but not perfect ranking of timbre.

These perceptual studies on the patients thus confirmed the findings on the experimental animal that electrical stimulation with the bionic ear was a 'bottle-neck' for information from the outside world to the central auditory pathways.

The first research to transmit information through the 'bottle-neck' was to select speech frequencies using fixed filters with similar properties to the tuning of the inner ear. When the outputs were used to stimulate the hearing nerves simultaneously, the

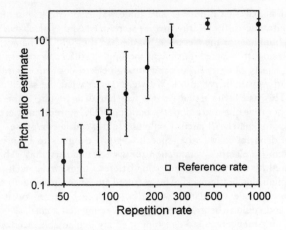

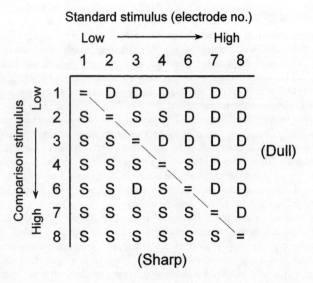

(Top) *Figure A9: The pitch ratio of the stimulus and a reference rate of 100 pulses/second on vertical scale is plotted against the stimulus rate on the horizontal scale. This shows no change in the ratios above 300 pulses/second. This indicated that rate of stimulation on a single electrode can only convey speech frequencies up to 300 cycles/second which is much less than the 4000 cycles/second for speech understanding.* (Bottom) *Figure A10: The ranking of timbre for place of stimulation in the cochlea. The electrodes are numbered from low to high according to their placement in the lower- or higher-frequency areas of the cochlea S-sharp and D-dull.*

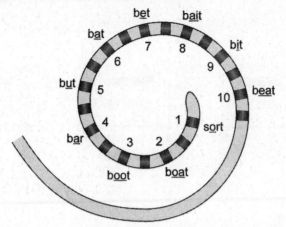

Figure A11: Different vowels were perceived according to site of stimulation along the inner ear. The vowels with the highest second formant frequency are perceived at the high-frequency end (at the base), and vice versa for the vowels with the lowest second formant (at the end).

result was poor. Simultaneous stimulation produced overlap of currents, resulting in unpredictable variations in loudness.

However, a speech processing strategy was discovered that gave the patients the ability to understand connected or running speech when presented with lip-reading or even using electrical stimulation alone. The clue to this speech processing strategy came when the first patient reported vowel sounds when each electrode was stimulated, as illustrated in Figure A11.

The vowels corresponded roughly with those perceived in hearing people when similar areas of the inner ear were excited by single formant frequencies. Formants are concentrations of frequency energy or vocal tract resonances that are important for intelligibility, especially the second formant. This is illustrated for the syllables /ba/, /da/ and /ga/ in Figure A12. These are the first and second formant frequencies, and a rising second formant transition produces a /b/, a falling formant /d/ and a steeply falling formant /g/.

As a result of this research, our inaugural speech processing strategy extracted the second formant frequency that is high in pitch using a filter. The voltages from the filter stimulated electrodes at appropriate frequency regions around the inner ear. The stimuli were perceived as timbre. The sound pressure for the formant frequency was coded as current level and perceived as loudness. The fundamental or voicing was coded as stimulus rate and perceived as pitch.

This speech processing strategy was trialled at a number of centres in the United States and Europe, and in 1985 was the first multiple-electrode cochlear implant to be approved by the US Food and Drug Administration (FDA). This inaugural speech processing strategy enabled our patients to understand running speech when combined with lip-reading, and some speech using electrical stimulation alone.

Our research then focused on which further speech elements to extract and present on a place-coding basis. It was found that picking the energy in the first (F1) as well as the second formant peak (F2), and presenting this non-simultaneously on a place-coding basis, gave improved results (Figure A13). Then it was discovered that selecting energy in the high-frequency bands in the third formant region, as well as

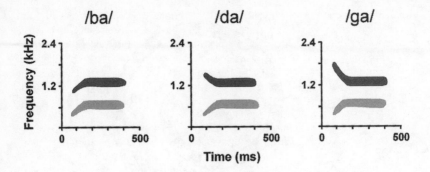

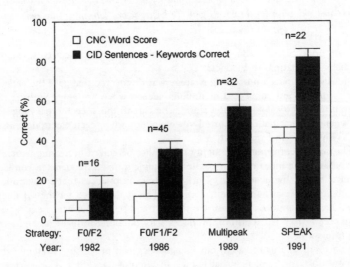

(Top) *Figure A12: The first and second formants (resonance frequencies) for the syllables /ba/, /da/ and /ga/ showing the importance of the change in the second formant frequency in syllable recognition.* (Bottom) *Figure A13: The average open-set word and sentence scores for the advances in the speech processing strategies as more speech frequencies are extracted and coded on a place of stimulation basis. F0/F2—voicing and second formant frequencies; F0/F1/F2—including first formants; Multipeak—including high frequency spectral peaks; SPEAK—spectral maxima.*

the first and second formants (Multipeak), gave a further improvement (Figure A13). The most recent strategy (SPEAK), implemented in the Nucleus 24 system, selects the six to eight frequency bands with the greatest energy from a 16–20 band pass filter bank, and presents the information as a place code. As the strategy selects the six to eight maximal outputs from the band pass filters, the sites of stimulation within the cochlea may lie close together leading to an overlap in the electrical current with unpredictable variations in loudness. These have been minimised by using a constant rate of stimulation on all electrodes. In this case, rate of stimulation is not used to convey voicing, but voicing is conveyed through the amplitude variations in the signal.

The present scores indicate that the average person can now communicate effectively over the telephone. Furthermore, they are now better than the average scores obtained by severely-to-profoundly deaf persons with some residual hearing using a hearing aid.

The fourth objection was that there wouldn't be enough residual hearing nerves in the inner ear after they died back through deafness for understanding speech. This was partly resolved when we found good results in a number of people. However, the residual hearing nerve population could have been responsible for the significant variability in the scores. The relation between the hearing nerve population and speech perception was studied by ranking speech perception scores versus the cause of deafness, and the hearing nerve population versus cause of deafness. The rankings for both speech perception and hearing nerve population versus cause of deafness were different, suggesting that speech perception is not strongly related to the population of nerves or ganglion cells. Therefore, dieback after deafness isn't a significant factor in performance with present cochlear implant systems.

The final major objection was that electrical stimulation would not be a substitute for sound in developing the nerve connections for hearing in a child's brain while it is still in the critical stage of being plastic or malleable. It was therefore essential to compare in implant subjects the speech perception of those children who had hearing before going deaf with that of those who had no previous exposure to sound (i.e. those born deaf). Their best perception skills ranged from mere detection of sound to recognition of words in sentences from an open set. The recognition of closed and open sets of words by children born without hearing (pre-linguistically deaf) and deaf after hearing (post-linguistically deaf) improved dramatically after operation. Although open-set recognition was better for the post-linguistic subjects, the performance for the children born deaf was sufficiently good to feel confident that prior exposure to sound wasn't necessary for good speech perception.

Our multiple-electrode cochlear implant was approved as safe and effective for deaf children from two years of age and above, by the US FDA in 1990. It was the first bionic ear to be approved by any world health regulatory body. It has been said that it was the first major advance in helping deaf children (those unable to get adequate assistance with a hearing aid) since Sign Language of the Deaf was developed 200 years ago.

Although the results showed that children born deaf could develop the right nerve-to-brain cell connections for speech understanding with a bionic ear, we still weren't clear how young they should be to get the best results. For this reason the sentence scores for a group of children at our clinic at the Royal Victorian Eye and Ear Hospital were plotted against age at implantation. There was considerable variability in responses, but on average performance improved the younger the age at operation (Figure A14). The responses also indicated they might be better if the operation was carried out under the age of two years.

There were special safety issues to be considered when implanting children under

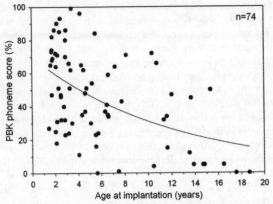

Figure A14: The speech perception scores versus age at implantation in a group of 74 congenitally deaf children at the Royal Victorian Eye and Ear Hospital Cochlear Implant Clinic.

two: (1) the effects of head growth; (2) middle ear infection, which is especially common at this age; and (3) electrical stimulation on a maturing nervous system. This research was undertaken through a five-year contract to the US National Institutes of Health and showed no cause for concern when operating on this group of children.

The research at the University of Melbourne and the Bionic Ear Institute has been germinal to the development of the multiple-electrode bionic ear produced by Nucleus and then Cochlear Limited, and helped them dominate the world market in the 1980s and into the 1990s.

Appendix 2

Testimonials and supplementary statements

TESTIMONIALS FROM RECIPIENTS

❖ Sue Zachariah, Melbourne, Australia, 1985

> To dear Professor Clark, surgeons, all your excellent staff, who have 'brought me back into the living world' I cannot thank you all enough for your patience and guidance that you all have given to me. I do hope you manage to have a break and a very Happy Christmas and may it bring ever more wonderful things. The people lucky enough to have had the implant should indeed be very, very ever grateful.
>
> Thank you to you all and a very happy Christmas.
>
> Kindest regards,
> SUE ZACHARIAH

❖ The story Anne Schmidt, Wylie, Texas, United States, wrote about her Mother, Muriel Bartholomew

> I can't help feeling that I'm experiencing a modern day miracle every time I talk to my mom on the phone. That's where I see the effects of her cochlear implant the most. Living some sixty miles away from my parents the telephone is an important communication link. Although mom is highly critical of herself; she notices the trivial mistakes more often than the vast amount of information she gets right, I am in total awe during every conversation. Sometimes I can't even respond readily. In my mind I'm thinking, 'I can't believe I'm actually talking to my mom over the phone!'
>
> The last time I talked to mom over the telephone, before the implant was when I was in the seventh grade. I called home from school and she couldn't recognize my voice. It was rather traumatic for both of us. Mostly, I felt badly for her knowing she would spend the rest of the afternoon wondering who had called and kicking herself for not knowing.
>
> Ever since I was very young I'd asked God to restore my mother's hearing. I would have settled for an average miracle. Her just waking up one day hearing perfectly well would have been acceptable. Instead, after wearing a hearing aid for nearly her whole life, she woke up one day not

able to hear anything. I was seventeen then and unable to cope with something that was not a black/white issue. I just hoped God had a better plan in mind.

And through twelve long years of silence, I guess He did. I've said for some time that if one is going to have significant trouble hearing with their ears, this is the time to be alive. But everyone who experiences this 'disability' knows how difficult it can be. I guess the telephone remains tops in my mind.

When I moved away to college we had to rely on other family members to translate our conversations. I would tell Dad or whoever else answered the phone what I wanted to tell Mom. Invariably, they would use their own interpretation of what I was saying. Meanwhile, I'd be on my end of the line saying 'No, no that's not what I meant!' Later, we located a TTY. That made all the difference in the world, except that the written word cannot express emotion like a voice can. And we always had so much to talk about our phone conversations were rather exhaustive.

When the idea of the cochlear implant came up, I was all for it. Mom was a little hesitant. After all, it was her head they would be cutting into. I didn't understand the technology of the thing. If she could simply hear some sound to fill the empty spaces in her day, say music on the radio during her drive to and from work, I felt it would be more than worthwhile. I truly never expected her to be able to talk to my children without looking at them, watch and understand the TV without captions, or to talk to me on the telephone!

My mom has come a long way since she heard her first word almost three years ago. I now have a better understanding of how the cochlear implant works, especially since two of my children have auditory processing problems. I know that it takes work to learn how to 'hear' with the implant. It isn't simply a matter of turning it on.

I can't put into words what my mom's ability to hear means to me. It has been pure joy to watch her notice new sounds: a newborn's cry, water dripping, computer noises. She made great strides even while dealing with total deafness, so hearing doesn't make her a better person. But I know it makes her life a whole lot more pleasant. And the day I called my mom at work and was able to tell her personally about the arrival of her ninth grand child will remain a most thrilling memory for me. As was the time she called me from out of town, some 1100 miles away, because she just needed to HEAR my voice. I think that God has finally answered my prayer!

❖ Jack Day, Washington, United States, 1990

Dear Dr Clark

I am writing this letter to personally thank you for your development of the Cochlear Implant.

It has truly been a blessing in my life.

I lost my hearing due to Juvenile Rheumatoid Arthritis (JRA) several years ago. My JRA has affected my entire body with crippling effects in my hands and limbs. I have had both hip and knee replacements and numerous other surgeries. I have lost the sight of one eye and have had a valve replaced in my heart. I have not been able to work and have had to curtail to some extent my travelling (which I dearly love). None of this has bothered me as much or so devastated me as did my hearing loss.

I completely withdrew from everything and felt totally isolated, and left out of everything. If not for the love, care and comfort of my wife and family I would have been truly lost.

Your implant and the work of Dr Skinner and the Washington University team has given me back my life. I never believed I would be able to hear anything again, but to hear not only sounds and voices again and to carry on a normal conversation with my wife is truly a miracle.

The voices I hear are not mechanical-like sounds but truly human voices as I once remember them. I do hear and understand people once again.

I wish that I could personally thank you for your work but Marge, who has been so wonderful to me over the years has kindly offered to hand deliver this to you.

I am most appreciative of your work and thank you from the bottom of my heart.

May God Bless You.

Sincerely
JACK DAY

❖ Patient, United States, 1990

For many years, church attendance has been very difficult for me. Even with the WSP, I found myself sitting close to the front so I could 'see what the pastor was saying.' Now I can easily sit halfway back in a sanctuary that seats more than 2000 people and hear the entire service.

As a child and youth, before completely losing my hearing, I was an active musician. One of life's greatest losses for me was not being able to listen to the world's great music. I was told up front that the WSP was not designed to give me the enjoyment of music I so badly wanted. Yet, with practice, I was able to recognize and enjoy various instruments within the orchestra, as well as solo music. Once more, I discovered that God had more in mind for me than I had anticipated. With the MSP, music has once again become an integral part of my life. I haven't attempted to pick up the drum sticks again, but the thrill and excitement of classical and church music is mine once more to enjoy. My church, Calvary Church of Grand Rapids, Michigan, presents a musical outreach each Christmas in which the combined efforts of a 200 voice choir and 65-piece orchestra tell in music and song the beautiful Christmas story. For the first time in 25 years, I was able to hear and understand this beautiful presentation.

❖ Jennine Brand, daughter of Peter Stewart, Bendigo, Australia, 1992

My father, Peter Stewart of Bendigo, was the recipient of an implant in July of 1985. I was very sceptical. Here I was, a twenty-four-year-old mother of two, who had grown up with a father who had never heard me speak. It was hard for me to adjust to the fact that he could now hear.

I didn't get to see my father as often as I would have liked because of the geographical difference, but I couldn't have been happier to notice the improvement in his hearing each and every time I saw him.

In July of 1989, my father became the first person in the world to receive a second cochlear implant (one in each ear). This second operation convinced me that my father could hear and was not just relying on lip-reading.

My greatest thrill was hearing my father answer a question he had heard my six-year-old son ask. I am very proud of my father.

❖ Claire White, Sydney, Australia, 1992

Four years after hearing her husband utter the words 'I do' at her wedding, Sydney woman Claire White could hear nothing. The deafness was a devastating blow to a woman who already suffered from severe cerebral palsy; it prevented her from participating in sign language.

'Claire regarded her hearing loss as her greatest social handicap. Everyone could see there was something wrong with her (physically) but the deafness was invisible,' said her husband. 'Now,' he confided, 'she can hear the rude remarks I make behind her back.'

❖ Andrew McHugh, Sydney, Australia, 1992

Andrew became deaf at 2½ years from meningitis, he grew up communicating with his family through sign language. At 9½ he was one of the first signing deaf children to have a cochlear implant, which his mother said he really wanted. 'Andrew always used to ignore the phone but the other day he picked it up and answered,' his mother said.

'He has gone from a school of 44 children to a school of 500,' his mother said.

'He has signed for 7 years and signing is his main natural language. He is like a pupil with school boy French who has had to go and live in Paris.' Andrew said, 'It is a little bit hard . . . But I like it.'

(Courtesy *The Manly Daily* and Tricia Dearden)

❖ Alice Brennan, Melbourne, Australia, 1999

My name is Alice Brennan and I just want to talk about what it was like without my Cochlear implant and what it was like when I got it. Before I had my Cochlear implant I missed out a lot of what people said. When my friends would say something I would say 'I beg your pardon', they would then say 'don't worry'. So I felt left out.

I often interrupted people when they were speaking to me because I didn't notice that they were talking. Sometimes that made me feel embarrassed especially with my teachers. Before my Cochlear implant it wasn't as much fun listening to my CD player, even though I could hear some music I couldn't understand the words.

When my Mum was calling me I wouldn't hear her and my sister or brother would have to tell me that my mum wanted me. I remember when I was on holidays in Queensland when I met a new friend, of course myself or my sister would tell them that I was hearing impaired and that they would have to face me for me to understand. Even with my hearing aids in I noticed after a while that some new friends found it easier to talk to my sister than to me. Sometimes this made me feel quite sad.

After I had done the tests and my mum and dad told me that I was going to get a cochlear implant at first I wasn't sure that I really wanted it. Even though I knew it would help me I suppose I was a bit scared of the operation and the things that could go wrong even though they told me that there was only a very little chance of anything bad happening. However when I talked about it with another girl called Katie who had just had the operation I felt a lot better. On the day before the operation I was a bit nervous but still really looking forward to what was going to happen.

When I woke up I was very very tired but happy that the operation was over. I was really looking forward to the day they would switch it on. When that day came my mum and dad were with me when Katie from the Cochlear clinic turned it on. The first voices I heard were strange and even though I knew it was mum and Katie it sounded like a big strong man talking under water. I thought at first that this would be only for a little while and then the sound would go back to normal. Bit by bit, day by day sounds got better and I really got excited when I started to hear new sounds that I had never heard before. Birds singing, words of the music on my CD player, the sound of curtains, the printer on the computer, waves at the beach, brushing my teeth, but most of all I could say the end of my words. I also heard people breaking wind!! It became so much easier now to talk to new friends even on the telephone and it was more enjoyable to meet new people.

I'm so happy to have been able to get a Cochlear implant, it has made my life so much better. Thanks to you Professor Clark for inventing such a wonderful thing and all the people who did my operation. Thanks also to Katie and all the people at the Eye and Ear Hospital for making it all come true.

❖ Rose Smith, Melbourne, Australia, 1999

Johnny Smith got the shock of his life when he returned from several months at sea with the merchant navy and said hello to his wife, Rose. She answered him. Deaf since the age of 11, Rose had a Cochlear implant fitted at the age of 60 while her husband was at sea in 1985. 'We had been married for 40 years and from my wife's side there had been nothing but silence', he said. Now aged 74, she said the operation was like a breath of fresh air. 'I still remember going to my niece's house and hearing her baby cry for the first time', Mrs Smith said. As well as enjoying activities such as the opera, Mrs Smith said it was the little things that made a difference. 'I can hear the birds and the sounds of the waves at the beach, just little things like that. It's just wonderful.'

(Courtesy The Herald & Weekly Times)

❖ Marlene Marriott, Melbourne, Australia, 2000

Dear Prof Clark,

As an implantee of four years, I thought it was time that I personally did something to say thank you for the wonderful work you have done and are still doing for the hearing impaired.

It's certainly an experience to be able to hear again.

I travel down from Shady Creek to participate in research at the Bionic Institute and the Royal Victorian Eye & Ear Hospital mainly on a fortnightly basis. The people I work with are very dedicated to their work. It's a great pleasure to be able to do something that will help other people who are deaf or partially so.

Living near bush and being on a dairy farm, hearing birds, cows, geese again is certainly a wonderful experience that is very hard to explain. I just love being out at the clothes line testing oneself on the sounds of different birds. I really love listening to the bell birds.

I have never acknowledged thanks to you in writing before, so I thought it was time to do so.

Please accept this gift in appreciation of the wonderful work that you have done for the hearing impaired, so we are all able to hear the birds.

I certainly enjoyed painting the picture.

Sincerely,
MARLENE MARRIOTT

SUPPLEMENTARY STATEMENTS

❖ Excerpt from Graeme Clark's PhD thesis, University of Sydney, 1969

If the answers to these questions indicate that stimulation of the auditory nerve fibres near their termination in the cochlea is important, then it will be necessary to know more about the internal resistances and lines of current flow within the cochlea, and whether the electrical responses normally recorded are a reflection of the transduction of sound into nerve discharges, or directly responsible for stimulating the nerve endings.

The final criterion of success will be whether the patient can hear, and understand speech. If pure tone reproduction is not perfect, meaningful speech may still be perceived if speech can be analyzed into its important components, and these used for electrical stimulation. More work is still needed to decide which signals are of greatest importance for speech.

❖ Excerpt from the Submission by Graeme Clark for establishing the Inaugural Chair in Otolaryngology at the University of Melbourne, 1969

Although I have had experience with all types of E.N.T. surgery and also with related specialities such as neurosurgery, I consider it is important to concentrate on an aspect of surgery that needs further development and would benefit from the resources of a university department. Such an aspect is the surgical treatment of perceptive deafness in which most advances in otological surgery in the next 10–20 years are likely to be made . . . The establishment of an Otoneurological Clinic at the Royal Victorian Eye and Ear Hospital could provide an important service to the community. One of its main aims would be the restoration of hearing and speech in children who have nerve deafness which is so severe that conventional hearing aids are ineffective. The methods now being used to help these children are still being developed, and as they are based on neurophysiological principles, the support of an auditory neurophysiological laboratory would be essential to the clinic.

❖ Welcome by Colleagues to the Chair of Otolaryngology at the University of Melbourne, 1970

On 13 March 1970 a welcoming dinner was held at the Windsor Hotel at which The Hon. Peter and Kitty Howson, Sir Sydney and Lady Sunderland, and Mrs George Swinburne were present. Dr George Gray gave the welcoming speech, an excerpt from which follows:

Thus far I have spoken of struggle and effort, but we are also celebrating success—success signified tonight by the presence of Graeme Clark, the Foundation Professor of Otolaryngology at the University of Melbourne and the only professor of otolaryngology in Australia.

He comes equipped with a remarkable history of rapid achievement. He graduated with honours in 1958 MB, BS, Sydney, FRCS (Edin) 1962, FRCS (Eng) 1963, FRACS 1966, MS (Sydney) 1969, PhD (Sydney) 1969. Now Professor of Otolaryngology, we were privileged to hear him contribute to the scientific program of the recent meeting of the Otolaryngological Society of Australia. We are all acquainted with his very many publications in the last few years. We can then have every expectation he will bring honour and achievement to his departments, the university and the speciality. It is not unusual at this point to recount an episode or two inconsistent with the image of the academician. As I glance at various friends among you, a variety of anecdotes varying from bawdy to much worse spring readily to mind. So I proceeded to dig and dig and dig and I couldn't believe it. Those of you in the audience I was referring to previously had been amateurs. Graeme's discretion had been phenomenal. I couldn't uncover a damn thing. He had covered his tracks too well.

Graeme, you have the goodwill of all us—you may be sure you have only to ask, to receive any assistance we can give you. As professor, we welcome you amongst us in this Society. I should now like to invite Professor Sunderland and Mr Peter Howson to join with the Society in extending a welcome to Graeme Clark.

❖ Preface to John Nathar's Bachelor of Medical Science thesis, completed 1971

As is usual with any form of investigation, there were many people instrumental in making this study possible. Foremost to be mentioned in this note of gratitude would be my supervisor, Professor G.M. Clark. He was always keenly and actively involved in the experiments, offering inspiration, invaluable advice and many constructive criticisms. He instilled the spirit, 'there is always a solution, if one searches hard enough, even until midnight or the next morning'. And true enough, there were many a night when the experiments were still in progress!

It (this research) reports the first ever attempt at using a behavioural method in an experimental animal to arrive at a difference limen threshold of frequencies of electrical stimulation and to interpret these findings in terms of the roles of the place and the rate theory. It hopes to highlight also the potential usefulness of using the laboratory animals in a combined neurophysiological-behavioral method of solving many of the basic problems in this area of research. Ultimately, it is hoped that in the not so distant future the malady of sensorineural deafness would not be a frustrating and hopeless one as it is at the moment, and this research would in some ways contribute to this achievement.

❖ Excerpt from summary of Harry Minas's Bachelor of Medical Science thesis, completed 1972

The method of fixation of the electrode socket to the skull of the animal was seriously deficient, and constituted one of the two major problems encountered in the experiment. An alternative method of fixation in future, similar experimentation is considered essential. Post-operative infection constituted a serious problem in one, but was adequately controlled in all the others.

❖ Letter from the parents and teachers of the Glendonald School for Deaf Children congratulating Channel 0 for the successful mini-telethon to support the development of a bionic ear

Dear Sir

At the request of the members of the School Committee of the above school, I am writing on their behalf to express our recognition of the Mini Telethon recently programmed on Channel 0, to aid the Nerve Deafness Fund.

Our committee is comprised of parents and teachers of deaf children and other members of the community interested in the education and welfare of deaf children and adults. Your efforts to support the Nerve Deafness Fund aroused considerable excitement and comment from members of the Committee. They fully appreciate the value of your support for the research work into the surgical treatment of perceptive deafness and of the implications this may have for deaf people in the future.

Yours sincerely
D. JONES
Chairman

❖ Letter from 3M Australia expressing interest in the development of the bionic ear

Dear Professor Clark,

I read with great interest the article in the Sydney press, a copy of which is attached, on the 'bionic ear', that you and your team have developed. You and your team must be very proud of this invention and the potential contributions it will make to medicine.

As a manufacturer and marketer in the health care industry, we would be interested to discuss with you the feasibility of manufacturing and marketing this new device in Australia. I will be glad to come to Melbourne to discuss this matter with you.

I look forward to hearing from you.

Yours sincerely,
ALFRED SHUM, B.SC., M.SC.,
Professional Services Manager,
Health Care Products & Services Group

❖ Letter to the Prime Minister, Malcolm Fraser, 20 July 1978, in support of funds

Dear Mr. Fraser,

During the last eight years the University of Melbourne has developed an artificial hearing device that can be surgically implanted into patients who are profoundly or completely deaf. This has amounted to something in the order of sixty man years work.

Recently the European Economic Community decided to fund a joint project at major centres in Western European countries with a view to a completion of the project in early 1980 and commercial development. The news item covering the matter is enclosed for your consideration; as it is copyright it should not be for general circulation. The National Institute of Health in America has also recently decided to commit substantial funds for a similar development.

The University of Melbourne project is at the moment ahead of developments in Europe & North America and is looking for avenues of commercial development. We have also applied to the Department of Productivity in the hope of obtaining appropriate governmental assistance to enable this Australian development to capture a significant proportion of the markets before the European & North American developments.

I would be very grateful if the Government could develop the project which I believe to be in the national interest for a number of sound reasons.

Yours sincerely,
GRAEME M. CLARK
Professor of Otolaryngology

❖ Reply from the Prime Minister, 28 August 1978

Dear Professor Clark,

Thank you for your letter of 20 July concerning the artificial hearing device developed by the University of Melbourne for surgical implantation into patients who are profoundly or completely deaf.

Your letter highlights the need to capitalise on Australia's current lead in this field, particularly in the light of planned developments in Europe and North America. In this respect, you will notice that the 1978/79 Budget provides for enhanced Government support for industrial research and development including the provision of support for the undertaking of 'public interest' research projects.

I am aware that the Minister for Productivity is giving careful consideration to providing appropriate assistance for the commercial development of this Australian innovation as a public interest project and I understand that a decision on your application is anticipated in the near future.

Finally, I would like to express my appreciation at your own research contribution to this potentially important development and also for your continuing effort towards transferring the results of this research to Australian industry.

Yours sincerely,
MALCOLM FRASER

Appendix 3

People associated with the development of the bionic ear, tickle talker and automatic brainwave audiometer

STAFF AND STUDENTS OF THE DEPARTMENT OF OTOLARYNGOLOGY, THE
UNIVERSITY OF MELBOURNE AND THE BIONIC EAR INSTITUTE

TT (Tickle Talker), BWA (Brainwave Audiometer)

Joseph Alcantara	1986–93
Caitrin-Jane Anderson	1988–90
David Au	1993–95
Quentin Bailey	1976–90
Dimitris Bairaktaris	1994–96
Elizabeth Barker	1993–
Jagir Baxi	1995–96
Rob Berkowitz	1984
Kim Berner	1971–72
Ray Black	1974–83
Peter Blamey	1979–
David Bloom	1980–86
Warwick Brennan	1985
Rob Briggs	1994–
Audrey Brock	1982–88
Gordon Brown	1988–94
Mel Brown	1992–99
Ian Bruce	1995–99
Christine Bunn	1981–82
Tony Burkitt	1997–
Martin Burton	1987, 1991
Peter Busby	1979–
H. Campbell	1981–82
Trevor Carter	1992–94
John Chow	1990–91

David Clarke	1981–82
Maria Clarke	1991–
Laurie Cohen	1982–
Barbara Cone-Wesson (BWA)	1995–
Greg Cook	1979–86
Liz Cossen	1998–
Vince Cousins	1982
Robert Cowan (TT)	1985–92
James Cox	1984
Noel Cranswick	1986
June Creighton	1973–76
Grant Da Costa	1981–84
Markus Dahm	1987–91, 1998–
Amy Dalgleish	1998
Sue Davine	1994–
Pam Dawson	1986–
John Delahunty	1971–75, 1977–83
Michael Denison	1985–89
Shani Dettman	1986–
David Dewhurst	1973–86
Martin Donnelly	1993–94
Gary Dooley	1988–94
Richard Dowell	1980–
Yvonne Duan	1997–
Alan Duffett	1973–75
Kerry Fairbank	1980–81
Alan Freeman	1980–83
Mark Flynn	1995–99
Ian Forster	1974–79
Burkhard Franz	1984–90
Karyn Galvin (TT)	1986–
Elvira Gerin	1991–92
Lisa Gillespie	1998–
Margaret Gilmour	1982–89
Michael Gordon	1992–95
Jacky Gray	1992–98
David Grayden	1997–
John Gwyther	1975–78
Rick Hallworth	1974–77
Chris Hammond	1999–2000
Natalie Hardie	1995–
Mark Harrison	1992–
Noelle Harron	1989–95
Alison Hennessy	1989–
Belinda Henry	1995–99
Noelene Hitchon	1997–
Helen Hodgens	1982–
Rod Hollow	1989–
Kate Hoogedure	1974–
Christie Huang	1996–
John Huigen	1987–

Leeanne Hurlston	1981–82
Laurence Irlicht	1994–97
Chris James	1995–
David Johnathon	1989
Peter Jones	1989–94
Alison King	1993–94
Howard Kranz	1971–76
Wai Kong Lai	1986–90
Rod Laird	1979–
Merran Larratt	1994–96
Katie Latus	1997–
David Lawrence	1998–
Alex Lia	1982
Brian Lithgow	1981–88
Andy Lim	1986–90
Neil Linahan	1996–99
Brian Little	1975–76
Xuguang Liu	1994–2000
Phillip Lukies	1982–86
Susan Luscombe	1982–83
Ken McAnally	1989–93
Hugh McDermott	1989–
Colette McKay	1988–
Gary McLeod (TT)	1979–80
Judith McNaughton	1986–94
Don McMahon	1971–80
Greg McPhee	1994–97
Coz Maffi	1986–94
Joan Maher	1975–82
Mike Marsh	1991–93
Angela Marshall	1977–79
Lois Martin	1979–86, 1999
Russell Martin	1990–92
Cameron Martland	1994
Phillip Marzella	1996–
Junichi Matsushima	1989–90
Jacqui Mellor	1996–
J. Bruce Millar	1974–
Rodney Millard	1985–
Harry Minas	1972
James Moxham	1992
Gaye Musgrave	1985–86
John Nathar	1971
G. Neill	1981–82
Terry Neinhuys	1974–78
Frank Nielsen	1986–
Jane Ng	1978–83
Daofeng Ni	1989–90
Margaret Noonan	1990–
Pauline Nott	1984
Michael Oerlemans	1993–97

Steve O'Leary	1982–89, 1999–
Bernard O'Loughlan	1976–79
Tony Paolini	1994–
Elvira Parisi	1992–94
Joanna Parker	1996–
Jim Patrick	1975–79
Cecil Pengilley	1972–77
Chris Phyland (TT)	1986–88
Simon Purser	1989
Brian Pyman	1975–
Gary Rance	1990–
Vanessa Raulings	1999–
Louise Richardson	1993–95
Field Rickards (BWA)	1973–93
Jonathan Ridler	1981–84
Helen Ried	1995–
Sue Roberts	1985–97
Jones Rhys	1974–77
Sue Rubenstein	1970–72
Cynthia Russell	1970–73
Alexander Sapozhnikov	1989
Julia Sarant	1986–
Elaine Saunders	1997–
David Scrimgeour	1971
Lee Seldon	1988–99
Peter Seligman	1979–80
Rob Shepherd	1975–76, 1980–
Simon Shute	1989
Marisa Skok	1993–96
Carole Smith	1988–90, 1995–96
Kaye Smith	1997–
Paul Sorenson	1986–90
Thomas Stainsby	1997–
Annette Steel	1981
Tania Thomas	1998–
Ivan Thrift	1993–97
Joe Tong	1971–92
Michael Tykocinski	1993–
Enid Utton	1980–89
Andrew Vandali	1989–
Richard Van Hoesel	1988–
John Vorrath	1971
Susan Walmsley	1994–95
Rodney Walkerden	1970–80
Chris Walters	1980–82
Rob Webb	1981–
Barbara Weight	1975–97
Lesley Whitford (TT)	1987–89
Aileen Williams	1973–76
Ross Wills	1986–92
Julia Wunderlich (BWA)	1997–

Jin Xu	1987–
Shi-Ang Xu	1984–94
Andy Zhang	1996–

COMMONWEALTH PUBLIC INTEREST GRANT COCHLEAR PTY LIMITED

PERSONNEL

Peter Crosby	1979–85
Mike Hirshorn	1979–85
Janesh Kusma	1980–85
Geoff Lavery	1981–82
David Money	1979–85
Jim Patrick	1980–85
Peter Seligman	1980–85

CO-OPERATIVE RESEARCH CENTRE FOR COCHLEAR IMPLANT, SPEECH & HEARING RESEARCH—COCHLEAR PTY LIMITED SECONDED AND FUNDED

PERSONNEL

Peter Baxter	1992–93
Hector Biondi	1992–93
Chris Daly	1992–94
Leigh Davey	1992–93
Ivan Dujmovik	1992–94
Neville Inglis	1993–96
Laini Kalnins	1998–99
Craig Laing	1992–94
Bruce Macaulay	1992–94
Andrew Mortlock	1992–94
John Parker	1998–99
Jim Patrick	1992–99
Kerry Plant	1994–99
Gary Ross	1992–94
Peter Seligman	1992–99
Stephanie Shaw	1993–99
Bruce Tabor	1997–98
Chula Thenuwara	1992–93
Claudiu Treaba	1994–99
Lesley Whitford	1989–99

Appendix 4

Contributors to The Bionic Ear Institute and The University of Melbourne

* Original members of the Board (formerly the Executive Committee) of the Bionic Ear Institute

PATRONS

*Professor Emeritus Sir Macfarlane Burnett, AK, OM, KBE, MD, PhD (Lond), FAA, FRS Nobel Laureate (Physiology & Medicine)   1984–86
His Excellency Dr Davis McCaughey, MA, DD, Hon LLD, FACE, Governor of Victoria   1986–92
His Excellency the Honourable Richard E. McGarvie, Governor of Victoria 1992–97
His Excellency the Honourable Sir James Augustine Gobbo, AC Kt cr, BA (Hons) (Melb), BA, MA (Oxon), Hon LLD (Monash), DUniv (Catholic), Hon FAIV, Governor of Victoria   1997–

BOARD OF DIRECTORS (FORMERLY EXECUTIVE COMMITTEE)

Presidents/Chairmen
*Dr James McBride White, RFD, ED   1984–92
Mr David J. Brydon   1992
Mr John A.C. Calvert-Jones   1992–98
Mr Michael Robinson   1998–

Vice-Presidents/Vice-Chairmen
*Mr James W.B. King   1984–91
Mr David J. Brydon   1991–92
Mr Bruce Teele   1992–98
Mr Jack Smorgon AM   1998–

Treasurers
*Mr James Beveridge   1984–89
Mr Ian T. Perkins   1989–

Executive
*Professor Graeme M. Clark, AO   1984–
*Dr James McBride White, RFD, ED   1984–92
*Mr James W.B. King   1986–91
*Mr James Beveridge   1984–92
*Mrs Joy Kemp   1984–86
*Mr Jack Riley   1984–86
Mr Graham Carrick   1986–88
Mrs Aline Darke, OAM   1986–93
Sir Cecil Looker   1986–88
Mr J. Gordon M. Moffatt, J.P.   1986–90
Mrs Cate Rozario   1986–88
Professor Field W. Rickards   1987–
Mr Bruce B. Teele   1988–92
Mr David J. Brydon   1988–91
Mr John A.C. Calvert-Jones   1988–92
Mr David Elsum, AM   1988–94
Sir David Zeidler, AC, CBE   1988–93
Mr James Beveridge   1989–92
Mr Roy Ricker   1993–98
Mr Michael Robinson   1993–98
Mrs Jennifer M.L. Prescott   1993–
Ms Jill E. Keyte   1994–97
Mr Jack Smorgon, AM   1996–
Professor Iven Mareels   1998–
Mr John Bryson   1998–
Ms Kathleen Jordan   1998–
Mr Gerald Moriarty   1999–

Research director and chief executive officer
Professor Graeme M. Clark, AO, FAA, FTSE, MBBS, (Syd), MS (Syd) Hon., MD
(Hann), Hon. MD (Syd), PhD (Syd), FRCS (Edin & Lond), FRACS   1984–

Executive manager
Mr John Huigen BSc, MSc, Dip Aud   1996–

Company secretaries and finance managers
Dr Gordon G. Brown, BMetE, MSc, PhD, Hon, FIMMA, FAusIMM,
CEng(UK)   1988–92
Mr Ivan B. Thrift, CPA   1992–97
Ms D. Kaye Smith, FCA, MAICD   1997–

Solicitors
McCracken & McCracken   1986–

Auditors
Kimberley Smith, Saward & Co   1986–
Saward, Dawson, Wright

MAJOR RESEARCH FUNDING AND DONORS

Government and industry
Australian Research Council—Human Communications Research Centre
National Health and Medical Research Council Program and Projects Grants
Commonwealth Government—Co-operative Research Centre for Cochlear Implant,
Speech and Hearing Research
Commonwealth Government—Co-operative Research Centre for Cochlear Implant
and Hearing Aid Innovation
Commonwealth Government—Public Interest Grant
US National Institutes of Health Grants and Contracts
State Government Grant

Ansell International
ANZ Banking Group
Arthur Robinson & Hedderwicks
Cochlear Limited
Nucleus Limited
Pacific Dunlop Ltd
PMP Communications Limited
The Herald & Weekly Times Limited
Telstra

Charitable trusts and foundations
The George Alexander Foundation
Estate of the Late William Charles Angliss
The Arthur Robinson & Hedderwicks Charitable Fund
Percy Baxter Charitable Trust
The Jack Brockhoff Foundation
Channel 0 (10) Nerve Deafness Telethon
Collier Charitable Trust
Deafness Foundation (Vic.)
Deafness Foundation Ladies Committee
The Felton Bequest
The George Hicks Foundation
The George Brook Hutchings Estate/Bequest
H. & L. Hecht Trust
Ladies Auxiliary of the Bionic Ear Institute
Lions Clubs International
Lions Deafness Research Fund
The Victorian Lions Foundation
Mazda Foundation
Perpetual Trustees
The Ian Potter Foundation
Sir Donald and Lady Trescowthick Foundation Ltd
The R.E. Ross Trust
Nell & Herman Slade Trust
The Executive Council of Auxiliaries, The Royal Victorian Eye & Ear Hospital
The Eric Smorgon Family Charitable Foundation
J.B. Were & Son Charitable Fund
The Joe White Bequest

The Hilton White Bequest
Estate of the Late James Francis Williams
Windemere Foundation Ltd

Major personal donors
Mr R. Albert, AM, RFD, RD
Mr Eric Bauer
Mr James Calver-Jones
Mr & Mrs John Calvert-Jones
Mr Peter Clemenger
Mr L. Gordon Darling, AO, CMG
Dame Elisabeth Murdoch, AC, DBE
Mr & Mrs John Prescott AO
Mrs Beth Smallwood
Mr Jack Smorgon AM
Mr Paul Trainor AO

Appendix 5

Common questions asked by school children

1. Where did you grow up?
2. What school did you go to?
3. What University did you study at?
4. Why did you come back to Melbourne?
5. When did you think up the idea?
6. Where did you receive inspiration from?
7. Where do you get the money to research the ear?
8. How long did it take to complete the bionic ear?
9. How many people were on the team?
10. Were you the boss or were several people involved?
11. What were the hardships?
12. Were you ever tempted to give up?
13. Were there any disputes/was it easy to get along with everyone?
14. What did you feel when the first implant actually worked?
15. What did you gain from this?
16. Who will benefit from it?
17. Are you happy with the outcome?
18. How many people have the cochlear implant?
19. How much did it cost to produce the bionic ear?
20. How much does the bionic ear cost?
21. How do you see the future for the bionic ear and what would be your ultimate dream?
22. Do you have any more ideas for new inventions?
23. What is the next advance?
24. How many people are currently involved/what occupations?
25. What do you do today/do you have a job/do lectures?
26. Do you think that the bionic ear will ever be placed under the skin?
27. Has the process of researching the bionic ear changed?

Glossary of terms

- The **bionic ear** bypasses the inner ear by electrically stimulating the hearing nerves and so brings hearing to severely and profoundly deaf people when they cannot get adequate help with a hearing aid. The bionic ear has multiple electrodes to provide a range of speech sounds.

- The **cochlea** is the technical term for the inner ear. The name is derived from a word for snail because it is coiled like a snail shell.

- A **cochlear implant** is the medical term for a bionic ear and refers to the implantation of a single or multiple electrode wires in the inner ear in order to stimulate the hearing nerve.

- **Electrode array** is a bundle of electrical wires that carry current to stimulate different groups of nerve fibres.

- **Formants** are speech frequencies that are especially important for intelligibility.

- The **frequency of sound** is the number of times sound energy oscillates back and forth in a second.

- The **inner ear** houses the hearing receptor. It is enclosed in a small snail shell-like cavity in the bone. It has cells that sit on a vibrating membrane. The cells have protruding hairs that move back and forth in time with the sound vibrations, thus converting sound to electrical signals.

- **Intensity** is the physical dimension of sound that is related to its energy and therefore loudness.

- **Loudness** is the sensation of a sound that depends on intensity and varies from low or soft to high or loud.

- The **middle ear** lies between the outer and inner ear. It contains three small bones of hearing that amplify the sound for transmission to the inner ear through a small opening called the oval window. Another opening, the round window, acts as a relief valve.

- **Open sets of words and sentences** are any from the language and selected without the person knowing or having rehearsed them beforehand.

- **Pitch** is the sensation that depends on the frequency and is experienced for different musical notes ranging from low to high.

- **Post-linguistic deafness** is deafness that occurs after language has developed.

- **Pre-linguistic deafness** is deafness that occurs before language has developed.

- **Timbre** is a complex sensation that is not strictly pitch but helps to give quality to a musical note, so that we can recognise a particular voice or instrument.

- **Voicing** is the low frequency of speech that differentiates sounds such as /b/ and /d/ from the unvoiced /p/ and /t/.

Index

Dreams can come true . . .

Twenty-one years ago, Professor Graeme Clark and his team pioneered the world's first Bionic Ear using ideas and techniques considered by many to be either outrageous or impossible. Since then, his dream to help people with hearing loss has continued to push the boundaries of medicine and bio-engineering, finding new ways to extend the gift of hearing to many thousands across the world.

We need your help to continue. Join us in achieving this aim by supporting The Bionic Ear Institute through a tax-deductible donation or by making provision in your Will to further extend the Institute's work.

If you would like to make a donation, receive information about making a Bequest or go on our mailing list to receive regular updates about the work of the Institute, please write to us at:

The Bionic Ear Institute
384–388 Albert Street
East Melbourne 3002 Victoria Australia
Tel: +61 3 9283 7500 Fax: +61 3 9283 7505

Thank you